The Ex-Prisoner's Dilemma

CRITICAL ISSUES IN CRIME AND SOCIETY
Raymond J. Michalowski, Series Editor

Critical Issues in Crime and Society is oriented toward critical analysis of contemporary problems in crime and justice. The series is open to a broad range of topics including specific types of crime, wrongful behavior by economically or politically powerful actors, controversies over justice system practices, and issues related to the intersection of identity, crime, and justice. It is committed to offering thoughtful works that will be accessible to scholars and professional criminologists, general readers, and students.

For a list of titles in the series, see the last page of the book.

The Ex-Prisoner's Dilemma

How Women Negotiate Competing Narratives of Reentry and Desistance

Andrea M. Leverentz

Rutgers University Press
New Brunswick, New Jersey, and London

LIBRARY OF CONGRESS CATALOGING-IN-PUBLICATION DATA

Leverentz, Andrea M., 1973–
    The ex-prisoner's dilemma : how women negotiate competing narratives of reentry and desistance / Andrea M. Leverentz.
        pages cm. — (Critical issues in crime and society)
    Includes bibliographical references and index.
    ISBN 978-0-8135-6228-5 (hardcover : alk. paper) — ISBN 978-0-8135-6227-8 (pbk. : alk. paper) — ISBN 978-0-8135-6229-2 (e-book)
        1. Women prisoners—Rehabilitation—United States. 2. Prisoners—Rehabilitation—United States. 3. Ex-convicts—Services for—United States. 4. Prisoners—Family relationships—United States. 5. Ex-convicts—United States—Longitudinal studies. I. Title.
    HV9304.L427 2014
    365'.660820973—dc23   2013027190

A British Cataloging-in-Publication record for this book is available
from the British Library.

Visit our website: http://rutgerspress.rutgers.edu

Manufactured in the United States of America

For the women of the Mercy Home

CONTENTS

ACKNOWLEDGMENTS

FIRST AND FOREMOST, I give my deepest thanks to the women who participated in this project. They generously gave their time and their stories, and the time I spent with them was incredibly rewarding. I continue to think of them often and fondly and wish them the best. Many of the women who participated did so because they hoped it would help others in similar places and help people to better understand them. I hope this book lives up to those goals and that the women recognize themselves in its pages. I also thank the staff of the Mercy Home for allowing me access and providing valuable assistance along the way, and the families and friends of the women who participated in interviews.

The National Institute of Justice, Office of Justice Programs, U.S. Department of Justice (2003-IJ-CX-1005) provided funding for this project. The points of view in this book are those of the author and do not necessarily represent the official position of the U.S. Department of Justice. The Center for the Study of Race, Politics, and Culture at the University of Chicago also provided funding.

Over the life of this project, I have received advice, feedback, and encouragement from a number of colleagues and friends. Andrew Abbott, Richard Taub, Robert Sampson, Andrew Papachristos, Shadd Maruna, Patrick Carr, Bianca Bersani, David Kirk, Katherine Irwin, and John Eason provided feedback on pieces of this project at different stages and helped me work through issues, sometimes frequently and at length and always with good humor. In addition to critiquing my arguments and words, they provided moral support and confidence in this project, even, and especially, when my own faltered. Credit for the title goes to Andy Abbott. I also thank Saundra Westervelt and Venezia Michalsen for their thoughtful, generous, and constructive comments on the manuscript. Peggy Giordano, Beth Richie, Patricia O'Brien, Meda Chesney-Lind, Russ Immarigeon, Bruce Arrigo, Mary Thomas, Lauren Krivo, and Ruth Peterson also provided advice and encouragement at key moments along the way. Mary Simmerling provided invaluable guidance in developing a methodologically sound research strategy that protected the privacy and rights of a very vulnerable population. I also thank Peter Mickulas of Rutgers University Press for his enthusiastic and patient support. Thanks to Willa

Speiser for meticulous copyediting. Many of my students over the years have heard these stories and listened to me work out the arguments represented in this book. They have all helped enrich the final product. Anna Andrews, Adam Collins, Dory Gayler, Whitney Gecker, Britta Hansen, Holly Jacobs, and Sean Sullivan deserve special mention for their enthusiastic critique of the methodological appendix.

Interviewing provides very rich data, but to fully maximize its use, the interviews need to be transformed into written transcripts. This is a time-consuming, often tedious, task and I thank Brendan Dooley, Lauren Haskell Donohue, Jessie Goldberg, Angela Cody, Xavier Lazcano, Jessica Callea, Maria Perrone, Whitney Gecker, Dory Gayler, and Erin Scott for their help.

Portions of chapter 4 previously appeared as "Being a Good Daughter and Sister: Families of Origin in the Reentry of African American Female Ex-Prisoners," in *Feminist Criminology* 6, no. 4 (2011): 239–267. Portions of chapter 5 previously appeared as "The Love of a Good Man? Romantic Relationships as a Source of Support or Hindrance for Female Ex-Offenders," in the *Journal of Research in Crime and Delinquency* 43, no. 4 (2006): 459–488. Portions of chapter 6 previously appeared as "People, Places, and Things: How Female Ex-Prisoners Negotiate Neighborhood," in the *Journal of Contemporary Ethnography* 39, no. 6 (2010): 646–681. I thank the publishers of these journals for their permission to include the material here and the reviewers and journals' editors for helping me clarify and strengthen my arguments.

I also thank those friends who never cared whether or not I finished this book. While less obviously connected to this project, and sometimes oblivious to its existence, they have provided a crucial escape from the pressures and anxieties of academia. Finally, I thank my parents, Charles and Sheila Leverentz, and my sister and brother-in-law, Terri and Mark Matthews, for humoring me even when they did not really understand what I was doing or why and for making sure I never take myself too seriously.

The Ex-Prisoner's Dilemma

Introduction

SHORTY D¹ WAS A thirty-eight-year-old African American mother of two. Her younger son was five and living with her mother; the other was nineteen and at a work release center. As a child, Shorty D was involved with school and extracurricular activities. She described her childhood as a good one and herself as having "had dreams" of a career. She was close with her father, who "was an alcoholic, but he wasn't an abusive alcoholic. You know, he was the type that would take a drink and give you all his money." In her teen years, she felt unloved by her mother. "I know the reasons why I felt like that today. My mother had six kids and some of her kids were going to jail and all that, so she focused on the ones that needed some help more so than the ones that was all right. You know, she had to give up a little more time to help the ones that needed the help, but, see, I didn't look at it like that. I used to look at it like, they always in trouble, why are they getting all the attention? When do I get a pat on the back?" She was "thrown" when she got pregnant with her older son when she was nineteen. She said that having a baby "played a part in me getting caught up, too, you know."

Shorty D had recently been released from prison after serving sixteen months. This was her only time in prison, though she had been arrested several times before, had spent short stints in jail, and had been on intensive probation. From prison, she went to the Mercy Home, a voluntary halfway house for women returning from prison. She first learned of the Mercy Home from her sister Lauren, who had stayed there several years earlier. All of Shorty D's law enforcement and criminal justice system involvement stemmed from drug use and selling. Prior to her incarceration, she had been "using drugs every day all day." Still, she did not begin using drugs until after the birth of her first child. "My mother never did drugs, you know what I'm saying? None of that, right. Everything I did, I did by choice. You know, when people say that it's somebody that—it's in a family? Drugs were never in my family. Matter of fact, I was in my twenties, early twenties, when I started getting high. I didn't know what cocaine looked like, you know, until I got on the street and hang, started hanging with the wrong crowd. You know, which my mama, you know, didn't approve of. . . . You don't even look at the time you wasted or how many years that went by, you know." Of Shorty D's five siblings, three had histories of drug use. One brother was in and out of the penitentiary. Another brother continued to use drugs, though "he's the type of person that get high once a month. You know, he don't be out there every day all day."

A few months after her release, she "gave up for a few days" and relapsed. Although she was ashamed of this, "it's all about if you fall you ain't gotta stay down. . . . I refused to let my pride and my guilt keep me out there, 'cause see that's what had me in my addiction." She spoke to her case manager at the single-room-occupancy (SRO) building where she was living at the time, and went into treatment. A few months after this, she said, "To be totally honest, I got high one time . . . it wasn't like I can really blame it on anything. I just got high for that day, but you know, it messed my nose up, my throat was all messed up, you know, so every time I make a decision that ain't right, you know what I'm saying, I always get disappointed out of it." This time, she talked to her sponsor. Over the course of her first year out of prison, she participated in two job-training programs, and was looking for work at the end.

Shorty D's sister, Lauren, was forty years old and had stayed at the Mercy Home about seven years prior. She had served three prison sentences, one jail sentence, and was arrested "numerous" times from age seventeen until her early thirties. Like Shorty D, she described her childhood as a good one. Her childhood neighborhood was close knit. "You know that saying where they say it take a neighborhood to raise a child? It puts you in a mind of that. Everybody knew everybody's mom and dad. Growing up over there was ideal. It was ideal. It's what happened after you grew up that became the problem." She began using marijuana as a teenager.

LAUREN: If I was at school, the girls I hung out with would smoke marijuana in the bathroom. Or on our lunch break, you smoke marijuana. Class, we smoking marijuana. When I got outta school, I hung out with another group of people. They smoked marijuana. You know, even when I was, when I used to go hang out in, all their friends in that house, you know, they smoke marijuana. Granted, you know, we did the things that you normally do. Like, you go to the dance classes, you take tennis lessons and you learn how to play chess. We weren't being deprived, you know, the extracurricular activities and stuff, and you know, didn't go, you know, to different events and all of that. You wasn't deprived, you just were on drugs.

Around age eighteen, she began using her drug of choice, heroin. She chose to go to the Mercy Home after a prison drug treatment counselor suggested that she try something different upon her release. "I think the message he gave, now that I'm able to comprehend a little bit better, is that you need to change your thinking about places and people, you know. It was just a way for me to think about the way I think about things."

When she first left the Mercy Home, she lived in a single-room-occupancy building for approximately a year. She then moved in with a boyfriend, before moving in with her mother. Eventually she moved to her current apartment, where she lived with her daughter and baby grandson. She was working as a drug counselor while in school to complete her CADC (certified addiction drug counselor) license and a third associate's degree, this one in addiction studies. She also helped care for her nephew, Shorty D's younger son.

LAUREN: I had my nephew for a while, because his mom was still in her addiction. I ended up with him because at the time I lived on the third floor, my mom lived on the first floor. When she had the baby I was living with my mom and then I moved on the third floor. And we knew we were going to have him. We just knew it. The day she [Shorty D] told her [our mother] she was pregnant, it was like you know you're going to have this baby when it comes. I guess we just took on the responsibility because we knew we had a baby coming. There's no getting around it. So we had to prepare ourselves. He was with me and my mom for, well he's still with my mom, but with us both together until he was four. That's when I moved.

Lauren said, "My relationship with my mom, it took her—I was living with her, it took her three years just to say that she was proud of me. Then I knew our relationship was mended. It took her a long time. And I was out of the joint for a while before that even came about." While Lauren and Shorty D both felt as children they did not get enough attention from their mother and had been closer to their fathers, both were now close with their mother.

Tammy was an African American woman in her early thirties. She was one of the few women at the Mercy Home who had no history of drug use; she decided to go there because "I have been gone for a while." Tammy first entered prison when she was nineteen; her only criminal justice system involvement was a first-degree murder conviction, for which she served fourteen years. She was shy and nervous when she was first released, and appreciated the security of being at the Mercy Home, though she would have preferred it to be more structured. She said, "I thought a lot of people would judge me. And a lot of people here understand and they're caring people. So I feel at home. I feel comfortable and relaxed and nonviolent and I haven't felt that way in a long time." She wanted to work on an assembly line while she went to college; instead she got a job as a facilitator for mentally ill clients at a day program. She enjoyed working with the clients, to her surprise, and stayed at that job for about a year. She then quit because "it was stressful with the coworkers, the atmosphere." She also completed her first semester of college.

She was initially hesitant to talk about the events that led to her incarceration, but eventually began opening up about them.

TAMMY: Well, I could just tell you just briefly how it probably came about. When I was young, about ten years old, up to my incarceration time, nineteen, my mother came up missing. And that's how I took it—that she came up missing. Later on, I found out she was murdered, from events that happened, and it made me realize that she just didn't leave, but she was murdered. I tried to go to the police and explain to them the things that I seen and heard, and my family members was talking about her and actually seeing her being abused. Later on, I couldn't get the help that I wanted or needed, so I took the law into my own hands. That's what led up to that.

This continued to be a source of strain among her siblings and other family members, and she struggled to establish relationships with them. Both she and her older sister Kristen talked about a divide between the three older siblings, who had clearer memories of their mother, and the three younger siblings. She had contact with two of her siblings: Kristen and a younger brother.

At the Mercy Home, she was particularly close with Danielle, who took on a maternal or sisterly role with her. Tammy described Danielle: "She's close to my mother's age, so I respect her and she, you know, give me advice. She like to go shopping with me, and, you know, I feel close to her." Tammy and Danielle moved to the same SRO building, and they remained close. Over time, Tammy said she maintained contact with her fellow Mercy Home residents, but "they're not doing too good, you know, because of the drug abuse, and I haven't used drugs. . . . Most of them have fell off, but they, this place here will get you help instead of kicking you out. If you relapse, they will get you help, send you to a rehabilitation center . . . they really do believe in helping the women here." She knew of three women who had relapsed and then went back into treatment, and had heard rumors about a few others.

TAMMY: At first, I was unable to tell if someone's using drugs. Now that my close friends have, yes, I can tell now. One that's very close to me, I can tell, because she stopped doing the things, you know, we used to hang out a lot and so we don't hang out that much. And I can tell by the mood swings, the reddish eyes, and forgetfulness and irritation, and asking me to loan her large sums of money. And then they weren't going to work, every other day, they was missing, and I was like, what's wrong? You like to work. "I'm tired, or doing other things," to the point where she just quit. And that was a big sign. . . . I never approached her about it, but I knew something was happening. She finally told me after she went to a counselor here to get treatment, said she needed help. So, she finally told me.

Tammy was wary and hurt by the experiences she had with the women who relapsed. She had begun to depend on Danielle to learn how to be a free adult. After her friends relapsed, she began doing more things on her own and continued to struggle with establishing a satisfying social life. Over time, she developed a closer friendship with Sunshine, another of the women from the Mercy Home who did not have a history of addiction. While Tammy never used drugs, she did occasionally attend Alcoholics Anonymous or Narcotics Anonymous groups and also helped start an Emotions Anonymous group at the SRO.

These vignettes introduce just three of the women who are the core of this study, and represent some of the range in their experiences. Shorty D and Lauren are, in many ways, illustrative of the experiences of many women who are in prison in the contemporary United States. They have extensive histories of drug addiction, and much of their offending and criminal justice system involvement is tied to this drug use. These addictions affect many areas of their lives, from their ability to parent effectively to their relationships with other family members, friends, and communities. Their attempts to stop offending and using drugs in the future are also strongly implicated in these relationships and in their social context. Tammy represents an important counterpoint—a reminder that not all prisoners and not all female offenders have histories of addiction and some also must contend with the impact of long periods of incarceration. Tammy was in prison at a time she might have been completing her college education, establishing a career, adult friendships, and romantic partnerships, starting a family, and other common adult transitions. All three of the women were learning what it meant to have this history of offending and incarceration, and how to reestablish their lives and their relationships on the other side of that history.

Research Approach

The Ex-Prisoner's Dilemma is based on repeated qualitative interviews with women who returned from prison to the Mercy Home and members of their social networks.[2] In the book, I analyze the narratives the women use to describe and define their lives as they reenter society and attempt to desist from offending and drug use. I went to the Mercy Home twice to formally recruit current residents to the study. I also mailed letters to all former residents for whom the Mercy Home had addresses and invited them to participate. Some of these women had only recently moved out of the Mercy Home, while others had lived there years earlier. The goal was to interview all women four times over the course of a year. Through these interviews, I tracked the women's progress and changes to their lives and perspectives. I also incorporated questions about emergent themes and issues. In all, I interviewed forty-nine women, who were evenly divided between current and former Mercy Home residents at the time we met. Of these, I interviewed thirty-three women four times, and the remainder between one and three times. The combination of current and former residents and multiple interviews over time allowed me to hear about a wide range of experiences with reentry and desistance as an ongoing process that evolves over the women's life course.

In the first interview, I asked the women to identify family, friends, romantic partners, or coworkers they would be comfortable with my interviewing. The goal of these interviews was to better understand the women's social context and relationships. Through this approach, I interviewed twenty-six people who were referred by fifteen women. While I draw on these interviews through the manuscript, they are particularly central to the analysis in chapters 4 and 5, which focus on family dynamics and relationships with romantic partners and friends. In addition to formal "network" interviews, the women were interconnected with one another and talked about one another.

In the pages that follow, I detail how women coming out of prison negotiate competing messages of who they are, who they should be, and how they should live their lives. They receive often-conflicting messages from prison staff, halfway house and drug treatment program staff, family members, romantic partners, friends, and acquaintances about how to be a "good" ex-offender, recovering drug user, mother, daughter, sister, romantic partner, and productive member of society. Many of these are incompatible with one another, and the women must learn to redefine themselves in light of these multiple and competing messages. The goal here is to understand not only what their narratives or stories are but also where they come from and how they are used.

Narratives that people construct provide an explanation of past behavior and a guide to future behavior (Gubrium and Holstein 1998; Laub and Sampson 2003; Maruna 2001; McAdams 2006). These narratives are strongly shaped by social and structural positions, relationships, and the various messages they receive about their roles in life. As Dan McAdams argues, "Narrative identities are stories we live by. We make them and remake them, we tell them and revise them not so much to arrive at an accurate record of the past as to create a coherent self that moves us forward in life with energy and purpose. Our stories are partly determined by the real circumstances of our lives—by family, class, gender, culture, and the historical moment into which we're thrown. But we also make choices, narrative choices" (2006, 98–99). The women's interpretations of their lives and their relationships represent a cognitive schema through which women account for who they are and the choices they have made. These narratives shape and are shaped by the women's interactions with individuals and institutions; as such, they tell us not only about the women but also about how contemporary U.S. society constructs gender, female criminality, and prisoner reentry.

In looking at the women's experiences before and after their incarcerations, I draw most heavily on the life course and symbolic interactionist perspectives (Berger and Luckman 1966; Elder 1998; Goffman 1963; Laub and Sampson 2003; Mead 1934). Specifically, from life course approaches, I recognize that these women's lives are embedded in and shaped by the historical and physical context, the timing of life events matters, lives are interdependent, and human agency plays a key role in constructing one's life (Elder 1998; Laub and Sampson 2003). In addition, I use the premises of symbolic interactionism, as laid out by Herbert Blumer: people act toward things on the basis of the meanings that the things have for them, these meanings come from social interaction and are handled and modified through an interpretive process, and the complex interlinkages of acts are dynamic, not static (1969, 50). In other words, the women's lives are socially contextualized and they actively construct a sense of their lives through their interactions with other individuals and institutions.

STRUCTURAL AND CONTEXTUAL FACTORS INFLUENCING FEMALE OFFENDING

The experiences of and reactions to women who offend or who are incarcerated are shaped by their role as women. Women who engage in offending are often looked upon as "doubly deviant," violating both gender and legal norms (Heimer and De Coster 1999; Owen 1998; Sterk 1999). In addition, the streets are one place in which gendered power relations play out (Miller 1995; 2008). For example, women in the drug economy most often remain in subordinate or peripheral positions and often acquire access to roles through their relationships with men (Fagan 1994; Maher and Hudson 2007; Miller 1995). However, while substantial research demonstrates their continued subordination, many women who are engaged in street life believe in their independence and efficacy within a street culture (Maher and Daly 1996; Maher and Hudson 2007; Miller 1995; Steffensmeier 1983; Stewart, Schreck, and Simons 2006). For women reentering the community after incarceration, race, gender, and power dynamics continue to shape the negotiation of neighborhood life (Huebner, DeJong, and Cobbina 2010; O'Brien 2007). When female prisoners return to the community, they, like men, return primarily to disadvantaged neighborhoods. The added stigma of being a female offender may make it more difficult to feel accepted and to access resources. As Beth Richie argues, "the sense of being marginalized within the context of a disenfranchised community has a profound impact on the ability of the women to successfully reintegrate into it" (2001, 383).

Many female prisoners have experienced victimization and trauma, often at the hands of family members (Chesney-Lind 2002; Gaarder and Belknap

2002; Gilfus 1992; Makarios 2007; McDaniels-Wilson and Belknap 2008; Richie 1996). They are much more likely to have been physically or sexually abused by family members or intimates as children and as adults than male prisoners (Harlow 1999; McDaniels-Wilson and Belknap 2008).[3] This abusiveness and violence is often related to additional problems and disruptions in the home. Both male and female prisoners reporting abuse were more likely to also report that their parent(s) abused drugs or alcohol or had been incarcerated; similarly, those who had been abused reported higher illegal drug and alcohol use themselves (Harlow 1999). While the relationship between abuse and substance use is true for both male and female prisoners, these findings are more pronounced for women (Harlow 1999; Makarios 2007).

The relationship between a dysfunctional or violent home life and later offending also is gendered. In some cases, involvement with the criminal justice system is a direct result of childhood victimization, as in the case of a runaway who flees an abusive home environment (Chesney-Lind 2002). In other cases, the connection may be more indirect. Girls often are more closely supervised and encouraged to spend more time in the home and with family than boys, so the behavior of relatives may be particularly important to their development, including their initiation into drug use and criminal activity (Blee and Tickamyer 1995; Bottcher 2001; M. Brown 2006; Covington 1985; Kane 2000). Because relationship goals are often more important for many girls and women than boys and men, problems in family relationships have a greater impact on them (Covington 1985). Given their high rates of abuse by family members, adult relationships with families of origin may be particularly fraught for female offenders, prisoners, and former prisoners, though they often rely on family members to care for their children while incarcerated (Hagan and Coleman 2001; Swann and Sheran Sylvester 2006). In addition, girls and women are socialized to see themselves as caregivers and often remain loyal to their parents and other relatives, even when those relatives were abusive, neglectful, or criminally involved (Gilfus 1992; O'Brien 2001).

The impact of structural disadvantage on criminal offending is particularly true for African American women (Hill and Crawford 1990). Crime, drug use, and violence are widespread in the neighborhoods from which female prisoners are drawn and to which they return. These neighborhoods also tend to have high rates of economic disadvantage and to be communities of color. Like men, women in these neighborhoods are affected by structural conditions that shape the nature and extent of their offending (Anderson 1999; Baskin and Sommers 1998; Hill and Crawford 1990; O'Brien 2007; Reckdenwald and Parker 2008; Simpson 1991; Sterk 1999). Rates of female offending and recidivism are related to the financial instability of women, especially single mothers in poor urban areas (Holtfreter, Reisig, and Morash

2004). African American women in urban contexts are more exposed to a cultural legitimacy of violence and are more likely to engage in violence than other women (Anderson 1999; Heimer and De Coster 1999; Hill and Crawford 1990; Miller 1998).

Beyond offending, we must also consider other aspects of women's lives. For example, race and class statuses influence women's roles within their families and communities. African Americans are less likely than whites or Hispanics to live in married-couple households, and African American women are less likely to be economically dependent on men (Kane 2000). Those who are unemployed (of any race) are particularly unlikely to marry, contributing to the argument that there is a dearth of "marriageable men" in the poor, inner-city neighborhoods from which most prisoners are drawn (Fitch and Ruggles 2000; Griffin and Armstrong 2003; Hill 2001; Wilson 1987). Although economically disadvantaged women of color may aspire to marriage, they are less likely to aspire to financial dependence on men (Edin and Kefalas 2005; Rogers-Dillon and Haney 2005). In addition to differences in marriage patterns, nearly half of black children are born in poverty and more than half are born to single mothers (Hill 2001; Jayakody, Chatters, and Taylor 1993). These experiences also are more likely among African American families than white families to lead to delinquency (Haynie and Payne 2006; Matsueda and Heimer 1987).

Black women commonly function as "othermothers" in their communities, creating an extended and fictive kin network of shared child care and "a more generalized ethic of caring and personal accountability" (Collins 2000, 189). African American women are central to kin networks, reflecting in part an adaptation to race, gender, and class oppression, though at the same time their self-reliance is valued and encouraged (Collins 2000; Hill 2001; Turner 1997). Thus, although traditional marital relationships may be less prevalent for contemporary African American women, families of origin and extended kin remain central, particularly among single mothers (Jayakody, Chatters, and Taylor 1993). These patterns suggest the necessity of looking beyond the "love of a good woman/man" argument when looking at the influence of relationships on contemporary African American female offending populations (Bottcher 2001; Giordano, Cernkovich, and Rudolph 2002; Laub, Nagin, and Sampson 1998; Leverentz 2006; 2011). Romantic relationships and marriage may be less central to their identity, and families of origin may be much more central into adulthood.

Desistance

One of our primary concerns in understanding prisoners' return to the community is whether they reoffend. Recidivism and reincarceration rates among returning prisoners are high and are thus a significant policy concern. Desistance from offending also is a key concept in life course criminology. It is interesting or relevant not only to understand why people begin committing crimes, but also why they stop. There are three dominant theoretical approaches to explain desistance, which differentially highlight social bonds, self-conceptions, and the interplay between the two. A commonality in all of these approaches is the recognition of desistance as a process, and one that often includes stops and starts, setbacks, and forward progress.

One of the prevalent approaches to understanding desistance is John Laub and Robert Sampson's age-graded theory of social control. Offenders stop offending when they develop social bonds to conventional society, which in turn increases the cost to offending (Laub and Sampson 2003). For Laub and Sampson a key element is the concept of "knifing off" offenders from their immediate environment; this may take the form of a residential move or physical removal (for example, prison, reform school, the military). In addition, desistance emerges from structured role stability, such as that provided by long-term marriage and employment and residential stability. Both knifing off and role stability result in changed social networks and routine activities, all of which contributes to continuing desistance from offending and new identities as desisting offenders, family men, workers, and providers. For many of the men studied by Laub and Sampson, this seemed to occur, at least initially, without a conscious decision to do so (2003).

In contrast, Shadd Maruna (2001) focuses on individual self-conceptions. Individuals "rebiograph," or rewrite their offending history to give their future, law-abiding lives meaning. Here, a change in identity drives a sustained change in behavior; a redemptive script "not only has to allow for desistance but also has to make desistance a logical necessity" (Maruna 2001, 86). A resulting redemptive script often takes the form of a "professional ex," such as a peer mentor or drug counselor, in which one's past is meaningful to now help others in similar situations (J. D. Brown 1991; Ebaugh 1988; Maruna 2001). Successful desisters see themselves as good people who may have done bad things, rather than being bad people at their core. In contrast, those who continue to offend often see themselves as victims of circumstance, with little hope of changing their lot.[4]

In spite of their different theoretical interpretations, there are striking parallels between the narratives of the Glueck men and those of the desisting men and women that Maruna interviewed. In both studies, desisters accepted responsibility for their actions, did not offer excuses, and did exhibit generativity, or a concern for and commitment to promoting the wellbeing of future generations (Erikson 1950; McAdams 2006). A key difference is the source of these changed narratives and changed behavior. For Laub and Sampson

(2003), an offender desists when "knifed off" from his offending environment and thereby offered a new script for the future. A man who marries, gets a job, and moves to a new neighborhood may stop offending and the offending past may become irrelevant to the present. For Maruna (2001), desistance begins with a cognitive change. "Knifing off" is neither necessary nor sufficient; rather, offending pasts are redefined as valuable for a generative future, and therefore remain relevant to the present (Maruna and Roy 2007).

Other theorists have argued, as I do here, for a middle position, in which desistance is shaped by an interplay between individual choices and social factors (Farrall et al. 2011; Giordano, Cernkovich, and Rudolph 2002; Paternoster and Bushway 2009). Peggy Giordano and colleagues, for example, develop a theory of cognitive transformation in which people's identities change in interaction with their environment. A person must be open to change and able to envision a "replacement self," and also must be exposed to socially controlling hooks for change like employment or marriage (Giordano, Cernkovich, and Rudolph 2002). In addition, there are emotional shifts that reflect an interaction between possible catalysts for change and the meaning ascribed to them by the individual (Giordano, Schroeder, and Cernkovich 2007). Ray Paternoster and Shawn Bushway (2009) develop the idea of the "feared possible self." In other words, people define themselves in terms of who they do *not* want to be, rather than who they do want to be. First pushed away from an offending lifestyle, desisting offenders will eventually feel pulled toward a crime-free lifestyle. While these changes reflect a changed identity, Paternoster and Bushway, like Laub and Sampson, argue that desistance requires a "break with the past."

A benefit of a symbolic interactionist approach to desistance is that it highlights the individual in interaction with his or her environment. Desistance is neither a decision nor a behavior that happens purely at the individual level. Wanting to "go straight" does not pay the bills or provide a roof over one's head absent an ability to get a legal job or some other source of financial support. Many former prisoners and would-be ex-offenders in the contemporary United States face significant legal and informal barriers to entering the paid workforce and the housing market. Stigma against people with criminal records is significant, and even more so for those who may look like stereotypical offenders (Flavin 2001; Pager 2007; Western 2006). And yet, in spite of these barriers, some people with extensive histories of drug addiction, criminal involvement, and related stigmas do desist, so they are clearly not entirely constrained by their structural positions.

I draw most extensively on a symbolic interactionist approach here, particularly in terms of the ways in which women with a history of criminal justice involvement make sense of their lives in interaction with others.

Several key aspects to their identities are reflected in their narratives, including their roles as mothers, daughters, and "normal" people. In addition, all of the women in this study are influenced by what they learn and with whom they interact at the Mercy Home, the halfway house in which they lived upon their release from prison. While desistance and recidivism are important aspects of their narratives, I also discuss extensively the nonoffending aspects of their lives and relationships. These are certainly necessary to understand the underlying themes of desistance and recidivism, but they are also crucial to understanding these women as people, not just as offenders or prisoners.

THE LANGUAGE OF SELF-HELP

Self-help and twelve-step programs are common approaches to drug treatment in contemporary U.S. prisons and in halfway and supportive housing programs, including the Mercy Home. Approximately 75 percent of drug treatment in U.S. prisons consists of self-help groups, like Alcoholics Anonymous and Narcotics Anonymous (Petersilia 2003). The rhetoric of the Mercy Home is infused with self-help messages, such as encouragements to avoid all people, places, and things related to offending and drug use. The women in turn use this language to talk about their experiences and their plans for the future.

All drug treatment and reentry programming develops a particular understanding of the problem and appropriate strategies to address it. Self-help programs' emphasis on identity transformation through group membership and empowerment, along with their widespread presence in prisons and transitional housing, makes the groups and their narratives of particular interest in understanding their connections to prisoner reentry and offender desistance. The goal of these groups is to foster cognitive restructuring, to change one's understanding of his or her problem and to thereby change the associated behaviors (Archibald 2007; Cain 1991; A. Katz 1993). Participants become empowered and gain a sense of self-efficacy, in part through group identity and group involvement (Archibald 2007). An important aspect of that is the mutuality of experience (Cain 1991). Participation in a self-help group means interacting with others who share at least some of the same experiences and aspects of a stigmatized identity (Goffman 1963).

Alcoholics Anonymous (AA) was founded in 1935 by a stockbroker and a surgeon and was influenced by the English Oxford Group, which "emphasized personal redemption through verbal honesty, admission of defects, reparations to others for past wrongs, and belief in God" (A. Katz 1993, 10; Swora 2004). A foundational idea of twelve-step programs is that individuals are powerless over their addiction, but that giving themselves over to a higher power will result in increased control and empowerment. In AA parlance, this apparent contradiction is summed up as "letting go and letting God"; "the alcoholic gains control over drinking not by exercising self-control, but by surrendering control to God or a Higher Power" (Swora 2004, 194). Twelve-step participants must then make a moral inventory, share that with another person, and try to make amends to those he or she has hurt. Making amends may be a direct restitution or apology for past wrongs, but it goes beyond this to change the way one relates to others (Swora 2004). The final step includes carrying the message in the "spiritual awakening" to other addicts (Swora 2004). Doing so not only helps others but also helps the individual maintain his or her sobriety. In these latter senses, self-help programs are fundamentally social at the same time they strive for individual transformation.

Twelve-step programs are a low-cost approach to drug treatment and often become popular when other support systems break down (Archibald 2007; Wuthnow 1994). Ideologically, self-help is a populist response to the widespread medicalization of psychological problems. The individual and small-group approach is consistent with U.S. cultural ideals of individualism, self-reliance, and mutual aid. Structurally, the expansion of self-help groups is a response to a need, both in terms of a breakdown of traditional informal support systems and a lack of formal medical and welfare supports. Among prisoners and former prisoners, many come from disadvantaged backgrounds, have attenuated social networks and therefore may lack informal support structures, and lack access to medical care or social services. In addition, the widespread expansion of incarceration, high rates of drug addiction and drug involvement among prisoners, and a lack of funding for prison programming means that a minority of state and federal inmates participate in other prison-based drug treatment (Petersilia 2003). In most cases, twelve-step programs are the only substance abuse treatment available.

Twelve-step programs universalize the problems participants face and thereby discourage a social or institutional critique (Carr 2011; Haney 2010; Sered and Norton-Hawk 2011). A participant's background and social differences among group members are less important than the group's shared experiences with alcohol, drugs, and addiction. The rhetoric does not acknowledge that drug or alcohol users may inhabit very different social contexts. Among these women, and many returning prisoners, for example, most have little choice but to live and spend time in neighborhoods high in crime and drug use. They are unlikely to easily avoid others in their lives who remind them of using, as this group often includes children and other family members, romantic partners, and neighbors. These relationships, in addition to being connected to histories of drug use, are central to their identities as women and as caregivers and may be important supports in their reentry and recovery.

While avoiding people, places, and things related to drug use may be feasible for a subset of drug users, it is done at significant cost and difficulty for many ex-prisoners, including these women.

While it is true that a disproportionate number of prisoners, and most of the women in this study, have problems with addiction, the relevance of self-help language goes beyond the specificities of addiction. Twelve-step programs and the language we use to talk about addiction parallels the ways in which we talk about prisoners and offenders. For example, an AA member remains an alcoholic for life. While one may abstain from drinking and be a "recovering alcoholic," one never stops being an alcoholic; it is an identity that is not reversible or removable (Cain 1991). In much the same way, once one has gone to prison, one can be an ex-prisoner or an ex-offender and one can stop offending, but one cannot return to a pre-prisoner identity (Ebaugh 1988; Maruna 2011). In both tangible and intangible ways, those convicted of criminal offenses continue to experience the invisible punishments or collateral consequences of their convictions (Travis 2002). In addition, spirituality, a cornerstone of twelve-step programs, is an important factor to which many ex-offenders attribute their desistance (Giordano, Cernkovich, and Rudolph 2002; Giordano et al. 2008; Maruna 2001; Terry 2003). Religious involvement is one way in which ex-offenders and prisoners can affiliate with "decent," rather than "street," identities (Anderson 1999; Giordano et al. 2008). Religious involvement also may foster positive coping strategies and pro-social relationships, and it can be a means through which former prisoners can demonstrate their commitment to desistance and reconnect with family. At the same time, the types of therapeutic discourse that twelve-step programs represent are entrenched in many contemporary social institutions, not just those connected to drug treatment or desistance from offending (Bellah et al. 1985; Carr 2011; Haney 2010; Illouz 2008; Silva 2012).

The nature of the Mercy Home, with its "professional ex" staff members and informal mentoring, parallels the social nature of twelve-step groups. The goal of the house is to transform its residents from "offenders" or "prisoners" to former or desisting offenders, much in the same way that AA and other twelve-step programs foster an identity shift from drinker to recovering alcoholic (Cain 1991). Much of the twelve-step language of addiction is incorporated into the way these women talk about their attempts at desistance and a "successful" life in the future. This does not mean that all the women accept the messages and the narrative forms that they learned in drug treatment and at the Mercy Home, but rather that they understood and could reframe their own experiences using the language (Carr 2011). They use the language of self-help programs, even while resisting or reframing the importance of the lessons of that particular view of their problems (Gubrium and Holstein 2000;

Maruna 2001; Miller and Silverman 1995). In doing so, participants may construct an identity that is consistent both with their identity as an "ex" drug user/prisoner/offender and their limited choices and competing needs. This negotiation is a major theme in this book.

OVERVIEW

The women in this study have two things in common: they all have a history of criminal justice system involvement and they all lived at the Mercy Home, a halfway house for returning female prisoners in Chicago. As a group, incarcerated women remain a minority among incarcerated populations and are often dismissed in much of mainstream criminology. Women are often seen as the wives of incarcerated men and the mothers of their children (Braman 2004; Comfort 2008; Western and Pettit 2010). It is true that many more men are incarcerated than women (approximately 90 percent of the prison population and 80 percent of the total correctional population, including probation and parole, is male), female prisoners are less likely than men to be convicted of violent offenses, and they do not correspond to our most common stereotypes of criminals. At the same time, women prisoners are more likely to be custodial parents than male prisoners, so issues of separation through incarceration are very real for this subset of women and their children (Greenfield and Snell 1999; Hagan and Coleman 2001). In addition, women take on important caregiving roles in families and communities, so their absence through incarceration has a significant effect on their families and communities (Collins 2000; Leverentz 2011; Richie 2002). Candace Kruttschnitt (2010, 39) argues that "the paradox of women's imprisonment, then, lies in the sizable repercussions it has on society given the small number of individuals in affects."

The first half of this book primarily addresses the experiences of the women, at the Mercy Home and beyond, as they reconstruct their sense of self and learn what it means to be "normal." In the first chapter, I introduce the Mercy Home, the halfway house through which the women were recruited to be a part of this study and one of the key sources of their understandings of what it means to be a returning prisoner and desisting offender. I then introduce the women themselves, including the common pathways through which they became residents of the Mercy Home. In the third chapter, I look at how the experiences and narratives of the women change over the course of the interview period. In this time, they experience and respond to successes and setbacks and revise their narratives based on these changing circumstances.

In the second half of the book, I begin to more explicitly look at the women as members of larger social worlds. Reentry takes place in a social context and is shaped by social relationships. It is through social interaction that the women learn who they are and who they are supposed to be (Blumer

1969; Mead 1934; Yeung and Martin 2003). In their relationships, self-help messages often come into conflict with the women's structural positions and their social expectations. One of the phrases most often repeated by the women is to avoid people, places, and things related to their offending. For these women, these people, places, and things often include family members who form central parts of their identity and social networks and neighborhoods that are the only ones they know and in which they feel comfortable. A key self-definitional issue the women must confront is how to negotiate these competing messages, such as how to be a good daughter, as defined by their mothers and other relatives, and a successfully recovering drug user, as defined through self-help programs. The women's narratives of their social relationships reflect both their social and cultural context and the messages they learned in drug treatment and at the Mercy Home.

In chapter 4, I focus on the women as members of family units. This represents key roles for them, of mother and daughter, and it also represents a site of conflict, as they attempt to be the mothers and daughters they want to be while also keeping a focus on their needs as individuals. In chapter 5, I look at "chosen" relationships with romantic partners and friends, the role these relationships play in the women's reentry, and how they learn about themselves through these relationships. Chapter 6 focuses on how they negotiate public life, in terms of pursuing education, employment, and neighborhood life. Here again they confront disparities between what they came to believe were the measures of success—working hard, getting an education and work experience—with the reality of their experiences. They wrestle with feeling out of place and feeling as though nothing they do will be enough to achieve true "success." The final chapter addresses what we can take away from this particular study to better understand prisoner reentry, desistance from offending, and female offenders and prisoners. In this final chapter, I also touch on new research questions this project raises as well as possible policy implications.

PART I

*Becoming an
Ex-Offender*

CHAPTER I

The Mercy Home and the Discourse of Reentry and Desistance

HALFWAY HOUSES PROVIDE a transition between prison and life in the community, to ease reentry challenges and to foster desistance from future offending. They also provide assistance with employment and housing, two issues at the forefront of reentry discussions. As such, halfway houses are sources of tangible support for those returning to the community. In addition, they provide one view of what reentry means and how former prisoners should understand their lives and experiences (Gubrium and Holstein 2000). This chapter describes how the women experienced their time at the Mercy Home, and so provides a context through which to read the rest of the book.[1] I argue that many of their experiences and ways of talking about their experiences parallel those of a broader ex-prisoner population, but still, their understanding of their lives was clearly influenced by their experiences at the Mercy Home.

The Mercy Home was the women's first stop out of prison and their experiences there shape the narratives with which they talk about their post-prison lives.[2] The women both accept and resist the messages they receive; regardless, they learn to use the language and narrative framework to explain their lives. The halfway house, through its programming and informal interactions, provides a narrative framework in which the women understand their reentry and construct their sense of self.

THE MERCY HOME

The Mercy Home was opened by a religious order in the 1990s, about a decade before this study began. There is a parallel men's facility, opened forty years earlier and serving three times as many men. The Mercy Home was created out of a recognition of the growing numbers of women being incarcerated and the need to provide services for them. The initial location was in a large building in a residential area on the South Side of Chicago. Angela, who first moved to the South Side location, described her trip there: "I remember just walking up and down the street just thinking, because nobody in the neighborhood knew where the Mercy Home was. And when I got off the bus, the bus driver said, 'It's over there on the corner.' So, it had this brick wall and it was real tall, so you couldn't see what was on the other side. I was like, okay, how do I get in there? I went on the other corner and they didn't know where the Mercy Home was. Since they didn't know what I was talking about, I asked one of them if I could use their phone. I called them and they said, 'You're right here.'"

Several years later, because of conflicts with the building owners over maintenance, the Mercy Home moved into adjoining townhouses on the West Side of the city, in a building reportedly owned previously by a major drug dealer. The building was redeveloped and transformed into a sixteen-bed half-way house. The West Side location was as discreet and low profile as the earlier location had been. A small plaque near the front door was all that marked it as a halfway house, and it blended in with the surrounding housing stock. From a distance, it looked like a private residence and the residents and staff likewise kept a low profile, rarely spending leisure time outside or in groups.

Both the old and new locations were in areas with high rates of crime and large numbers of returning prisoners (La Vigne et al. 2003). The new location was in a gentrifying area on the Near West Side. It was near both areas of high drug use, with which many of the women were intimately familiar, and new private housing developments and recreational facilities. The immediate area was quiet, though it was within a short walk or drive of areas with an active street life. Some women were wary of staying there because of its location and their connections to area drug markets, although many also appreciated the quiet and peaceful neighborhood.

A house manager or a secretary sat at a reception desk in the front lobby and buzzed residents and visitors in. Residents filled out a log with their destinations and times in and out; visitors also signed in and out. To the left of the reception area was a lounge/smoking room, where many of the women spent their free time. The room contained mismatched sofas and chairs, a TV, and videos. The women were allowed to smoke, since, according to the director, "you can't expect them to give up everything." Also on the first floor was a library with a small collection of books, the office of the executive director, and a meeting room in which most of the group meetings were held. The second and third floors contained staff offices and resident rooms, with a shared phone in the hallway. A kitchen was located in the basement; a staff cook prepared many of the meals and the women prepared their own meals when the cook was not working. The building was well maintained and clean, with a slightly institutional feel.

Getting to the Mercy Home

About three hundred women stayed at the Mercy Home during its first decade in existence. Almost all of them had a history of substance use; most also had extensive criminal histories. The program was voluntary; women must choose to come there on their own and it was never a condition of probation, parole, or supervised release. Most first heard of the Mercy Home when in prison, either through inmates who were former residents or through prison program staff. Others knew of it because family members had stayed there. The women had to apply, and the program director interviewed prospective residents, looking for signs they were sincere about wanting to change. Beyond their knowledge of the Mercy Home and their ability to demonstrate to the program director that they wanted to change, their acceptance was contingent on timing—a bed had to be available at the time the woman was being released from the penitentiary.

While there were few formal criteria for entry, the Mercy Home typically excluded women with histories of arson, extensive records of behavioral problems in prison, records of child abuse, or extreme cases of mental illness. These issues were of concern because of the group nature of the house and the possible impact on the safety of the residents and staff. Children were not allowed to stay at the Mercy Home; however, most of the women did have children, who could visit. Women who engaged in drug use, criminal activity, or excessive violations of house rules may be asked to leave.

Their first milestone—tied to the emphasis on women *choosing* to stay there—was arriving at the halfway house of their own accord when expected, immediately after their prison release. Gertrude, a resident in the late 1990s, described this process:

GERTRUDE: [The program director] wasn't really hard core or any of that. She just had rules that worked. But she suggested that after leaving prison, on your day out, they give us fifty dollars and to use that fifty dollars to get on the train, to get a cab outside the Amtrak station and come straight to the Mercy Home with it. Don't go to McDonald's. Don't go to Payless. Don't go shopping. Don't go to your boyfriend's. None of that. She knew what time we were leaving, the girls that were coming in. She knew what time we were leaving the prison, what time the train left, and what time it arrived in Chicago. The information that she gathered was important because she needed to know about the commitment we were making and whether we were serious enough to do what the rules were. We got there and for the first week there was no contact with people. Our family and friends couldn't come see us.

After passing the milestones of arriving and being in the house for a week, they began acquiring privileges.

In my interviews with the women, many mentioned a desire for a new way of life. Many of the women described themselves as physically and emotionally tired and old, regardless of their current chronological age. Heidi, who at twenty-eight was the youngest participant, described herself as "getting old," and said that she changed "because I got tired of being who I was. I was selfish. You know, I didn't care. I was coldhearted when I was out there because I just used and I didn't care about people." Similarly, Sugar said that this time was different because "this time I'm thirty years old and I have absolutely nothing, as far as material things. I don't have a place to stay. I have hardly any relationships. It's been like that my whole life, though. I've never had any real roots or any real lasting relationships. Just the lifestyle that I led, I was tired of it." Sheila described her reasons for coming to the Mercy Home: "What made me decide to come here is my cousin [Adena] told me about the place. I knew I wasn't going to go back to prison. I was going to give myself a chance. I've been incarcerated three times and I'm in the age in my life where I need to change. You know, because I'm not getting younger; I'm getting older. I need to get things together before it's too late. So I decided to give myself a chance and work this program." Sheila felt, at age forty-eight, that she was too old to continue living the life she had been.

Many of the women cited the opportunity for a change in environment as a benefit and a motivation. Sweetness decided while incarcerated that "I didn't want to, uh, go back to live the lifestyle I was living, that I wanted to change my life for the better and do something different altogether this time. I wanted to be in a different environment, period." Typically, they framed their desire to change as connected to their families, but ultimately self-driven. They wanted to do right by their parents, siblings, and children, prove they could change, and strengthen relationships. Usually, this was not driven by an ultimatum, though occasionally they were pressured by family or loved ones to make a change. For example, Danielle came to the halfway house after her fourth attempt at drug treatment. This time was different, she said, because "part of it was because my family had told me, 'It's on.'" That they made this choice signaled to family members that "this time is different" and that the women were serious about changing their lives.

The women stayed for an average of eight months. This length of stay was in constant negotiation with funding agencies. Funders wanted to serve as many people as possible, pushing the halfway house to have women move on after four months, while the administrators wanted women to stay until they believed they were ready to live on their own. At a minimum, women were allowed to stay, barring behavioral problems or drug relapse, until they had alternative stable housing (often single-room-occupancy buildings and other supportive housing programs) and a source of income. According to an internal evaluation, they had a 50 percent completion rate, meaning that half the women who stayed there remained until they had housing and a source of income. Approximately 17 to 20 percent of the women eventually returned to state prison.[3]

Fostering Social Mobility

The Mercy Home helps meet the immediate needs of women exiting prison. Two of the most immediate and talked about needs are employment and housing (see, for example, Travis 2005), and the halfway house helps with both. Residents live there, rent-free, until they secure stable and affordable housing elsewhere. The women often later moved into other subsidized housing programs, most often paying a third of their income in rent, and most residents were employed before leaving the halfway house. The Mercy Home provides computers to create and update resumes, job search guidance, long-standing relationships with employers willing to hire those with a criminal record, and contacts at education and employment programs. They provide more resources than many other programs, which many of the residents had experienced firsthand. Shelly detailed the differences between the Mercy Home and other halfway and recovery homes:

AL: What appealed to you about it [the Mercy Home]? What made you want to come here?

SHELLY: Well, number one, it's a place for women coming home from the penitentiary back out into society, that are starting all over again. This is my third time coming home from the penitentiary. I have experienced other recovery homes that they have and what appealed to me was that you are able to stay here and save your money. They help you with housing, they have different, more, resources than the other places have for women that was incarcerated. The other places that I've been to it's like after the state gets through paying for you to be there they want you to get out and find a job and pay like three hundred, four hundred dollars a month for rent. For rent, which, you're not going to stay there for the rest of your life so you need to save money so you can get out there on your own. Most of the jobs were minimum wage so I didn't see how that was helping women starting out all over again. It kind of like puts you in a bind.

In addition to benefitting from the support of transitional housing, the women are taught to take a long view of their reentry. Much of their time is spent in structured activities, first predominantly in the home and increasingly in community-based programs and jobs. This includes not only drug treatment, self-help groups, and individual counseling but also time in an alternative high school, job training programs, and employment. The connections they develop at the Mercy Home serve as "hooks for change" and social capital that also may be useful in fostering future opportunities (Giordano,

Cernkovich, and Rudolph 2002). These aspects of the program are frequently mentioned as strengths of the house. Sheila, for example, described what she liked best about her experience at the Mercy Home: "Oh, the meetings and stuff that they have. You know, it's a drug program but we have life skills. But it's a lot more things. You can get your education down here. I've got my high school diploma but that's been thirty years ago. I need to go back. I want to be going back to school." Many of the women enrolled in a GED or alternative high school program and then college. Education was encouraged by the staff and highly valued by many of the women. The halfway house staff and volunteers also helped the women negotiate educational institutions, through their connections with GED programs and alternative high schools, their familiarity with financial aid and application forms, and computer access to complete the forms. Several of the women had defaulted student loans from previous attempts to go to college, and staff helped negotiate these barriers.

Many women enjoyed the pursuit of education, both because of the challenge and because they felt they were working toward a more successful and stable future. The opportunities available to the women at the Mercy Home were primarily targeted to women with low levels of prior education and work experience. For the small number of women who had achieved higher levels of either prior to their incarceration, there was little available, and these women were often dissatisfied with the available services and programs. Carolyn, for example, had a master's degree and a long professional career before she went to prison. She felt that job-training services and the entry-level jobs that were available to the women were unhelpful for someone with her background.

CAROLYN: Prison is after. You know, so, you don't even know. It's after you get out is where the struggle is, because you can't just pick up. See, the work I do is certified and licensed, and that's cut off. . . . I'm angry. It's [prohibited jobs] like a list, two pages. I was going to get a Ph.D. in social work. And I thought F-you. I can't work in a health care facility. There's so many places you can't work. So, come on. If there are, how can you get in? You get in by somebody knowing you, not by the education you got. I got enough paper [credentials]. Why is it that I have to get more paper? You know, I got enough paper. I got enough life experiences but the people that write the laws, they just closed it off. I didn't realize, I didn't have any idea of what was coming after [prison]. . . . So it's designed to hurt you forever.

The administrators recognized the struggles of people like Carolyn. They believed that one group who tended not to succeed were those with higher education, who had a job and an apartment before, because these women were unwilling to accept their current circumstances and "don't want to take responsibility for what happened to them." An alternative explanation is that they are more acutely aware of the structural constraints they face and more quickly reached a ceiling to the opportunities available to them. Carolyn had long since achieved many of the firsts—degrees and jobs or careers—that the other women were working toward. While many of the barriers Carolyn faced apply to all of the women, she was one of the few to frame her experiences in terms of structural constraints and barriers. In part, this may reflect her pre-incarceration educational and professional accomplishments, which were unusually high among Mercy Home residents and among incarcerated populations. At the same time, the women at the Mercy Home are taught to take an individual view of their problems, a framework I turn to later in this chapter.

Daily Life at the Mercy Home

In the Mercy Home, life is "hectic" as the women participate in numerous groups and activities. They are in structured activities for most of their days and into the evenings. In the early days of their stay, they spend most of their time in home-based activities, groups, and classes and in off-site outpatient drug treatment. Shorty D described the classes and programs as helping her become more responsible, "giving me a stable foundation, you know, to be able to stay sober and focus on society and life terms." Marie credited the structure with making her a better person. She said that she changed because of "the structure. The different programming: self-esteem, employment. Just a lot of programming. The women's issues, individual counseling. Just a lot of different things and the programming that they had." These are common explanations the women give of the benefits of the Mercy Home: the Mercy Home exposes them to hooks for change and to different perspectives on their lives and choices.

Over time, they gain increasing freedom of movement and individualized activities. Once they finish outpatient drug treatment, the women seek employment. Most women do find work, often through the contacts and relationships the halfway house has set up. This work is often part time and temporary, as the women participate in welfare-to-work type programs or work in the service industry. Many women I interviewed cited the jobs they got while living at the Mercy Home as an important stepping-stone. This type of job was consistent with the long-term view that they were taught to take at the Mercy Home, and consistent with their stated needs to be persistent and patient in order to succeed. They gained valuable work experience, which they had often lacked or which was in the distant past. The jobs also provided another form of structure to their days. Regardless of the type of employment, it got them out of the house during the day, away from the Mercy Home (though in some jobs, there are several residents working at the same organization). They gained freedom and responsibility while maintaining the structure and the safety of the Mercy Home.

Being at the Mercy Home is a luxury for these women. It affords them a reprieve from many of the responsibilities of everyday life. They did not have to provide daily care to children, and although they eventually work and maintain savings accounts, they did not need to worry about paying bills or rent or how to spend their time. When they did have unstructured time, they could spend it in the common room, where they could watch movies and talk. Eventually, they earned weekend passes and were able to leave the house from Friday to Sunday afternoons. They often spent these passes with family or a boyfriend. This also gave them a break from the treatment and therapeutic groups. Caprice, after saying she got burned out on groups, added "And thank God it's Friday, because at four o'clock we out the door!" Still, while the Mercy Home provides shelter from many of the demands of daily life, the programming is intended to prepare the women for life outside.

A Safe Space

The most important aspects of the Mercy Home for many of the women are the more amorphous benefits, like the opportunity to reflect on their lives and goals and to develop relationships with other women with similar experiences and challenges. Bennie, who described her stay at the Mercy Home as a "spiritual experience," detailed changes in herself as a result of her stay: "I was able to reacquire some of my good attributes, you know, talent wise, my socialization skills. I was able to share my experiences, my hopes and dreams with other people, you know, which only enhances me as a person. I was able to give back and raise my level of consciousness, my self-esteem, you know, that had been dormant for so long. So, yeah, it helped. It made me aware of emotions in life that I was just not familiar with. Like, I had grief for a long time and I didn't even know what it was. It just gave me an element of wisdom and intelligence. It made me a wiser person. It made me more wiser." Bennie's focus, like that of many of the women, was on how she changed as a person, or her cognitive and emotional shifts (Giordano, Cernkovich, and Rudolph 2002; Giordano, Schroeder, and Cernkovich 2007; Maruna 2001). This was not distinct from the tangible benefits of housing and employment—having these concrete supports provided the women the time and space to focus on themselves without many of the responsibilities they otherwise faced. As Adena described it, "That seven-month period when I was out at the Mercy Home, I did more in that seven-month period than I had done the last ten years of my life." This included both developing ties to mainstream society, through employment and other activities, and cognitive and emotional changes in worldview.

Being at the Mercy Home gives women the time, energy, and structure to think about their lives, to process their past experiences, and make pro-social goals for the future. Most appreciated that they did not need to move immediately from the deprivations of prison to the responsibilities of free life. Women who had served long sentences needed transitional support to the "free world." Caprice, who had just been released after ten years in prison, said that "trying to cope" was the hardest thing she was dealing with. She said, "I'm not really ready to go out there. I'm going to have to go and I don't want to." Tammy, who had been incarcerated for fourteen years, wished there was more structure; she too welcomed the transition period between her lengthy time in prison and the free world.

Many of those with shorter sentences were often trying to restructure their lives away from drug use and from social networks with high criminal and drug involvement. For many, the adjustment was daunting and the Mercy Home helped to ease it. Sugar said, "You know, it's a lot different when you're getting high all the time and you're around people that are doing the same thing, and then to try to be around normal people that do normal things, you know, it was just that transition and it was hard." I asked Edie, who had served approximately four years in prison across two sentences, what she expected at the Mercy Home. She highlighted the practical aspects, but what she appreciated the most was much different.

EDIE: I thought it was going to be a place where you go and stay; they can find you a place to stay. But, it was totally different, actually. They really, you know, it's an individual thing. I'm not going to say everybody wants the same thing, but if you have the desire. See, they showed me things that I hadn't ever seen before, you know, about myself. You know, that I too could. They sat people in front of me that had been addicts and alcoholics, like, "Oh, no they wasn't!" There was one lady there, Lisa D, you probably know her. She's my best friend now. But I seen her and I mimicked her. I used her as a—well, I couldn't stand it at first, but when you see people who have what you want, it kind of makes you resent them, actually, because you wonder if they can do, why I can't. See, I had never tried to do it. It gave me role models.

Edie emphasized a common concern among the women; she said, "By me not having been on out into the streets sober, I didn't want to go into the streets until I was pretty much, until I was in the house for three months. I didn't take the prison braids out, didn't do anything, actually, except go to groups. . . . They just gave me time, as I was getting myself to adjusted to coming and going at will. It was a good transition." Many of the women felt that they were out of touch with what "normal" meant and they needed to readjust their expectations and their ways of interacting with the world.

Vivian said she most liked "to have a lot of peace and they control me. Because this is the place. I just be grateful and thankful that I am here again. And I hope that when I leave I don't mess up again because I think that will be it for me." Vivian had previously stayed at the Mercy Home, and relapsed after she moved out. Of this experience, she said, "I did the program and everything and I left and I started using. I guess I didn't take my tools with me." After her first release from the Mercy Home, Vivian moved in with a cousin. She said, "I started using, using drugs and going crazy in the street because I was wild. And then the last time I was down and depressed, nobody to talk to so I tried to take some pills. And I tried to, you know, kill myself and I ended up in the hospital. So I was in the hospital and they were to release me so I called the Mercy Home to see if they could give me help. And that's why I came back again this time." It was relatively unusual for the Mercy Home to allow a woman to come back a second time. For Vivian, this provided a welcome respite from managing her own life.

The structure is seen as both a strength of the house and a frustration for some women. Those who welcome the structure see it as a protective factor in their reentry and desistance attempts. Danielle emphasized structure as the best part of her experience at the Mercy Home, "because it doesn't give me time to think of negative things or time to get involved with anything negative." For Danielle, the structure made the Mercy Home a safe place for her; she was "protected" from the dangers of free time and the temptations that come with it. She was anxious about her ability to desist from crime and drug use, and the Mercy Home took some of this out of her control. Other women also valued the structure, because it protected them from boredom, loneliness, and temptation and because it sheltered them from some of the realities of life on their own. For Winifred, the structure allowed her time to reflect: "Uh, what do I like best—the structure I'd say, giving me time to rethink my steps." The women's appreciation of the structure and the rules reflect their own insecurities. The Mercy Home provides a safe place for them to adjust to and control their freedom.

Not surprising among a group that had recently spent time incarcerated, the structured activities and lack of privacy were also frequency cited as frustrations of the Mercy Home. Caprice complained that "it's hectic, very hectic.... It's like groups ... you get kind of burnt out." While some women appreciated the ability to ease back into the free world, others bristled at the slow pace of their reentry. Winifred was impatient to feel established and successful. She felt the groups were a distraction: "I think I could be doing something more, maybe living what we're talking about and trying to apply what we come up with in the groups."

The Mercy Home allows the women to adjust to increasing freedoms and responsibilities and to changed lifestyles and relationships. Many women feared going back to their neighborhoods—or any neighborhood—and lacked confidence in their ability to succeed. Their stay at the Mercy Home allowed many of them to develop that confidence, through the security of being there and the role models they were exposed to. Edie said, "Matter of fact, I think after the first four months, I realized I could stay sober." Sugar also described the house: "As far as how the house is and the people that work here, it makes you actually feel like you have some choices. You know, like you're not in an institution setting. You are in an institution, but they don't make you feel like it." Most of the women appreciate both the opportunities and the "safe space" the Mercy Home provides.

THE DISCOURSE OF REENTRY AND DESISTANCE

The Mercy Home provides the women with supports and alternative perspectives for their futures. It brings together peer supports and professional support services, including drug treatment, education, and employment opportunities. Both embed the women in valuable networks. Educational, employment, and housing opportunities are hooks for change that tie them into mainstream society (Giordano, Cernkovich, and Rudolph 2002; Laub and Sampson 2003; Warr 1998). Their importance goes beyond the tangible, though, to how they are built into the women's narratives. While the women maintain different perspectives on their lives and how to live them, they share a common language. This language is shaped by their shared experiences in the Mercy Home, through the way the programming rhetoric defines their offending pasts and recovery futures.

While supporting the women through transitional housing, drug treatment, education, and connections to employment, the halfway house staff also are teaching them, explicitly and implicitly, the "right" way to approach their new lives (Gubrium and Holstein 2000). The halfway house, its staff, and its residents construct a particular understanding of incarceration, reentry, and desistance. For example, Bennie described her own new worry-free approach to life: "I don't worry. I just thank God, because it's not me. You know, I'm just starting to realize that I'm powerless over things that unfold in my life. You know, I thank God for the things that did unfold because it empowered me, you know, and it gave me insight so where I can help others who are at the threshold of where I come from or children or orphans or wards of the state or adults or children on drugs, abused. I say that because I've had to walk in those shoes and I have a feel or compassion for that type of tragedy." Bennie surrendered the power in her life to God, which in turn empowered her. Here she clearly mirrors the twelve-step approach. She continued to use twelve-step language to highlight the importance of using her past experience to help others in the future, thereby giving her past victimization and offending positive meaning. In the remainder of this chapter, I detail some of the key themes and concepts of the twelve-step rhetoric in the women's narratives. In later chapters, I draw on this rhetoric to illustrate how the women accomplish their reentry and how they understand it.

According to the Mercy Home's executive director, the keys to success for the women are that they accept what happened to them, accept why they were incarcerated, internalize their value and goodness, and establish independence from both men and drugs. There is recognition of the victimization many experienced and the difficult environments in which they lived, but, ultimately, they are responsible for their past actions and their future selves. In addition, they are encouraged to develop self-esteem and a cognitive frame that allows for a redeemed and pro-social sense of self. In many ways, these messages are consistent with academic research on phenomenological approaches to understanding desistance from criminal activity (see, for example, Giordano, Cernkovich, and Rudolph 2002; Giordano, Schroeder, and Cernkovich, 2007; Maruna 2001; Shover 1996). Central to these approaches is the ability of a desisting offender to envision a replacement self, one that allows her to see herself as a *former* offender or as someone who may have done bad things but is not at her core a bad person.

The house rules include no sex, no drugs, and no violence. Staff members see the biggest cause of relapse to be relationships, and so encourage the women to avoid romantic relationships, especially early in their recovery. This is counter to a growing literature on the positive role of marriage on desistance, especially among male offenders (Bersani, Laub, and Nieuwbeerta 2009; King, Massoglia, and MacMillan 2007; Laub, Nagin, and Sampson 1998; Warr 1998). This rhetoric of dependence—on the "wrong" men, on drugs, on government aid—is commonly used to explain women's criminality and poverty, and getting out of such relationships is a primary way in which the women are encouraged to be independent (McCorkel 2004). Independence and self-efficacy are central to their ability to succeed. This message is reinforced through the twelve-step programs and other drug treatment that the women have participated in, both at the halfway house and in other treatment settings. Many of the women embrace this message. Others struggle or resist it, remaining in existing relationships, sometimes temporarily until they decide the relationship no longer works, or developing new relationships, often with people they meet through their outpatient drug treatment or other programming. Occasionally, two of the residents become romantically involved with one another, which may result in dismissal from the house.

A House Full of Women: Interpersonal Dynamics and Peer Support

The group of women at the Mercy Home forms a community. Each member of that community plays a role in socializing the others, and each fulfills certain roles and expectations. This structure, with its emphasis on peer support, illustrates reentry as a process. It also parallels the twelve-step model of mutual aid and the redefinition of self through group membership. As Adena described it, "When we was at the Mercy Home, it was about sisterhood, you know? Helping each other." The residents and staff form a hierarchy, with professional staff at the top and the newest residents at the bottom. New residents come into the house and are socialized by longer-term residents who are in turn socialized by staff members, many of whom are former residents. Allison described it as "different pieces of the puzzle fitting together."

ALLISON: It was like all different, you know how different pieces of the puzzle fit together. We had a good softhearted individual there. . . . Then we had a stern one that didn't play, . . . and then we had a director . . . that had to have a lot of acceptance in the way she ran things. And then a lot of the case managers, we had to learn how to deal with a lot of different people because all of us had different attitudes and personalities and that's how you have to deal with people in the work force. So it was just like pieces of the puzzle being put together.

The professional staff members are experts who have educational and work backgrounds to guide the women through this transition. Typically the women respect the professional staff for their expertise, though their roles and backgrounds also set them somewhat apart from the rest of the staff and the residents. According to Bennie, professional staff "are good for food, clothing, shelter, you know, a network of connections and things like that." When it came to cognitive and emotional changes, their experience and knowledge was less valuable. Bennie described the limitations of "book knowledge."

BENNIE: That's like, you could have all the education in the world, and you're dealing with an addict, okay, and you're a drug counselor but if you don't have the hands on experience of being a drug addict and they present a situation to you, you can't really deal with it. I mean, you can deal with it, theoretically, from a book, but you can't deal with it psychologically, from where that person is, you know. You can't meet them where they're at. . . . I mean, you've got prostitutes, murderers. You got robbers. And they might be in a vulnerable place. You could suggest some things, pray about it, whatever, but it's an individual plight. You know, you got to really pull yourself out, or you know, just go through what you got to go through and in a lot of instances people can't.

Women need to change, cognitively and emotionally, with the support of their peers, more so than the formal expertise of the professional staff. Peers can "meet them where they're at," because they were once in the same place. The former-resident staff members and longer-term residents can draw on their firsthand experience to guide and encourage the current and new residents in ways that professional staff cannot. Importantly, this group also sees themselves as best equipped to call the residents out on their "slick and devious behaviors" when they try to bend the rules and hustle staff members or other residents. This emphasizes the important roles that the residents can evolve into, to help future generations of residents and others in similar positions.

At its best, the Mercy Home is credited with creating a "sisterhood" and a culture of peer support. Angela said her favorite part of being at the Mercy Home was "all the girls in the house. It was great for support." In addition, she said, "another empowering thing was getting to talk to the house managers because they were a success story. So that really helped a lot." Strong value was placed on mentorship and the value of firsthand experience. Both informal relationships and the twelve step and counseling groups at the house are a framework for making a "moral inventory," and making amends by changing the way that the women relate to others. In addition, the structure of the house and the relationships within it embody the twelfth step of carrying the message forward to others. Linnette, a woman who had recently moved out of the halfway house, described the value of the peer support: "They act like they've known you all your life. It's like an open arms place . . . it's like everything, anything those ladies can do for you they'll do. . . . That made me feel like there is somebody that cares about me; you know, I'm not alone; there is somebody that's walking in my shoes. And then there are those that are not actually walking in my shoes but have walked in my shoes. They understand and have been through the things that I've been through. And that made me feel real comfortable. . . . They make you feel like you're a part of their family." Many residents particularly valued those staff members who shared a similar history, and more readily accepted their guidance and advice because of that experience. The women commonly mentioned a few popular staff members as friends, and many cited the value of staff mentors. These staff members are a manifestation of a realistic "replacement self" that the current residents can envision for themselves (Giordano, Cernkovich, and Rudolph 2002).

That the Mercy Home was a structured residential home for women with an almost all-female staff led to some comparisons with prison. Albany, in answering the question of what she liked least about the Mercy Home, said, "So many women. Women again, like jail [laughing]. Surrounded with women, all day, all night." EJ first said there was not anything she did not like about the Mercy Home, but then added "maybe being around a bunch of women."[4] Sharon similarly equated the Mercy Home's all-female environment with prison: "I really had a problem being around women, although I was in prison, I was forced to be around women. I didn't think I could make it in an environment like this." It was not only the parallels to prison that made her wary, however. When asked why she did not like being around women, Sharon said, "I never really, most of my relatives that I grew up around were guys. I just relate better to guys as opposed to women. I never had any—I had a few close girlfriends, but, you know, nothing major. So I never really been able to relate to women." This is a common attitude, especially among women who have been involved in urban street life, where gender inequality is high, and striving to be "one of the guys" can be a survival strategy (Miller 2001). Shelly, who had served three prison sentences and had been in several other halfway houses, recognized possible tensions in the group nature of the home, but said, "I mean when you're staying around a lot of ladies and you've been around a lot of ladies going in and out of jail and different treatment centers, recovery homes, you learn how to deal with the women. So the women isn't even my problem no more, it's me. Everything about this place, I like it." While Shelly also equated being at the Mercy Home with the all-female settings of prison and other treatment centers, she had adjusted to these dynamics. Similarly, while Allison's least favorite part of the Mercy Home was "being around certain ladies all the time . . . Just the different attitudes," she recognized, "but that's a part of life."

Another source of tension in the house was negotiating personalities and group conflict. Danielle complained about the "different personalities" of the women. Heidi described "some of the conflicts that be going on between the sisters here. You know, we all supposed to be here to change. . . . I try not to include myself, but sometimes I fall short too." Several women complained specifically about "negative women" who are a barrier to those who are more sincere in their attempts at recovery. Part of this tension is that women come to the Mercy Home one by one, rather than in cohorts or groups. Thus women in the house at any one time are often at different stages of their reentry. While this allows them to help socialize one another, it also contributes to a hierarchy among residents and tension resulting from being in different places and with different perspectives. In addition, many of the staff members are former residents. These two factors mean there are always women at different stages in their reentry and recovery, which can lead to tension. Melvina also complained about women less dedicated to their recovery.

MELVINA: When the new girls come in, you know, and they act like they don't want no help. That bothers me.

AL: Does that happen often?

MELVINA: Well there's always going to be someone in the crew that don't want to act right.

AL: How do you respond to them? How do you respond when that happens?

MELVINA: Sometimes I just tell them just don't leave before the miracle happen. And then after that I don't say nothing else to them.

In addition, the group nature of the home meant living closely with others, so other residents might learn intimate and painful details of their lives. Women complained about other residents "knowing their business," and said they often would not say things in house-based groups because they did not want other residents to know. Some were more likely to open up in one-on-one sessions than in groups. Some sought out twelve-step groups that were off-site when possible.

These relationships and dynamics also are significant for the women who are working at the Mercy Home. The staff members serve as "professional exes" and value their role as positive role models for current residents (J. D. Brown 1991; Ebaugh 1988; Maruna 2001). It is in this role that they "carry the message" to others. Their offending and drug using pasts and desisting presents are meaningful and useful to serve as a model for newer residents. Although many of the staff members I interviewed had been working at the halfway house for a while at the time of the interviews, Dee Dee was a recent resident who was hired as a house manager during the interview period. She waited for several months to become eligible, as all of her fellow residents had to move out before she could be work there. The more established employees spoke confidently about themselves and their roles at the halfway house. In Dee Dee's case, I could see and hear about the impact that her new part-time position had on her. Dee Dee reflected on some of the things she had learned about herself and her job, such as setting boundaries and maintaining professionalism. For example, in the third interview, she said, "I get to work around people that are just like me. Trying to build they life. I don't have to feel intimidated. There are no big I's and little you's, you know, 'cause they teach me like I teach them, you know. At the beginning, I guess the transition of being a staff member instead of a resident, you know, I had some lessons to learn [laughs]. . . . I can take criticism today without taking it personally. You know, like I have done in the past. Because I've never held no job down, you know, so my professionalism, it's not good. You know, but I'm learning."

Dee Dee illustrates the tensions many former offenders and prisoners feel in trying to adjust to a mainstream lifestyle. She was then in her late thirties. In the past fifteen years, she had spent close to five years in prison (across several sentences); she had completed one year of college and had a limited work history. She was aware of her lack of professional experience and was intimidated about making inroads into mainstream life. In addition to the generative aspects of working at the halfway house, the job gave her a safe place to develop a work history and professionalism. Dee Dee was transitioning into her new role, in what she perceived as a safe place, and was gaining self-assurance as she did so. A similar pattern is seen among other former residents who work in the Mercy Home house or similar environments that allow them to be a "professional ex."

These transitions and the corresponding hierarchy of residents and staff are not always smooth. Occasionally a staff member gets involved in illegal activity. More commonly, residents perceive a sense of superiority from staff members or longer-term residents. Staff members are aware of this accusation, though they deny the intention. Andrea, for example, said her least favorite aspect of the halfway house was "Some of the attitudes of the staff. . . . Sometimes it's just the way they speak to you, the staff, talk down to you like it was nothing, you know." Dee Dee offered a common staff interpretation of this dynamic.

DEE DEE: You know, some people come here and they don't always comply with the program. They half-step and they do what they need to do just to get by. And I think a lot of them take for granted, because I am an ex-resident, that they can do things in my face and think I'm not supposed to do my job. So when I reprimand them in any kind of way, they take that personal and twist it around to say that I am picking on 'em, or that I don't like 'em or, you know, things like that, which I am not gonna even let them twist it up like that. You know, you doing something you had no business doing, and I'm just making you aware of it, 'cause you say you didn't know. Now you know, you know? And then they'll tell you a further step, "Well you don't have to say it like that." You know, how am I supposed to say it? I mean, I wasn't, I don't think I degraded anyone, you know. . . . I'm really not trying to make anyone's stay here worse than it has to be, or however they want to look at it, you know.

These tensions are closely tied to all of the women negotiating new senses of self. The interactions in the Mercy Home are an important way that both staff and residents re-create their identities and try out new aspects of their personalities. In addition, while the conditions are not like prison, the similarities do cause some women to resist the structure and other residents or staff. As former residents/staff members become more settled in their new roles, they may lose patience for the same behavior or attitudes that they may have engaged in as residents.

All of these conditions can lead to seemingly petty conflicts. For example, the specific incident that Dee Dee alludes to in the previous quote—and one for which she was tempted to call the police—was over what I saw as a fairly minor rule violation but that she saw as a sign of something more significant.

AL: So what exactly did she do?

DEE DEE: She used the staff bathroom. And my thing is, is that a lot of people still doing little slick and devious stuff, you know, and I have to be alert and watchful, and at some point, she got into that bathroom without me knowing, you know. So, if she did that, she done it sneaky, 'cause she had to get past me. So, now I'm like, I've gotta watch this lady. . . . I just think that when you come in here, you supposed to come in here because you ready to change who you are. If other people can comply, what makes you any different that you don't have to?

This sort of tension is heightened between residents and staff members who are former residents. The director said that while staff members occasionally have to raise their voices at residents, residents rarely disrespect administrative staff members, who are typically not former residents. Their social distance and "professional standing" affords them respect, whereas the former-resident staff members must earn respect. Former-resident staff members, however, walk a fine line between serving as positive role models and empathetic supports and "acting superior." Other women express similar tensions when they return to old neighborhoods and strive to maintain cordial, or even inspiring, relationships with others in their neighborhood who may be former drug associates and active drug users.

Defining and Achieving Success

The most basic measures of success at the Mercy Home are desisting from drug use and illegal activity, following house rules, and securing employment and a stable and safe place to live. Women who do this successfully graduate from the Mercy Home, usually in about six months. The women themselves typically see success as maintaining a crime- and drug-free life, but also achieving financial independence. Heidi summarized her goals: "Well, one of my goals is to get my GED. To stay sober. Two, I want to take up school and do a CNA [certified nursing assistant], but now they say you have to have a high school diploma or GED. . . . And I just want to live life on life terms because I came from a dysfunctional family and I don't know the meaning of life on life's terms, because every time I turned around there was some action some crime, some drinking and this and that and that's the way I lived my whole life." Heidi's goals were a combination of practical (education and career) and cognitive (living life on life's terms). "Living life on life's term" is a phrase learned in twelve-step programs and ties back to the ideas of "letting go and letting God" and taking responsibility for their actions. This also relates to their desire to live a "normal" life and accepting that normality. Similarly, the women stress the importance of appreciating small pleasures, remaining humble, and working hard.

The women were expected to accept their past and present realities, learn what "normal" life entails, and change their approach in order to achieve that normality. Figuring out what "normal" meant—and how to enjoy it—was one of the primary cognitive shifts the women were working toward. For many, normal meant having a job, being able to support themselves and their families, and shedding some of the stigma of their histories of offending, drug use, and criminal justice system involvement. Linnette said that she went to the Mercy Home because "I want to be a part of society instead of being looked at differently." Mary said that her goals included, "Stay clean and sober. And just live life like it's supposed to be lived. Because I've been out there so many years on drugs and alcohol to where I really felt that that was living." For many, that first meant figuring out how life was supposed to be lived, and what that meant for them. Danielle described a normal life; she strove for a "simple life, live like a normal person. That's right. Get up, go to work, come home, and enjoy it."

Although many strove to fit in with mainstream life, they often did not want or expect to "knife themselves off" from their offending pasts. As Lauren explained, that was also an important part of who she was, and one that shaped her ability to accept simple pleasures.

LAUREN: The most important experience that I have had would be building a relationship with my daughter. Raising my nephew. Being able to just learn how to be humble and appreciative. Being appreciative of life in general. I like to think that that was very important to me, to just wake up and, you know, just appreciate the day. You know, that the sun is shining. That there's leaves on the trees and some grass out there. Things that I just never, things that I've always, that I had always taken for granted. You know, just being humble about a situation. What's really most important is me looking at me and just understanding me and being grateful of who I am in spite of the things that I had to go through to get to this point. And I'm not gonna take anything away from the negativity of my life because I believe without those negative aspects, I probably wouldn't be able to appreciate life in general. You know, I wouldn't have a sudden respect for, you know, just interacting with others. So, some of the things that might be in my negativity—and I'm not, you know, I'm not proud of those things—they were life experiences. And they served a purpose in getting me to this point where I'm at now.

Lauren accepted her offending past as a meaningful part of who she then was. While she was careful to not glorify the "negative aspects" of her life, she accepted them as a necessary part of appreciating the simple things in life. Redefining success and a happy life allowed her to appreciate her relationships and simple pleasures.

The women's ability to construct a sense of success in manageable and achievable terms was important for their ability to navigate the challenges and the barriers they faced. Achieving some level of normalcy also meant that the women had to accept the mundane and tedious aspects of the life that had been held up as an ideal standard. In order to do so, they needed to redefine what was enjoyable or desirable about their lives, and to remember the difficulties of their previous lives. For those who had long histories of drug addiction, the latter was not difficult. As Danielle learned, life was much simpler and more mundane that she had previously thought. She said, "I realize that my life is, that this is just life. You go to work, you pay your bills, you make yourself comfortable in your house, you come in, you watch TV, you eat, you bathe, you go to bed and you get up and that's it, you know what I'm saying? And that's all life is supposed to be, to make yourself comfortable, happy, you know, content. And all this time, I don't know what I was looking for to make my life what I thought it was supposed to be, and wasn't doing nothing but screwing it. Now my life is so simple, and I'm happy."

When the women were asked what it would take for them to achieve their goals, they emphasized patience, persistence, and hard work. Winifred said, "Persistence, patience no matter how scary it gets don't give up and just believe I can do this—yeah, believe I can do it and resist temptations." They were taught to take a long view of their reentry, that they may have to build a new life over time. Sharon said that to reach her goals she would have to "just continue the path that I'm on. I'm working toward every one of the goals. It just takes some time." An important theme in their understandings of success was that success is based in their own efforts. As Shadd Maruna wrote, an "essential characteristic of the redemption script is the narrator's strong sense that he or she is in control of his or her destiny" (2001, 147). This is evident in the women's descriptions of their own anticipated paths to success. Very rarely did they mention structural barriers to success, such as employment restrictions or stigma against former prisoners, although these are often very real barriers. In part, this can be attributed to the relatively high level of resources and connections they received at the halfway house, but even more so to the narratives they learned about their own efficacy and the necessity of their own hard work and perseverance. In addition, they echoed the executive director's emphasis on the importance of self-esteem and confidence.

The women frequently used the phrase "stepping-stone" to describe their current housing, employment, or relationship situations and emphasized the need for patience in achieving their goals. This also reflected their experience in self-help groups, as they focused on reaching their goals "one day at a time" and developing a relationship with a "higher power." This framework allowed them to feel satisfied in the short term, in spite of limited employment or housing stability and relationships that were often in flux. The women aspired to accomplish mainstream success, including a career, custody of their children, and living in a stable and low-crime neighborhood. Early in their reentry, the women experienced many changes and felt a strong sense of accomplishment and momentum. Maintaining this patience and optimism over time, however, as they come up against structural barriers, was the source of frequent struggles and frustrations.

CONCLUSION

The Mercy Home provided the women shelter and connections to employment. Importantly, it also gave them a safe place to develop goals for the future and the confidence to work toward them. The Mercy Home, along with other treatment, provides a socio-cognitive blueprint through which the women understand their options and their possible futures. The narratives that the women learned at the Mercy Home were infused with self-help and twelve-step ideology. They were taught to become empowered by giving themselves over to a higher power. Doing so provided a framework and an expectation to be patient, in spite of the many challenges, barriers, and setbacks they face. It also encouraged humility, a common view of their problems, and a strong group identity. Much of their time at the Mercy Home was spent making a "moral inventory," sharing that with others at the house, and learning to interact with others in a new way. They were expected to take responsibility for their own behaviors, past and future. This also encouraged a sense of self-efficacy. In addition, many carried their "miracle" forward to others by mentoring newer residents and by becoming staff members at the Mercy Home.

Key twelve-step themes that were infused in the women's narratives are the importance of avoiding people, places, and things related to their offending and drug use, the importance of spirituality and God, and the value of peer support. Beyond explicitly twelve-step rhetoric, the women learned the importance of education for social mobility, the value of independence, and the need for patience and persistence in developing a successful post prison life. These themes taught the women what they could expect from their post-prison lives and shaped their own future goals. In this way, the Mercy Home encouraged replacement selves, but sometimes in ways that were structurally difficult for them to accomplish, especially outside the halfway house support system. As Adena said, "Anything is possible when you're in the Mercy Home." Once they leave the halfway house they must develop new expectations. In the chapters that follow, I show how the women negotiated what they learned at the halfway house within the broader context of their lives.

CHAPTER 2

Introducing the Women and
Their Pathways to Offending

ALTHOUGH THERE IS CONSIDERABLE diversity in the experiences of women in this study, in important ways they represent those who are most affected by incarceration today. Like male prisoners, female prisoners are disproportionately poor, African American, and from disadvantaged urban communities (Richie 2001). A majority of female prisoners have children, and they often are stigmatized not only because of their offending and incarceration histories but also for being "bad women" and "bad mothers" (Flavin 2001; Greenfield and Snell 1999; Owen 1998). Female prisoners have high rates of drug use and drug addiction, and women have been particularly hard hit by the War on Drugs (Chesney-Lind 2002). They also tend to have even more limited work histories than male prisoners (Greenfield and Snell 1999). All of these trends were prevalent among the women in this study. This chapter provides a basic overview and description of the women who formed the core of the study, and the lives that led to their stay at the Mercy Home.

The pathways perspective argues that gender matters significantly in shaping criminality and that women's criminality is often based on survival of abuse, poverty, and substance abuse (Bloom, Owen, and Covington 2004; Chesney-Lind 1997; S. Covington 2003; Owen 1998; Richie 2001). In addition, women's incarceration has been shaped by policies related to the War on Drugs, welfare reform, and public housing that disproportionately affect drug-using women (Bloom, Owen, and Covington 2004). There were two common pathways to offending among these women. Many experienced a childhood and early adulthood characterized by abuse and addiction. Histories of family dysfunction, substance use, criminal activity and incarceration, material disadvantage, abuse, and violence were all common in their childhoods and young adulthoods and were often closely connected to their own substance use and offending histories. Another common pathway was for the women's offending to follow drug use that began casually but developed into addiction over time. Once the addiction was entrenched, these women began engaging in criminal activity to support their drug use and to compensate for their increasing difficulty maintaining employment. These women typically came from less disadvantaged or traumatic backgrounds and were often still embedded in neighborhoods and friendship circles in which drugs were widespread and available. In a few cases, the women's incarceration was a result of an isolated incident rather than a lifestyle that included a pattern of substance use and criminal activity.

Demographic Overview

By virtue of making the choice to go to the Mercy Home, all of the women in this study demonstrated a commitment to "going straight" and changing the aspects of their lives that led to criminal justice system involvement. Most of the women were from the neighborhoods in Chicago with the greatest concentration of crime, incarceration, and prisoner reentry (La Vigne et al. 2003; Sampson and Loeffler 2010), though a few were from outside Chicago and/or from middle-class communities. Most were African American; a few were white or Latina. The women ranged in age from twenty-eight to fifty-seven years old. Most had children; just over half had children under the age of eighteen.

Most of the women had extensive histories of criminal and criminal justice system involvement. About a third of the women had been incarcerated on drug-related charges, three-quarters self-reported drug-related offenses, and almost all reported drug use. Many others were convicted of offenses like theft and forgery that they committed in support of a drug addiction. They had served an average of 40.5 months in prison across 2.5 sentences. Three women had never been incarcerated but had served time on probation, and a few had served lengthy sentences of ten or more years. Nearly two-thirds reported having spent time in a city or county jail five or more times (see appendix A for descriptive tables).

Family "Dysfunction"

Drug use, criminal activity, and violence were common in the households in which these women grew up. For example, nearly half of the women reported drug or excessive alcohol use among their family members, and about a third of the respondents reported physical and/or sexual abuse by family members while they were growing up. Most often, this was abuse by fathers or stepfathers, though occasionally by other (most often male) relatives. An additional 15 percent reported witnessing the abuse of their mother by their father or stepfather, though they themselves were not abused. It also was common for the women to have no relationship with their fathers, with 15 percent having little to no contact with them throughout their lives, either not knowing who they were or meeting them only briefly in adulthood. Several of their fathers were imprisoned for long periods.

Bennie's story follows a common female pathway into delinquency. At the time of the interviews, she was a forty-eight year-old African American woman living with her husband of twenty-five years, Joe. When she was born, her mother "went insane" and she and her siblings lived with her grandmother and an aunt. After a fire, when Bennie was seven years old, her grandmother and aunt were no longer able to care for her and her youngest brother.

BENNIE: And I went to the Audy Home[1] and then I went to a foster home and then I went to another foster home. Stay in 'em for about a year, if you're not beat up or badgered or molested at it. Then I went to another one. Then I went to another one. Then I went to another one [laughs]. You don't know. And then I went to a boarding school, the Rockford Children's Home. Then I got, I was, must been about ten, or going on eleven, or eleven, or something like, then I went there and got brutally raped. Then I got on a bus, or the man who raped me put me on a bus, and I was to Chicago and I was [at the] bus, the Greyhound bus station, soaked in blood and a policeman came and got me and they tried to find out who I was and where I came from, la, la, la, la. And they managed to find my sister, who I went to live with. Then I lived with her. And she further abused me [laughs]. Used me and abused me. And that's when I met the man, you know. But, in the process I was educated. I went to school. I made good grades. I wasn't a bad person. I just had bad circumstances and I was a good, decent child who just had, who was cursed [laughs]. You know, so, and then, and then after that you learn, you know, you survive and you adapt and you try not to shut down and you just thank God for, you know, keeping you strong. So, that's, that's the tale of my two cities.

The "man" that Bennie refers to is her oldest child's father, through whom she became involved with criminal activity. Earlier in the interview, she described her initiation into criminal involvement.

BENNIE: I ran away from home. I was probably about sixteen. Well, you know, I came up in boarding school and foster homes, so . . . but, you know, it was, it was, you know, you can, you can, even though people have to go through that type of upbringing there's still a light in the tunnel and you can survive that. Many people have. But, when I got back with my family after a traumatic incident, I got back with my family; well, my sister anyway, I was looking for love in all the wrong places. I gotta put it like that. He was, he was what was behind door number one and that's what I got, so. What I interpreted to be love was, was a cruel deception of it. So, with that came everything on the dark side. And I got familiar and acquainted with it. So.

AL: How did you feel about that when you first started getting involved with illegal activity?

BENNIE: I thought it was the thing to do. You know, I was, I was recruited. I was in it for the long haul. I was in it for eleven years. It became a way of life and I didn't know anything different. I didn't desire anything different. You know, I was true, loyal, dedicated to it and I learned it from backwards, up, down, sideways and around the corner [laughs]. So, and he was a darn good teacher. May he rest in peace wherever the hell he at [laughs].

Through him, she learned "robbery, prostitution, drugs—taking, selling. Stealing, scamming, conning." After he was incarcerated, she "was just an outlaw by myself. And I discovered I didn't need nobody. And I was self-sufficient. I, you know, I can do everything and anything alone. So, that's what I did for some years. And I was quite successful at it [laughs]."

Bennie's story has many of the aspects of a gendered pathway into offending. She experienced a traumatic childhood, with multiple experiences being abused and raped. She ran away to escape this violence, several times, and eventually got involved in criminal activity through a boyfriend. She stayed involved in street life, drug use, and offending, though over time she gained independence from her oldest child's father. Bennie was careful to take responsibility for her actions. She described her family as "mildly dysfunctional" and emphasized that many people who experience similar traumas do not get involved in criminal activity. Although her boyfriend taught her criminal skills, she was committed to the lifestyle at the time. Still, she separated her actions and her criminal lifestyle from her core self as a "good, decent child who was cursed" (Maruna 2001). When she went to the Mercy Home years later, she was able to "reacquire some of my good attributes."

Other women had similar experiences of abuse, responding to that abuse by running away, then getting involved in illegal activity. For example, Sugar was a thirty-one-year-old white woman who had been involved with the criminal justice system for the past decade. While Sugar first attributed her criminal activity to her drug addiction, she then traced it back further, to shoplifting in early childhood. She lived with her stepfather after her mother left when Sugar was seven. She described her childhood:

AL: What do you remember most clearly from your childhood?
SUGAR: Him, him [her stepfather]. That's what I remember the most. He used to beat me all the time. He never sexually abused me, but it was emotional and physical. I was terrified through my whole childhood . . . terrified and miserable.
AL: After your mom left, did you see her at all?
SUGAR: Ah, occasionally. No, let me see. When I was like thirteen, I think, and my babysitter helped me find her. And then when I found her it lasted maybe two or three months, and she just was not, I was always the one

putting all the effort into it, like meeting her, and coming to her house and calling her and stuff like that. She would tell me, "Oh I'm gonna go and get custody of you," and she never did any of that. And after a while, after always trying so hard, I was only thirteen you know, I kinda got the hint she didn't want to see me, so I just stopped. Then I got ahold of her again when I was, maybe a year or two later, I called her. I had ran away, and I was crying and I wanted to come and live with her, she told me no. . . . I think that she just didn't want me in her life at all. There was no, she never put forth any effort ever, it was always me.

AL: So how did you end up going to foster homes?

SUGAR: My stepdad, like I said, he beat me all the time, and one time when I was eleven years old, I finally got tired of it, and he had thrown me through the window in the door, and he left to go get new glass for the window and I ran next door to the neighbors and told 'em. So they called whoever they call. I think they knew. My neighbors were a bit old, I used to go over there a lot with 'em, on both sides of me. I think they knew something, you know, but I don't know . . . that especially, it was like twenty years ago, they don't like to get involved. 'Cause that night they were scared, even when I ran over there they were scared that he was gonna come over there and do something, so.

AL: Then after you left there did you have any contact with him?

SUGAR: Yeah. Yup, it was sporadic. For a while there I didn't want anything to do with him, and then, well I ended up going to live with his sister. 'Cause see, his family is the only family I knew . . .

Sugar began shoplifting at age five, because her stepfather "was just a real ass, he never let me have anything." She ran away as a teenager, and "wrote some bad checks, on my own, like just to do it, 'cause I wanted stuff." She began using cocaine at age seventeen with friends and had been drinking alcohol prior to that. She first used heroin ten years later with a woman she had met in a drug rehabilitation program. Her offending increased during her period of addiction. "Everything that I have done has stemmed from either being drunk, high, or trying to get money to get high." Sugar primarily attributed her offending and incarceration history to her drug abuse. She did not link this directly to her abusive childhood but rather to the influence of friends. Still, she did attribute much of her early offending and delinquency, including running away, to the abuse and neglect she experienced from her parents.

Often, one or both of the women's parents was a problem drinker, drug user, or drug seller. Commonly, the women witnessed drug or heavy alcohol use by their parents. In some cases, the women ended up using the same drugs as their parents, occasionally stealing it from them. Other times, they purposely avoided those particular substances because of the problems their parents endured but used other drugs instead. For example, Heidi was a twenty-eight-year-old African American woman and mother of four. She had recently been released from her only incarceration for a Class X felony drug-related charge.[2] She went to the Mercy Home because her mother had been a resident several years earlier and continued to do well. Heidi's mother, aunt, and other relatives used cocaine and heroin, "because I ain't never used no dope or no cocaine and that's due to them, my family members. My auntie and them, they used to use crack cocaine and heroin. The only reason why I didn't use." Heidi did, however, drink alcohol heavily, beginning at age thirteen.

In many cases, the women's parents were troubled with abusive relationships, drug use, and incarceration and they often lived in high-crime neighborhoods in which drug use, gang activity, and violence were common. Sharon, a thirty-four-year-old African American woman who had spent nine months incarcerated after receiving a new charge while on probation, described her home environment as "dysfunctional." She was in her twenties when she first began using heroin and cocaine, "Every drug or alcohol. Everything I ever used I was introduced to by a family member." She also was involved in a gang during her teen years. "Basically, it was like, mostly my family was involved in gangs. So it was like, you know, a family kind of thing. I can remember carrying guns. We had a lot of gang fights—more like family fights. Basically that's it. I was less involved than other people were because I was younger." She first started engaging in illegal activity "as a ways and means to get money to use drugs. Support my family, you know, because my children always have been in my custody. Helping family members." Both she and her family members saw this as acceptable, "because they were all dysfunctional and doing the same thing." Sharon's mother had been in an abusive relationship with her stepfather and had used drugs, Sharon estimated, at least from the time that Sharon and her brothers were teenagers.

Sharon did not know her father until her teen years. Her relationship with her mother was strained, because of her mother's drug use and abusive relationship, and the effects these had on Sharon's childhood, and because her mother kept information about her father from her.

AL: What do you like least about your life until this point?

SHARON: Not having a closer relationship with my mother. It started out close, then it ended up real distant. Not really having the opportunity to know my father.

AL: Did you ever know your father?

SHARON: Yes. Later on in my life, after the age of sixteen. He was in the penitentiary, which is something that was kept from me for years. Then when I found out the truth I started going and visiting him in the prison system. He did quite a few years behind bars and we developed a relationship with him behind bars and, after I had kids, you know, I used to take my kids to visit him. But that was the relationship we had, and it was, you know, behind bars. Then when he came home, he died about two years after he came home.

AL: Then what happened?

SHARON: I held resentments against my mother because all those years that they didn't tell me. I felt like whatever had happened with them or in his life or what they were trying to keep from me, I felt like at some point I should have been told the truth.

AL: How did you find out the truth?

SHARON: Actually, I had got into a pretty bad fight, where I got stabbed several times, and I was in the hospital. I guess he had heard about it, you know, in the penitentiary, and he sent a letter to my mom. . . . Sitting in my room one day, and she came in and handed me a letter, and then I started reading and I found out. At first I didn't know what to do; I was okay, okay, what's this about. She never communicated much to me about the situation, so I took it upon myself because I was at the age where, you know, I could do some things myself. I made contact with him, and I made contact with his family, and that's how our relationship really started.

Despite their difficult childhood, her younger brother Samuel said he was surprised when he first learned that Sharon was involved with illegal activity. He said, "She was so smart, a straight-A student. She stayed in school, and had a real ambitious attitude." When he found out she was involved with illegal activity, he "couldn't believe it. It wasn't her type of situation, her type of crowd . . . I was shocked. I didn't want to accept it, for her to go that route, to have an 'X' on her back, and be marked." Samuel also had a history of drug use and illegal activity, and he had been incarcerated four times. According to Samuel, he and Sharon had occasionally used drugs together but did not commit any offenses together.

The women also were exposed to drug and alcohol use and offending through their own generation, either siblings or cousins. This often goes hand in hand with parental drug use and offending. For example, Tasha, a thirty-two-year-old African American woman who had first been incarcerated at age twenty-one, explained that a cousin first exposed her to shoplifting and drug use, and she in turn exposed her younger cousin, Sarah. Sarah said, "Coming from a poor family, her mom didn't have much. Tasha wanted nice clothes, and so began stealing. She turned me out. I didn't steal till we started hanging out. It was a rush for me, like getting high." While Tasha "turned out" Sarah, and the cousins frequently offended together, both she and Sarah also talked extensively about the problems in their families growing up. Tasha's father was incarcerated at the time of the interviews. Tasha also had a volatile relationship with her mother, Ms. Lewis, whom she accused of emotional abuse. Ms. Lewis considered herself a good influence, though Tasha's father, his family, and Tasha's boyfriends were all bad influences. When I asked Ms. Lewis about things she had done or could do to help Tasha, she said that she could "keep her from her father's family. There are some bad apples there."

Still, Tasha's mother said she was a good kid and she was "upset" when she learned about teenaged Tasha's illegal activity. She said, "I talked to her about it and told her things that she was involved in wasn't right." Tasha described her mother's reaction when she first saw Tasha bringing stolen clothing into their house, "She used to always tell me I was going to jail. That I was gonna wind up going to jail. I was gonna be like my daddy, 'cause he used to go to jail all the time." Her cousin Sarah was also upset, though for more personal reasons: "It just, like, mainly was trying to tell me something. You know, if I didn't stop, because even though she was in jail, I still was stealing. You know, trying to get away with stuff. That used to be always in the back of my mind. I was, if I get caught, I could be there too. I was just trying to make a different plan about how I was gonna go about doing something to keep from going to prison. But it didn't stop me." Neither Tasha nor Sarah was particularly concerned with getting arrested as juveniles. As Tasha said, "When I was a minor, I didn't even care, you know. 'Cause I knew that, I was like, back then, when you was a minor and you got caught stealing they didn't really didn't do much to you. They just call, you go to jail and your parents had to come and pick you up." They were, however, more concerned with adult incarceration.

Tasha described her relationship with her cousin Sarah: "We are real close. We have a lot of similarities. Her father and my father are brothers. Her father doesn't know how to be a father. Her mother used to be in and out of the penitentiary. We can relate on the parent perspective." All of Tasha's cousins have been to prison, though they are "not trying to go back." Sarah also said that many of her aunts, uncles (including Tasha's father), her own parents, and other relatives have been involved with illegal activity in the past and present. Sarah explained Tasha's childhood: "Her mother was in a lot of abusive relationships. . . . Her father was in and out of jail. She's the type who wanted to be grown early, and if she wouldn't abide by her mother's rules, she'd leave." Sarah's father molested her and her brother when they were children; both her parents were in and out of jail. Several of Sarah's siblings had drug problems, and several had no contact with either of their parents. Sarah also talked about several examples of incestuous relationships among her relatives, much of which she attributed to their drug use.

Aspects of these stories were quite common. While in some ways Heidi resisted her parents' behaviors, many of these women developed lifestyles similar to those of their parents, cousins, and siblings. This was by no means guaranteed, as some siblings and cousins avoided this and lived mainstream and law-abiding lives, but drug use, violence, and criminal activity were normative in many of the women's families and neighborhoods when they were growing up. Narratives of abuse, violence, and addiction were all common, and, for many, their offending was, at least in part, a reaction to the violence they experienced or witnessed in their homes (Chesney-Lind 1997; 2002). The "dysfunction" they experienced at home led them to "want to be grown early," leading to rebellion, drug use, and offending. It was common, especially among cross-sex siblings or cousins, to not use drugs or offend together, even when they were aware of the behavior of the other. Rather, offending and drug use most commonly happened in same-sex groups of family and friends, or with romantic partners.

DRUG EXPERIMENTATION

While experiences of abuse and victimization were common among these women, they were not universal. Many talked about good and stable childhoods and did not reveal abusive or traumatic experiences from this time in their lives. Nearly a third of the respondents reported first being exposed to and experimenting with drugs with their friends, consistent with differential association and other network-based theories of offending (Haynie 2001; Haynie and Payne 2006; Matsueda and Heimer 1987; Sutherland 1947). These women reported common drug use among their peer groups, and a resulting curiosity. For these women, the experimentation eventually crossed into addiction, which led to additional problems, including difficulty maintaining employment, problems in social relationships, offending, and incarceration. The experiences of Shorty D and Lauren, described in the introduction, are consistent with this pathway. Both emphasized the bad choices they made as adults, and stressed that their home life—in spite of drug use among several siblings—was good.

Cousins Sheila and Adena's experiences also illustrate this pathway. Sheila and Adena were African American, both in their late forties, and had each served approximately two years in prison. By all accounts, Sheila and Adena came from good and stable homes. Adena's parents now owned several buildings on the West Side of Chicago, and she "had everything" growing up. She grew up in the ABLA homes, a public housing development in Chicago, until the family moved to their current house on the West Side when Adena was fourteen years old. When asked what she remembered most about her childhood, she said, "having to go to church. My parents didn't play; education was a priority. I had both my parents—a lot of my friends didn't. There was a lot they could get away with that I couldn't." Similarly, Sheila said, "My upbringing was real good. My mom raised me right, with morals, standards, church. My upbringing didn't put me where I am. . . . I am a high school graduate;

I come from a large family and was the third to graduate. I went to summer camps, the Boys and Girls Club. . . . I did it to myself when grown." Sheila also grew up in the ABLA homes. "It was fine. We were in row houses. We respected our parents. There was grass. We slept outside in lawn chairs and left the doors open." Her parents divorced when she was a child, but her grand-mother lived next door, and her mother kept her involved in activities. Their cousin Joanne described Adena and Sheila as having a "good background. It shows it could happen to anyone."

Sheila began experimenting with drugs in her late teens.

SHEILA: Well, I was like nineteen, twenty years old. It's something I did on my own. I wanted to try it. It wasn't like somebody influenced me or nothing like that. I actually went and got it, purchased it myself. I wanted to try it.

AL: What made you want to try it?

SHEILA: I wanted to see what was the high like.

AL: How did you know what you were looking for?

SHEILA: That's it, I didn't [laughs]. I actually didn't because I started off tooting cocaine 'cause, well my girlfriends, and they were tooting it, and telling me it just made them feel so good and relaxed, but when I tooted it and stuff and it didn't make me feel the way they feel. So basically I left it alone until I heard about freebasing, then I went back to the cocaine. So, I can smoke it, I liked the effect that it gave me by smoking it much better than tooting.

While Sheila did not feel pressured into drug use, she had friends who used cocaine, which influenced which drug and method of administration she initially chose.

For many years, Sheila continued to work until "basically I started doing real crazy stuff like after fifteen years I was into my addiction." By this point, she had two children, and her relatives tried to intervene. Sheila attributed one change in her drug use and offending to the deaths of her abusive common-law husband and her mother. She said, "I think that basically I grew wild because he was gone, I didn't have to worry about the threat of him looking over my shoulder, nothin' like that. Then my mother was gone, so I was like basically I ain't gotta get clean, I ain't gotta answer to nobody no more, my mamma's gone too. So I started just really runnin' wild out on the streets." Sheila first went to prison in the late 1990s at the age of forty-four, several years after she "grew wild" and approximately twenty-five years into her drug use. Over the next several years, she served time on three charges for a total of twenty-eight months. After her third sentence, she came to the Mercy Home.

Adena's young adulthood developed much like her cousin Sheila's. She earned an associate's degree and then married and had several children. She explained the development of her drug use:

ADENA: [I first used heroin] with some friends, some girlfriends of mine. Yeah, that was about 1980, '81, something like that. Yeah, I had a girlfriend that would snort heroin and I used to always go around her and her friends. She's dead now. I started using with them.

AL: And so how old were you then?

ADENA: I'm forty-eight now, maybe like twenty-eight, twenty-nine, something like that. And it was just, like, occasional use then. I had, my babies were small, so I stopped because I did have, I stopped because of my children, you know. After they grew up, well, after my oldest one was sixteen, she was about fourteen. I was kind of going through changes with my marriage, that's when my disease progressed. That's when I got a habit. I gave up, I just stopped caring.

AL: What was going on in your marriage at that time?

ADENA: Well, me and my husband just didn't see eye to eye on things. He was, you know, cheating on me, stuff like that. Yeah, wasn't spending no time with me and the kids. Because I always just wanted to get married and have children, you know, I was one of those types of girls.

As with Sheila, Adena's drug use began casually, with friends, and continued for years before it became more serious and led to additional criminal activity. Also like Sheila, she attributed a shift in her drug using behavior to a stressor in her life. In Adena's case, this was a conflict in her marriage.

ADENA: It [other criminal activity] started when I first started with my addiction, not when I first started, but the second time, when I really got heavy into my addiction. This girl I used to get high with, she used to steal and she showed me the tricks of the trade. You know the first time I ever went to the penitentiary I was thirty-nine years old, in 1995.

AL: So how old were you when you feel that the addiction really—

ADENA: Really progressed? Started getting bad? Like maybe thirty-one, thirty-two.

AL: Okay, so there were, like, several years—

ADENA: Yeah because I was just like a recreational, a recreational user. Yeah. Maybe like once a month or if I go out or something like that. Yeah. And I, because of therapy and stuff, I understand when I crossed that line, at what point I crossed that line, you know. You know, you just look up one day and you there, you know.

Adena's mother, Ms. Banks, was shocked when she first learned of Adena's drug use. She said, "Oh, I went crazy. Oh geez. I couldn't believe, you know, how you in denial. I couldn't believe it. . . . Oh that killed me." Adena's parents were married, both worked, and they sent Adena to summer camp and

Catholic school as a child. At the same time, in their neighborhood, they experienced white flight, neighborhood decline, and an influx of drugs.

Sheila and Adena's experiences were common in several ways. First, their drug use started independently of romantic relationships, family, and trauma, and it began with several years of occasional or casual use. While they may not have been in a family with widespread drug use, they did have friends who used drugs and gave them the initial idea to try a particular drug. They did not feel pressured to use the drugs, but their friends' use gave them an idea of what to do and what to expect (Becker 1963). Then, their use escalated; they attributed this escalation to a response to personal trauma. The escalation led to additional offending to support their drug use and their families, and to eventual incarceration. The progression from initial use to first incarceration might span fifteen or twenty years. It also was common among these women for drug use to begin relatively late in life, in their twenties or thirties.

Another common theme in these narratives is the women's agency in choosing to use drugs. While they were exposed to drug use through many people in their social circles, they initiated the use. The people around them influenced what drugs they had access to and what methods of administration they chose. While not overly pressured to use drugs, Lisa D, a forty-six-year-old African American woman, described an indirect peer pressure. She said, "And I wasn't raised that way and that was the thing that hit like a ton of bricks. You know, I was not raised—. Those were choices I made. It wasn't like I came from a dysfunctional family and I lived in this neighborhood and that. It didn't happen like that. I made a bunch of bad choices trying to be a part of a crowd and for what? I paid a heck of a price for it." Lisa D served two sentences in prison, beginning at age thirty-eight. She denied both negative influences from her family and neighborhood context. Both of these as explanations for drug use or criminal involvement are prevalent, in academic and popular discourse, and in the treatment narratives she heard in prison, drug treatment, and the Mercy Home. Likewise, Shorty D, who first went to prison at age thirty-six, described her childhood as "not a bad childhood; I made bad decisions." She was exposed to drug use through her siblings, friends, and acquaintances, though she began using cocaine and heroin through curiosity and mistaken knowledge of the effects. She first began using cocaine in her mid-twenties, followed by heroin a few years later.

SHORTY D: First, I had smoked cocaine. My first son's father's sister used to snort cocaine. . . . Then my older brother he used to have cocaine, he had it cooked. . . . And I asked him could I have a snort and he had a hundred dollars of the stuff and he wouldn't give me a line to snort. I wanted to use it, I had to do it the way he did it, and I was smoking it, you know.

So, that's how I got interested in smoking cocaine. Okay, now as far as the heroin, I knew people that used to do heroin. And the ones that used to do heroin, it seemed like they was more manageable than the ones that did cocaine as far as they kept their appearance up, they kept money, you know. Uh, they kept themselves up, you know. . . . My sister was using heroin, so I asked her could I have some heroin. It was cool for a long time, I was getting it free and it didn't take that much.

While many people around her were using drugs, Shorty D took the initiative to ask if she could try some. She learned about types of drugs, possible methods of administration, and the likely effects (some of which she later learned were inaccurate) from those around her. Based on this, she made conscious decisions to experiment.

Many women in these first two pathways share a history of drug addiction and other offending that is often tied to their drug addiction, though they differ in their pathways to that addiction. Women who experimented with drugs did not experience the levels of abuse, neglect, and trauma that most of the women in the first group did. Although some began using drugs at a young age, this did not lead to other offending or "criminal lifestyles" until much later. Some of the women experienced trauma later in their lives, which led to an escalation in drug use. Others slowly lost control over their lives as their drug use progressed into addiction. By the time they went to prison and the Mercy Home, their lifestyles often looked very similar to those who had experienced "family dysfunction," but they reached that point through different experiences and mechanisms. They also understood their own histories, criminal and otherwise, differently, and did not attribute any of their problems to early childhood difficulties, abuse, or victimization.

Isolated Offending

A consistent theme in both of the first two pathways into offending narratives is the role of drug use and drug addiction in the women's offending. Most of the women had a history of drug addiction and most of them directly connected their drug use and their offending. This is true regardless of why or how they initially began using drugs. For a few women, however, drug use was not an issue. Tammy, one of the women who introduced this book, had never used drugs or committed an illegal act until she committed murder. Hers was an unusual and extreme case. She described a happy early childhood, though she and her sister also talked about their father's abuse of their mother. She felt isolated and unheard, and said, "I couldn't get the help that I wanted or needed, so I took the law into my own hands." Her sister Kristen described the aftermath of her mother's disappearance.

KRISTEN: That's really all we needed was counseling and maybe she wouldn't never done what she did. . . . And Tammy just missed her so much and she wrote about it in her journal. . . . "Oh, I miss my mama." Every page, every day for years. "Oh, I want my mama to come home." So that built up in her. She held onto it. And that's the result. So, that's why I can have a relationship with her because I know, not know, believe, I know something was wrong with her. She didn't go out like normal teenage girls. She wasn't into makeup and all that stuff. She did go to school. She had As and Bs. She was into sports. But, she stayed in the house. She hardly ever went anywhere. Then she became like a mother to my other sister and brothers. She, those kids, they listened to her before they listened to my father. She's the one that made sure they did they homework. That their clothes was ready for school. She disciplined them. They had to do book reports every week and turn 'em in to her. She was, a lot of responsibility for a seventeen-year-old. And then let them tell it, oh I was the party girl. Yeah, I was the one that wanted to be outside. "Why can't you be like your sister?" And "you need to be more like her." And then it [the murder] happened. Ain't nobody have anything to say. And then what really bothered me is that everybody thought I was quote unquote wild and fast. You know what that mean, fast? You know? How we say that? When really I just didn't wanna be at home. Who wanna be in the house where the father's not speaking to the daughter and then there was a lot of favoritism. Lot of people don't talk about that. The younger sister and brothers got more stuff and better stuff and they just got treated better than we did. And I know why. It's because they couldn't and did not remember what he did and we did.

According to both their accounts, Tammy and Kristen's home life deteriorated after the disappearance of their mother. They felt their father favored their younger siblings, and they were upset by their mother's absence. Their response to this trauma was very different. In some ways, Kristen's response was more typical of female offenders as described in the pathways research. She rebelled, avoided being at home, and partied. Kristen said, "Oh yeah. I smoked cigarettes. I hung out late. I drank. I did things, you know. I was out there." She dropped out of high school, shoplifted, stayed on the street, and avoided being in her "dysfunctional" home. She had been arrested a few times, but never convicted and never incarcerated. In contrast, Tammy, the "good" and responsible daughter, served fourteen years for homicide. The trauma in her childhood did not lead to a pattern of delinquent or criminal behavior, but it did lead to a single violent incident.

While Carolyn admitted to long-term occasional and recreational heroin use, she rejected the idea that drug use led to her incarceration. She was an

African American woman in her fifties who had earned a master's degree and had a long professional career. In her late forties, she committed several armed robberies over a short span of time and went to prison as a result. She described her reasons as, "I went crazy . . . I was going through the menopause. I was having family problems. I was crying out for help." Like Tammy, Carolyn had experienced trauma prior to this offending. She was abused by her sister as a child and had been in a long-term emotionally abusive relationship with the father of one of her children. However, she maintained a long-lasting "mainstream" and largely law-abiding life; her offending did not form a long-term pattern, and the only connection she made between her history of abuse and her offending was the "family problems" she was experiencing in the time just before committing her crimes.

With both Tammy and Carolyn, there was a "cry for help." This did not form a pattern of behavior but did lead to isolated offenses. Their experiences fit most closely with the "square john" in John Irwin's criminal identity typology (Irwin 1970). Given the severity of the crimes committed, Tammy and Carolyn had to contend with the impact of incarceration, both in terms of socialization and the stigma associated with it, but less so with the barriers related to addiction and accompanying lifestyles that many of the women had to face.

CONCLUSION

Many of the women began or escalated their drug use as a result of trauma, often at the hands of family members. This is a common pathway into addiction and offending, particularly for girls and women. However, many also began drug use casually, with friends or family members. In most cases, they were widely exposed to drug use through friends, family, and community. Drug use was common and they learned about various drugs and reasons for trying them through these networks. Their drug use often continued for years before leading to addiction, interpersonal problems, additional offending, or criminal justice system involvement. Occasionally, the women did not exhibit a pattern of illegal behavior, but rather committed isolated offenses.

There is overlap in these sets of narratives. One primary distinguishing factor between the first two is how the women frame their childhoods, particularly in the level of chaos and "dysfunction" in their homes A second key difference is the level of responsibility they accept for their choices. Sometimes there are clear differences in the level of trauma they experienced, though sometimes it is primarily a difference in interpretation. Both Heidi and Shorty D, for example, talked about widespread drug use among family members. In Heidi's case, however, she frames hers as a "dysfunctional" home environment to which she responded with heavy alcohol use and gang involvement, while Shorty D talks about a happy home and bad choices on her part. Sheila and

Adena talk about happy, secure childhoods with stable role models, though they both grew up in public housing and in neighborhoods that were undergoing racial and economic changes. While they experienced some structural disadvantages, they did not see this as a meaningful part of their history. Sheila lived with an abusive romantic partner and Adena experienced significant strains in her marriage. These strains led to heightened drug use but did not initiate it. In many ways, Tammy and Carolyn were conventionally successful and did not exhibit patterns of offending before those offenses that led to their single incarcerations.

The pathways presented are typologies. Most of the women's experiences do not fit neatly into one box or the other, and they could be summarized differently than as presented here. Still, these three narratives of their pathways to offending illustrate commonalities and differences among these women. The focus on how they construct their pasts also illustrates how they understand their own experiences with offending and drug use, how their pasts connect to their criminal justice involvement, and their current efforts at reentry into the community and desistance from offending.

CHAPTER 3

A Year in the Life

EVOLVING PERSPECTIVES
ON REENTRY AND DESISTANCE

MOST CONTEMPORARY RESEARCH AGREES that desistance is a process, not a single moment in time in which someone switches from being an "offender" to an "ex-offender" or "non-offender."[1] Becoming a desisting offender often means deciding to go straight, not offending for a period of time, perhaps until hitting a roadblock, followed by a step back into offending, a new resolve to desist, perhaps another setback and a new resolve, and so on until one sustains a more extended period of desistance. In order to take seriously the idea of reentry and desistance as processes, not finite moments or single turning points, we must look at this process as people experience it. Most of the women in this project made great strides in the time I knew them, though their path to desistance was often not smooth. Many struggled, with relapses, wavering confidence, strained relationships, stalled efforts, and setbacks.

Desistance as a process is difficult to capture, so we are often left to measure it as though it were a moment in time. Repeated interviews, however, allow us to see it better as it unfolds. In this chapter, I look at how the women saw themselves, their attempts at desistance, and how these played out over time, including periods of relapse and renewed resolve. The focus in this chapter is on their first year or two out of prison, a time that is characterized by the most disruption and redefinition of self. Recidivism rates are highest in the first year (Langan and Levin 2002), and particularly among those who are trying to desist, the first year or two is a time of redefining who they are, what they want, and how to achieve their goals. The focus is on how the women spend their time, how their daily lives shape their sense of self and personal agency, and how these issues may contribute to drug relapse, future offending, and continued desistance. In this chapter, I focus primarily on the women's sense of self. In subsequent chapters, I shift focus to the women as social beings and how they negotiate relationships and social institutions.

With the first interviews, we begin to see how the women constructed their own reentry and plans for desistance. They would have to work hard, follow Mercy Home lessons, and through this effort they would be able to lead a "normal" life. This is a satisfying narrative, both for the women and for society, as it implies that the women have full responsibility for and control over their success. Looking only at a single point in time, we have relatively little evidence about whether they come to embody these narratives. By looking at them over period of time we can see whether they were able to enact some of the changes they hoped for, and to see how these experiences shaped their narratives.

Moving Out and Managing Life after the Mercy Home

Leaving the Mercy Home is a significant transition. Once they leave, more variation emerges in the women's daily patterns and they are left to structure their daily lives according to their own needs, responsibilities, and desires. The majority of women in this study received referrals, facilitated by the Mercy Home, to housing programs that provided them more independence yet were still recovery communities that provided rent subsidies and case management. Some continued with the jobs that they had while at the Mercy Home; others left or lost these jobs and sought new employment, and a few had health problems that prevented them from working. While those in subsidized programs continued to have group attendance requirements, they typically had more unstructured time than they had at the Mercy Home. This was a new challenge for many of the women as they worked to fill their days in productive ways. Some women remained extremely busy, juggling employment, often at great physical distance and for which they relied on complex systems of public transportation, with taking care of personal needs and reestablishing relationships.

The Mercy Home provides a stable but short-term first step outside of prison. Moving out was the next step in their developing sense of self and confidence, as they adjusted to increasing control over their lives. Still, most of the women moved into other subsidized housing programs: over half of the recent Mercy Home residents moved into single-room-occupancy (SRO) or subsidized apartment buildings and 14 percent moved to scattered-site apartments that were part of subsidized housing programs. Most of the units that were available to them were studio apartments, and the programs were typically designed to help adults out of homelessness. These programs provided another helpful stepping-stone for the women. They allowed more privacy and independence than the Mercy Home but still provided some programming and case management. They also provided an important financial cushion; rent was typically calculated at one-third of their income and accommodations could be made if the women were out of work. The terms of these programs varied by site; some were permanent housing while others had stricter time limits. The particular program in which the women were placed depended largely on availability at the time the woman was ready to move.

Nine of the women moved together into the Refuge Apartments, a newly opened development for homeless women with special needs (for example, HIV/AIDS, chemical dependency, mental illness), with approximately 30 percent of the units reserved for female former prisoners. The complex consisted of more than sixty single-room-occupancy apartments and half a dozen townhouses. Eight of the women moved into SRO units, while Sharon moved into a townhouse with her four children. The women remained significant members of each other's social circle, as they continued to live in close proximity and participate in groups and programming together. While many of the women maintained close ties with the Mercy Home and other residents, particularly in the early days after their release, the women who went to the Refuge Apartments had a particularly strong social connection. After living in the close confines of prison and the Mercy Home, they appreciated their increased privacy. Danielle said, laughing, "Oh God, I like it! I've never lived by myself, never! Never, ever in my life have I ever lived by myself and I'm loving it." She also appreciated the safety net of the case management but did not feel she was truly living independently. She was frustrated with what she saw as the overinvolvement of case managers. "I think I'd be more comfortable if they weren't so involved in my life." Still, she appreciated having her own apartment and greater control over her time.

Moving out of the Mercy Home also meant that some women had to confront fears they had about being on their own. One of their significant concerns, particularly among those not working, was boredom. Winifred got involved with volunteer work because she got "tired of watching TV twenty-four hours." She wanted to go back to school and to work in a paying job, though she was struggling with both. This boredom was not inconsequential.

WINIFRED: I been trying to stay away from a lot of things that'll, you know, that'll send me back to where I been, so. Other than that I just sit at home and watch television, sometimes with the neighbor.

AL: So, what sorts of things do you, are you trying to stay away from?

WINIFRED: People, places, and things.

For Winifred and for others with a history of drug addiction, being bored was not merely a matter of entertaining themselves. There was also a concern that boredom would lead to old patterns of behavior and might trigger a relapse. Even with the volunteer work, Winifred remained bored and frustrated with her life.

AL: So, what's been going on?

WINIFRED: Nothing. Bored half to death.

AL: Yeah?

WINIFRED: Yeah, I've been working [volunteering] for the Marillac House [a Vincentian social service center in Chicago] two days out of the week, and, uh, going to meetings and trying to get in school . . .

AL: So, what school do you want to go to?

WINIFRED: I wanna go to Roosevelt [University], but my scores ain't good enough.

Winifred continued to look for paid work, but she said that "I got kinda discouraged because every time I look there's nothing." She said she would continue to volunteer, which was financially possible because she also was receiving social security payments and because she was living at the Refuge Apartments. She paid a fixed portion of her income on rent, which was well below market rate. She wanted to work although it was not financially necessary at the time. Beyond occupying her time, Winifred wanted to feel productive and that she was living a meaningful life. She said, "I'm not doing anything. I'm not creating nothing . . . I would like to do something that's a rewarding day job." Winifred struggled to fill her time without work or school obligations; other women had similar concerns while working. For example, Tasha, who was working, said, "See, I don't have no kids, I'm not married, so I have a lot of quality time by myself. And to me sometimes when I be by myself, I feel like sometimes I can be boring."

EJ experienced both too little and too much free time over the course of the year. While still at the Mercy Home, she began working approximately thirty hours a week at a telemarketing firm in suburban Chicago and spent nearly three hours commuting each way on public transit. She did not like the job, but said, "It's something to help me get by for now." She planned to stay there until she found another job but did not have the time to look for another one and could not afford to take time off. She also was dealing with several significant health issues; she was diabetic and anemic and spent much of the year trying to arrange surgery to remove fibroids. This was delayed several times because of problems related to her other health conditions, like blood sugar levels and blood pressure. She also had recently been diagnosed with depression. She said, "As soon as I got sober, everything in my body started breaking down." EJ's debilitating health problems exacerbated the problems with the job itself. She said, "I can't be going to Buffalo Grove, I've got bleeding fibroids. By the time I'd get there I'd be flooded and have to go home and change. I'd spend more time in the restroom than working." As a resident of the Refuge Apartments, she was required to attend twelve-step meetings.

She found them helpful, but went "when I can fit them in." Since she was on parole, visiting her incarcerated son took additional accommodations. She had been trying to arrange to visit him for months. In January, she said, "Since July of last year, I've been trying to see my child, to get a pass to see him. She [her parole officer] never did it. Now he's at a work release center. I've left messages. I've left messages for her supervisor. I went over to her office and left a nasty note." By our third interview, her son had been released from prison; she had never been able to arrange to visit him while he was incarcerated.

After working at the telemarketing job for approximately five months, and three months after moving out of the Mercy Home, EJ quit the job in the suburbs. She said it was not worth the commute, and "it costs more than I bring in, with lunch." She worried about her health and being unemployed. She said, "I hate asking for something. My mom is on a fixed income. I learned through the years that if you have a man, and ask for money, he runs your life. My marriage was like that. I depend on no one but me, and God." Later, when asked if she was healthy enough to work, she said, "I have no choice. I am tired of asking my mom. She's on a fixed income. My husband will only help if I come back, and that ain't gonna happen." She continued to look for a new job, with the help of her Refuge Apartments case manager, job boards, and personal contacts. She said, "I am not healthy, but I am still looking. I have to. I am stuck. I have time on my hands, which is something I don't need."

The challenges faced by Winifred and EJ are common among these women as they adjusted to life on their own. If they had free time, they feared the effects that boredom would have on their attempts to avoid drug use. Those women who were working often faced long commutes on public transportation. Finding employment was difficult, and even more difficult if they wanted it to be fulfilling or well compensated. Many had significant physical and mental health issues, which were often both frustrating and time consuming. The women maintained a strong desire for independence, but they struggled to achieve it. Nearly all of them wanted to work and to be able to support themselves and their families financially. While they appreciated the supports they received, they wanted to be in a position to not need them. Coming to terms with some of these challenges and barriers was one thing many attempted to do in their first year out of prison.

FLUCTUATIONS IN SELF-PRESENTATION AND CONFIDENCE

Self-confidence is a key aspect of the cognitive changes that can lead to desistance. Desisters need to believe in the possibility of an alternative law abiding self and their ability to create such a self, often absent structural supports to do so (Giordano, Cernkovich, and Rudolph 2002; Maruna 2001). Once women left the Mercy Home, they had to face more of the daily struggles of being ex-prisoners and ex-offenders. Events and changing circumstances led to sometimes dramatic changes in their self-confidence and self-presentation, for both the better and the worse. The women who exhibited confidence felt that they were working toward something, and were proud of their accomplishments. When they hit stumbling blocks, they often experienced lost enthusiasm, confidence, and self-efficacy. Many prisoners are hopeful about their ability to take a different direction and change their lives when they are released. Many of those fail in their attempts once they face the significant barriers that ex-prisoners typically face. John Irwin (1970) wrote, "The impact of release is often dramatic. After months of anticipation, planning, and dreaming, the felon leaves the confined, routinized, slow-paced setting of the prison and steps into the "streets" as an adult-citizen. The problems of the first weeks are usually staggering and sometimes insurmountable. Becoming accustomed to the outside world, coping with parole, finding a good job—perhaps finding any job—and getting started toward a gratifying lifestyle are at least difficult and for many impossible" (107). Even the most well intentioned prisoners may falter when confronted with the reality of their lives, and many of the women faced such struggles and frustrations.

Many women were wary of their ability to get along or feel comfortable in mainstream life. This took many forms, from a sense of actual or anticipated social and physical isolation in suburban or middle-class communities to fears of working for some employers. Given the recent history of these women, this is not surprising. Most of them had lengthy histories of drug use and incarceration and a resulting distancing from mainstream life. They had to adjust to new people and new ways of living their lives, and the Mercy Home and transitional housing helped them ease into these changes. In addition, many had grown up and lived in highly segregated low-income African American communities. Staying at the Mercy Home gave these women a safe space, with people who understood and often shared significant aspects of their personal histories. This socialization helped many women gain confidence in their ability to fit in outside that environment and outside "street" life; this is one of the ways in which it was designed to be a stepping-stone for the women.

Mercy Home staff members encouraged and supported positive behavior and changes and contributed to increased self-assurance. Self-confidence also came from the very real successes they were experiencing; this led to visible and dramatic changes in self-presentation. For example, Dee Dee was hired as a part-time house manager between our first and second interview. The first time I interviewed her, she was not working. Field notes from the second interview described the changes I perceived in her once she started working at the Mercy Home: "She sounded confident and sure of herself, both in what she said and how she said it. Last time, I had gotten the sense that she was waiting for things to happen to her, and that didn't seem to be the case now, maybe because at least some things have been going her way."

By the second interview, she was working and going to school part time, and was enthusiastic about her experiences in both areas. Dee Dee's self confidence increased dramatically over the course of the year, and this was reflected in how she physically and verbally presented herself. In subsequent interviews, she was even more self-possessed and continued to reflect on some of the things she had learned about herself and her job, such as setting boundaries and maintaining professionalism. Dee Dee talked about how she had changed since living at and then working at the Mercy Home. In our fourth interview, she said, "I know in the past, my presentation of myself is intimidating and I work daily on it. I am well aware of what is going on with Dee Dee. Because I used to be prone to negativity and stuff like that. A lot of times things happen here, and my first reaction is sometimes to be, to do what I probably would have done a couple of years ago. But, I've also learned to think. And that's what the blessing is, because now I am able to think on my feet. Before I would kind of react, you know." The Mercy Home gave her a needed place to develop as a worker in ways that also would serve her well in other jobs. She was conscious of the changes in her approach and perspective, and in the changes she still needed to make.

In contrast, Erica's experience illustrates wavering confidence, even several years after her release. Erica was a thirty-three-year-old African American woman with two children. She had stayed at the Mercy Home several years before and had transitioned from there to a single-room-occupancy building. After three years in the SRO, she moved into an apartment though a program that subsidized the rent for women going to college. I was very impressed when I first met her; she was dynamic and involved, and she had excellent communication skills and self-presentation. In my field notes, I described her as "welcoming and friendly, and I liked her from the start." She believed she had changed since her last incarceration and her stay at the Mercy Home.

ERICA: Self-esteem wise. I had very low self-esteem from different issues in my childhood. I was able to grow and work through those events that happened in my life that made me want to use drugs or not want to deal with reality and what's going on in my life. I was able to work through those issues and get some self-esteem. I realized a lot of different things.

AL: What are some of the things you realized?

ERICA: I didn't realize that I could do what I'm doing today. I didn't realize that it was okay that my mother was a drug addict. You know, I didn't realize that it's okay if you're alone with no sister and brother. I realized that all that's okay, just don't get mad about it.

Erica's acceptance of her childhood and her drug addiction was a common expression of developing self-esteem among the women from the Mercy Home. They were taught to accept and to take responsibility for their pasts, but also to forgive themselves and their families for those pasts. They were careful to not blame others, but also to not stay mired in their pasts and their past mistakes. These things, including their drug use, addictions, offending, and victimization, had happened, but need not fully define them in the future. While many asserted this, they still struggled with insecurities about their pasts and their current status.

At the time I met her, Erica sat on the board of several social service agencies, including the Mercy Home. She had been laid off a few months before from a job as an outreach worker and court advocate. She had recently transferred to a four-year university from a community college. "I feel like I'm in kindergarten right now. . . . It's a big difference from a city college and a university. I just want to be able to sit in and do good, not disappoint myself and others. It makes me feel good when I get a B. It doesn't have to be an A. I feel good if I apply myself and get something out of the class." In the first interview, Erica was primarily focused on school. However, she did talk about her job experiences and goals.

AL: [Is] finding a job [a goal]?

ERICA: I want to say that's a problem because of the "X" that I have on my back. I'm limited in what I can do. So I have to be real careful with what I want to do in social work because that's basically where a lot of recovering people are.

AL: So you want to be in the social work field, or . . . ?

ERICA: I found a niche that I like in social work. I like HIV testing, health education, counseling for HIV-infected people. I've done some work in there. So I think I have a better niche in there besides substance abuse counseling. I think that that's my niche. I feel real comfortable with that.

While her goal was to work in HIV testing and counseling, she described herself as "real humble when it comes to working. I've had to work at McDonald's and working at the hotel. I didn't have a problem with none of that." Still, like many of the women, she made a distinction between a job and a career and aspired to the latter.

While Erica remained friendly over subsequent interviews, she also became more withdrawn. She described herself as "stressed" in the second interview and was becoming increasingly concerned about finding work. Her housing program paid her rent, but she was worried. "Money. Bills. [Laughs]. What's gonna get cut off." At the time of the interview, she had just found out that someone else had been hired for a position for which she had applied: "They chose someone that had more experience basically." At the same time, Erica was adjusting to her new university. She had begun college at a two-year school and had some difficulty transitioning to a university. Erica was enjoying her experience, though she also felt more comfortable around other nontraditional students. She said "It's getting better. I can tell that it's getting better. I noticed that too, in the daytime, a lot more teenagers go to college, so I'm, I'm better off going at night, too, 'cause I wasn't really comfortable in the daytime." More generally, she said that she struggled to feel comfortable around others who didn't share her background. "I think a lot of times when I'm interacting with a lot of different people that don't have the background and such that I do, I feel like they, I can't say anything or they can't, they're just not saying anything that relates to me. I, I just seem, sometimes it just comes like I got this big 'X' on my forehead and I know it's really not any different, but I just don't feel the same."

Self-doubt continued to plague Erica, particularly when she was faced with setbacks or with new "mainstream" experiences. During our third interview, she talked of distancing herself from others so as not to burden them. Erica felt isolated and depressed. She distanced herself from the Mercy Home, saying, "I just want to work and I feel like I'm all alone. . . . I think that I'm isolating myself because I, I go out, even when I go out to my daughters' it's like I stay gone. I never want my kids to see what I'm going through." Erica wondered aloud how she would be able to afford traveling to a new job until she got paid. When I asked if there was anyone who could help her with that, she acknowledged that one of the programs probably could. She also ended a romantic relationship during this time, because "I think that I ended it because of my self-esteem and me not having anything. I don't feel like it helps for a relationship for one person to take on everything, then I end up blaming the person for stuff that's going on. So it's not healthy right now, and there was not bitterness, it's just not healthy right now. My choice."

Erica felt as if she were failing, and she did not want to burden anyone else with her struggles. She was in a car accident prior to the third interview, which resulted in her missing several of her final exams. Her affect was flat during this interview, while she described her struggles with looking for work and her experiences in school. She was actively applying and interviewing for work in the field of HIV/AIDS prevention or casework. She felt her biggest barrier to a job in this field was her lack of a college degree. She said, "When they say, like, a master's degree is required, sometimes they say the bachelor's, I'll say well I have enough experience in life experience, so maybe they'll give me a chance." Many of the women depended on just such a chance being taken on them, and many of those who did succeed experienced such breaks. Erica's mindset changed from the first interview, in which she felt everything was going well and she was just experiencing a minor setback of a lost job—sure to be replaced soon—to approximately nine months later, when she was still unemployed, missing exams, and withdrawing from loved ones.

By the fourth interview, Erica had received the break she was hoping for, and her mood improved dramatically. In field notes after this interview, I wrote "She was friendly and all smiles. She said she is doing much better, and looks it. She was upbeat and had lost the melancholy that she had the last two times I had interviewed her. . . . Erica is polished, projects professionalism and friendliness." She told me immediately that she had a new job: "Have a job. I'm finally working. So much better. So not stressed like I was. It's good." She was working as an outreach worker for the Department of Children and Family Services–involved clients. She had heard about the opening from a friend, and enjoyed the work a lot, in part because she worked independently, without a lot of supervision. She was taking one evening course and was finishing the work on the incompletes she had received the previous semester. Although she was making less money than she had at her previous job, she was very happy with the change. She said, "So, it's a lot less then what I had gotten used to, but I think that I have a lot more peace and I'm able to get through my homework if I need to. So, it's very much laid back. And me and my coworkers, we communicate very well. So, that makes up for the difference, so if I had to be there late or whatever. Right now, the money's real good. I would take more if I could, for like, a part-time job, but I wouldn't leave this." This seemed to be a positive turning point for her and she was "getting back on track now."

Still, Erica felt that not having a degree and not having certification as a counselor was a limitation in her career, particularly in light of her criminal record. She wanted to get her certification not only to increase her marketability but also to give her credibility among her coworkers. In describing why getting the additional credential was important to her, she emphasized the perceived impact on her job prospects.

ERICA: What makes that important for me? Because it makes me more marketable [laughs]. It makes me more aware of the disease or addiction and dealing with the population that I deal with, you know. And also, it would not make my coworkers feel as though [laughs], 'cause I have a coworker already I could tell because she has a master's, a bachelor's, LDAC [licensed drug and alcohol counselor] that a lot of times—. And I had to tell, you know, . . . I've been at this some time. You know, even me. I have to look like, you know, I've been there. You know, I don't disclose a lot to them but I told her I had been to jail or whatever. And I said, sometimes I feel like, you know, you use that as a weight with me. You know, you're always checking me in. I've been here for, like, a month—this is when I had been there for, like, a month. And I need my job. But, I was like, so, I would appreciate it—[laughs]. So, that's like a little conflict.

Erica took a very instrumental view of her goal of being certified as a counselor. She continued to wrestle with the relative values of credentials and her own lived experience, and she hoped the former would lessen her perceived stigmatized status as an ex-prisoner. Getting a degree or certification would give her greater credibility with coworkers and would lessen the extent to which they could use her past as a "weight" against her.

The examples of both Dee Dee and Erica illustrate how fleeting and changeable one's confidence and resolve could be, particularly in the early days of reentry. Many prisoners and the newly released share Erica's early resolve and lose their confidence when faced by common challenges and roadblocks. At the same time, getting a break and experiencing successes can have dramatic positive effects on the sense of what one may achieve. Both Dee Dee and Erica had been released from prison relatively recently. Dee Dee had lived at the Mercy Home a few months before I began the interviews. Erica had lived at the Mercy Home roughly three years before. Those women who had been lived at the Mercy Home relatively recently were typically most active in their self-definition, and often were more influenced by successes and setbacks. So although people who had been out longer relayed extreme swings in their life histories as they first attempted to desist from offending and drug use, their lives in the present were fairly stable. Bennie had lived at the Mercy Home approximately seven years before. She still considered herself as evolving; she said, in our first interview, "I'm still feeling my way through that, you know, of everyday interaction with people, you know. My social skills. I'm still feeling my way through that, but it's improved tremendously through the years. I'm just a regular Joe-Ann." Her sense of self and her life were much more stable than many of the newer releasees, however, and than her own life in the 1990s.

TAKING THE LONG VIEW

A goal of both the Mercy Home and the transitional housing programs that the women often moved to next was to serve as a stepping-stone. They provided temporary support and guidance so the women could eventually support themselves with legal employment and remain drug- and crime-free. This was welcomed by most of the women. Danielle summarized her goals: "So, it's reestablishing myself, period. To being self-supporting all the way around because you don't have this place [the Mercy Home] anymore. So, I'm going to have to provide all that stuff on my own." Danielle, like most of the women, appreciated the help and security of the Mercy Home, but they also looked forward to a moment in which they could meet all of their needs on their own. In our second interview, Danielle described how she changed while at the Mercy Home. She said, "I can sit down now. I can actually stay in the house by myself. I used to couldn't do that. Always had to have somebody around me. I don't always have to be going somewhere, doing something, you know. It slowed me down a lot."

These ways of thinking extend beyond their time at the Mercy Home. In our last interview, Danielle described the shift in what she thought life should be. "Like I said, I'm a simple person, all I want to do is get up, go to work, come home and relax. I just want me a bigger place, I see myself in a bigger apartment. I see myself owning a vehicle, for sure, I love to ride. That's it, you know, I'm not looking for, I'm too old to be talking about going out there and looking for the perfect career, you know at this moment in my life, so you know I'm not looking for anything outstanding out there, you know, something simple. I just want a simple life, live like a normal person. That's right, get up, go to work, come home and enjoy it." Danielle, over time, adjusted her expectations and appreciated being on her own for the first time. This shift in perspective was not seamless. It required both changes in behavior and a redefinition of what a good life meant. Danielle talked about life with some wistfulness, not because she missed her old life, but because of the "simplicity" of her current life. She strove to embrace that her life now consisted of working, paying bills, and watching television. Those who wanted to avoid people, places, and things related to their offending and drug use had to replace them with something, or be faced with long stretches of unstructured time and boredom. In addition to these changes in behavior—staying off the streets, staying away from old acquaintances—they had to find enjoyment in the new behavior.

Many women credited the Mercy Home with allowing them the time and space to make the transition from street and prison to a straight life. For those who went on to work there, this continued after they moved out. But again, this was not a seamless transition for most. Many of the women struggled to maintain a "long view" of their recovery and to understand that achieving their goals was a long and fraught process. When asked what it would take to reach their goals, most of the women said something like Jeanette: "Patience, perseverance, to put one foot in front of the other. To help myself." Yet many struggled with this and became frustrated by and impatient with a perceived lack of positive change or independence.

Some realized, accepted, and appreciated the mundane aspects of their present and future life. Others experienced life at the Mercy Home and after as a holding pattern, in which they must wait for their "real" life to begin. Winifred continued to struggle with her perceived lack of independence. When she moved into a subsidized housing program following her stay the Mercy Home, she was frustrated with her inability to afford to live in private housing.

WINIFRED: Well, what made me want to live here was: the rent was cheap and my credit is so messed up. I don't think I would have gotten an apartment nowhere else, honestly. You know how they do the credit check and that kind of thing. I didn't want, I wanted to pay market rent. . . . You know I thought I would be paying market rent, you know doing the things normal people do. I'm tired of people taking care of me. You know, the help is nice, but it makes me feel like, you know, it takes something from me. It keeps you feeling strange. . . . It's like, I feel like that I'm not doing enough. You know, and you put that in your mind and it works out like that, but I feel like, you know, I need to work, I need to be able to pay market rent like normal people, you know be part of the in crowd, not part of the problem.

Winifred was then receiving social security and looking for work ("but I'm not putting the effort that I could or should put in.") She feared she was more "laid back" in her job search than she should be. Her goal was to find a data entry job, a change from her past work in hospitals. She was hoping the change in career path would help her commit to her job, unlike in the past: "If I get something like data entry, I'm pretty sure that it would keep me hanging in there, but if I go back to doing what I used to do I'm scared that it might . . . what I did in the past: not commit, you know, stay two or three months or six months and move on to another one like that, you know, the cycle continues, and I don't want to do that."

Winifred's biggest concern was "getting stuck in this spot." She struggled with considering the Mercy Home, the subsidized housing, and other less "independent" or successful aspects of her life as useful supports, rather than as signs she was not "normal." Her perspective parallels that of Dee Dee in our first interview, in that she lacked a sense of agency and control over her fate. In reflecting on a past stay in a subsidized housing program, Winifred said, "It was a stepping-stone, and I took it for an insult." She acknowledged the self-defeating nature of this thinking but continued to struggle with feeling helpless and dependent. Her career goals changed to working as a switchboard operator at a hotel. One thing that remained consistent across interviews was her fear of "getting stuck." In my field notes after the third interview, I wrote, "She seems interested in doing things, but lacks of the follow-through to make it happen. Each time I talk to her, she says she's afraid of getting stuck where she is, but she hasn't made much progress at moving herself along. . . . She has a plan, but doesn't make much progress at achieving it." She hated feeling dependent, but got discouraged when she did not find a job. In the fourth interview, she said, "I just get stuck in these apartments. It bothers me. I'm try-ing to do the best I can, but I just can't control myself: too much television, no friends, no male partner, you know, to go out on a date. It wears thin with me, but then sometimes it's very rewarding. I just don't want to feel like I'm missing anything. . . . I don't want to feel like I'm missing stuff. I know I'm missing a lot to me, but it's more fun if you can live it, you know?"

Adena had similar frustrations. "I had to find out what made me do what I did and it was really a lot of fears of not having to deal with what I needed to deal with while I was at the Mercy Home, you know, being an ex-offender at my age, jack-of-all-trades but master of none, you know, trying to find a job. . . . I try to understand why I did what I did. There was really a lot of shame. Shame kept me there for a minute." Adena described the Mercy Home as being "about sisterhood, you know, helping each other." She helped a few of the women, including Jeanette, move into properties owned by her parents. When Adena relapsed after leaving the Mercy Home, Jeanette was the first person she told.

ADENA: Like when I relapsed, she's really the first person I told, right? And she was like, "You know, we all had dreams when we were at the Mercy Home." But I said, "You know what, Jeanette? I still got mine. You know, it ain't over . . ."

AL: So, you said that she said you all had dreams when you were at the Mercy Home. What did she mean by that? What do you think she was saying?

ADENA: There's things we wanted to accomplish and do. See, that seven-month period when I was at the Mercy Home, I did more in that seven-month period than I had done the last ten years of my life, you know, because of my addiction and everything. . . . You know, we got what we needed to get but we're not the same as before and I think it's the same with her. But, like I said, I have those fears of my age, having a couple Xs on my back, not being able to find a job.

Having goals and dreams while in the safety of the Mercy Home and realizing those dreams while on their own were two very different things. The reverse of having time to reflect and make plans while at the Mercy Home is that they often did not have that luxury once they left. Adena, Erica, and other women faced significant challenges and barriers to success, which wore them down. In addition, many felt insecure about their abilities and the stigma they would likely face, and shame in the face of these setbacks. These insecurities and shame limited Adena's willingness to admit defeat or to ask for help.

This shame in facing a setback reflects many of the women's insecurities from the start. Many were afraid to be in Chicago, afraid because of their past setbacks and relapses, and afraid of their ability to meet the challenges they would face. Being at the Mercy Home was a reprieve from some of these fears. Most women internalized their fears. The women commonly cited the difficulty of finding a job with "an X on their back," but they also typically claimed personal responsibility for their failures and missteps. Winifred, for example, attributed her inability to find a job to not trying hard enough. On the one hand, this is a potentially useful perspective, as it emphasizes the woman's efficacy and control over her fate. This sense of efficacy, even in the face of real structural constraints, may make successful desistance more likely (Maruna 2001). In contrast, someone who feels the inevitability of his or her own failure has less incentive to try. The women were all attempting to desist, with varying levels of success. Through them, we see the consequences of their optimism and efficacy, fostered at the Mercy Home, coming up against repeated barriers.

Those women who were longer out of prison were often still working to stabilize their lives. Lauren, eight years after her Mercy Home stay, reflected on her own steps forward and back. "What I learned is that you have to start over at one time or another at some point in time in your recovery. And that's not to say that you have to relapse in order to start over. So, at this point in my recovery I've begun. I'm in the middle phase of the starting over, because I did the mess up thing with the financial aspect of it. The relationship aspect of the recovery. I've fought that off. So you learn, you live and move on. And I'm moving on, so. And, basically everything I've said, I'm in the midst of right now." Lauren had accepted, and many women experienced, that their recovery and desistance efforts would include mistakes, setbacks, and barriers. These setbacks may include drug use or offending, but they also may involve financial decisions, employment problems, or relationship strains. Most expected that they would make their own mistakes or not work hard enough. Others came up against, or feared, social stigma. When this happened, they needed to regain their footing, without letting shame or disappointment derail them.

RELAPSES

A very common setback among these women, and those struggling with addiction more broadly, was a relapse back into drug use. Many of the women had experienced relapses at various points in their histories, and several relapsed during the course of this study. In several cases, this was at least partly connected to their health struggles and the pressures of their reentry. Shorty D was the first person to tell me about a relapse, in our second interview.

SHORTY D: I was going through some changes with the relationship, with this guy here . . . because he was in recovery. And we was together for like seven months. And he fell off. And I should have quit him then, but I didn't. Then I started having problems with my nineteen-year-old son, and I got really stressed out, you know. And then I got slacking off on my meetings and stuff. . . . Had I put him outta my life, you know what I'm saying, I wouldn't have relapsed the day I relapsed, you know. I'm not saying it wouldn't never have happened, because by having it, it woulda kinda happened because I wasn't dealing with my problems very well, you know. After I relapsed and I went to a meeting, and it's like, you know, I had two years clean. And, um, they said stand up for your time, your clean time, and I couldn't stand up because I knew I had relapsed. And at the same time, I felt shame and guilty. But when I came home, here, to my house, I just prayed on it, you know, and I thought about it, you know what I'm saying? And do I want to do something about it, or do I want to hide behind the shame and guilt which is just gonna make everything worse, you know.

A few months later, Shorty D again used drugs, just once. She was one of the women who had moved into the Refuge Apartments, and first sought help from her case manager and then her twelve-step sponsor. The second time she relapsed, she was one of at least five former Mercy Home residents, all of whom had moved into the Refuge Apartments, to tell me about their own relapses.[2]

EJ was in her mid-forties and said she used to "drink as much beer as I could get" and "use as much [heroin] as money would allow for twenty-seven or twenty-eight years. That was my drug." In addition, she occasionally used cocaine. She had been to prison once and while at the Mercy Home was in recovery for the first time. She relapsed a little more than a year after her release from prison. She described this in our fourth interview:

AL: So, what's been going on?

EJ: I relapsed. I just got out of detox yesterday. It wasn't constant, but I didn't want it to lead to that.

AL: So, what happened? How did you end up relapsing?

EJ: Depression. I got tired. . . . First of all, I led me to relapse. I got tired of getting turned down, I got tired. My health is failing. I thought, I wasn't this sick when I was getting high.

AL: When did this happen? How long before you went into treatment?

EJ: Almost three months. I took a month to get into a place. I didn't use that much—a dime bag would last me two or three days. I kept calling, and kept calling. I hurt my mother real bad. . . .

AL: When you relapsed, did you go to the same place [to buy drugs] as you did before, or where did you go to get it?

EJ: No, I went someplace different. . . . I knew about it. I just had to catch the bus. I didn't want anyone to know that I was using. I knew where it was going to lead me. I didn't want that. I came too far to give up.

When EJ decided to get help, she called someone at the Mercy Home. She said, "I had to talk to somebody; spiritually we connect." She also told Danielle, "my buddy," and the staff at the Refuge Apartments, but not other residents, because "I didn't feel it was their business." Danielle encouraged EJ:

"She [Danielle] said I've gotta get some help. She was real supportive. She bugged me every day to see if I had called to get treatment. She got on my nerves. That's a friend."

Around the same time, Danielle also relapsed. She said, "Wasn't taking my medication, got depressed, tried to commit suicide." She stopped taking the medication about a month before her overdose attempt. While she first said she got tired of taking the medication, for depression, she elaborated:

DANIELLE: It wasn't by choice. I didn't have the medication and I couldn't just find a doctor, which was, it was dumb because I could have went to the County [Hospital] and I didn't. You know, trying to get into private clinics around here, you know, so I didn't have to go to the County, and wound up being without my medication for a while.

Danielle had spoken to her Refuge Apartments counselor, who had tried to help her get a doctor's appointment, but it was too far in the future. She said, "It had gotten bad at that point. I need to recognize the fact that when I get to that point, go to the doctor. I could have went anywhere and gotten it. I didn't know that, you know, I could have. I guess I should educate myself more on my depression." Danielle was then in her late forties. While she estimated that she had suffered from depression since her late teens or early adulthood, she had only been treating it for three or four years. She had previously gone into treatment and used drugs again, because "I just wasn't ready to stop using." This time was different; she said, "I just let myself go into a depression that I couldn't control anymore. Believe me, life is much less stressful sober. It's hard work getting high every day, it's very hard work." Danielle complained that the staff at the Refuge Apartments who knew about her relapse treated her "like a damned disgrace," but that "I'm not going to let their attitudes stop me from doing what I have to do. They're human, you know, and I have to make myself get through them, you know. They don't make or break me."

Winifred also used drugs twice. When I first asked if she had used any since our last interview, she hesitated, then answered, "No. Yeah, I did. I messed around and I'm scared that I'll make a habit of it. I'm trying to stay clean. [I used] out of boredom." The first time she used, she wondered if it would feel the same as it did before. The second time, another resident brought drugs to her and she used them. She wondered why she could put the effort in to find heroin, but not put the same effort into looking for a job. A few years prior, she had been sober for five and half years. Then, "I had left one job to find another, but I never did find a job, so I ended up doing nothing, sitting around doing nothing, and I decided to have a drink. I had a drink or two, then the drinks started escalating into my drug of choice [heroin], then the vicious cycle started all over again." This time, she said "I don't think I'll be curious again. After this time, I don't think I'll go there again. I had a chance to know Winifred a little bit."

In our third interview, Melvina complained about other women in the house using drugs. This was a common story I heard when visiting the Refuge Apartments during the latter months of interviewing. Melvina emphasized that she did not want to be around these women. Still, during the fourth interview, she told me about her own relapses, which had started about a month and a half before. She said, "I started back using. After I talk with you, I'm gonna go down there, in to tell the case manager, but I'm going to tell her." While she knew about the drug use of several other women at Refuge Apartments, she used with her boyfriend and said this was not related to the other women's drug use.

MELVINA: It's just coincidence. For the last couple of months, I was back and forth to the hospital because you know I take an injection for my liver once a week, and the side effects made sores on my breasts. So I started going back and forth to the doctor just about that. And I still gotta go back to the doctor 'cause it's taking a long time to heal. So I wasn't going to no meetings. So I was up in here doing nothing, a lot of free time. Then with him [her boyfriend] coming around and I see him, that's all he wants. He say he want to get better, but I guess by the time he gonna get into that place he only care to get high.

Melvina talks about the competing concerns of being too busy with doctors' appointments to fit in twelve-step meetings and having too much free time, which led to boredom, which could lead to relapse. Melvina said that the women from the Mercy Home who had relapsed "all talk about we need to stop." She wanted to talk to her case manager to get help because "I'm getting tired of lying to everybody. . . . I tell girls from the Mercy Home what's going on. Really what could they tell me, they in the same boat I'm in. We all try-ing to get ourself back together." This was an ongoing benefit of peer support, even when they were struggling.

Winifred was the only women at Refuge Apartments who connected her own drug use with another resident, though Corrina talked about a friend bringing drugs into her supportive-housing building. Most women were ashamed of their own use and tried to keep it a secret until they asked for help. At the same time, gossiping about others' drug use was common. I often heard about suspected drug use during interviews, both with the women at the Refuge Apartments and with former residents who were working at the Mercy Home. Lisa D, who was working as a case manager at the Mercy Home, said she occasionally ran into a woman on the street "and when I saw her, I knew." She also heard stories.

LISA D.: By word of mouth. . . . And then you have the, you may have one or
    two that just connected to the Mercy Home, where, what I mean by that
    is they come in to the Mercy Home. So I usually find out by them. . . .
    And people tell you what's going on. Or drugs make you lose all sense of
    direction, so you'll have that one or two that may do something that some
    people say why did they do that, but they don't understand drugs. So you
    have those that come back to the Mercy Home while they are high, and
    attempt to do things that they know, they wouldn't normally do if they
    were in their right minds. So you find out various different ways.

While gossip channels meant that word of relapses spread quickly, the supportive housing programs also provided assistance. Tammy, who did not use drugs
herself but saw the drug use around her, described the Refuge Apartments'
response to the drug use: "Most of them have fell off, but they, this place here
will get you help instead of kicking you out. If you relapse, they will get you
help, send you to a rehabilitation center at least for a month or a couple of
weeks, whichever one the person needs. And a lot of them come back, they
continue to work with you. They might take some of your privileges away
from you, but they continue to help you. So that's one good thing about this
place, you know, they really do believe in helping the women here." Shorty
D, EJ, and Danielle all went into detox programs and then returned to the
Refuge Apartments and planned to stay. This was Melvina's plan as well. All
of the women with whom I spoke after their relapse remained committed to
their desistance and recovery efforts. Many others spoke of previous attempts
and renewed commitment in the past. Although this makes recovery from
addiction a difficult process for which to measure success, these setbacks are
common (Paternoster and Bushway 2009; Vaillant 1988). The Refuge Apartments understood this and responded in ways to minimize the damage that
the relapses had done to the women and the facility. This did not prevent
feelings of shame or tensions within families, but they did help foster that
recommitment.

BEYOND TWELVE-STEP

While twelve-step programs are meant to be part of a long-term lifestyle,
the women had varying responses to the programs as they established their
independence post-Mercy Home. Twelve-step meetings helped the women
develop social networks of people who are "doing what I'm doing and doing
things that I would like to." Some women continued to attend meetings long
after they left the Mercy Home and other programs where meeting attendance was required. Others took the lessons they learned from their twelve-
step involvement, and often retained their language, but found alternative
support systems and either purposely avoided meetings or scaled back their

attendance. They were fairly evenly split in their approaches; those with formal connections to drug treatment (for example, drug counselors, Mercy Home staff, those in other generative fields) also fell into both groups.

Some women found that they still received valuable support and fellow-ship through their involvement with twelve-step groups. April, who had been at the Mercy Home eight years earlier, still went to meetings every other day and described them as "enlightening. Very spiritual. It calms me down in a miraculous way." Dee Dee, who was a much more recent Mercy Home resi-dent, said, "I find that I need to have something. . . . I even started going back to church. 'Cause I find that I find that I'm missing those things." Blanche also went to multiple meetings a week. She had lived at the Mercy Home nearly a decade before, though she had gone back to prison on a drug charge after that. She felt "stuck" and then sought a new sponsor: "It was like, I wasn't using drugs or alcohol, but I was hurting, you know inside . . . I was like, man, you know what, I saw him at the elevator and I was like, man, I need a spon-sor." Her sponsor required her to attend several meetings a week. She liked going to the same meetings "because I look forward to fellowshipping with not just my sponsee sisters and brothers, but with other people in the fellow-ship that I've come close with, you know, and then if I, if I miss a meeting a couple weeks, they're calling me on my phone, 'What's going on?' You know, 'You okay?'" Blanche also tried to provide structure and guidance to other women she worked with and who were new to recovery. Some appreciated being a mentor to others through twelve-step or similar meetings. Bennie, who had also been out of the Mercy Home for about eight years, participated in a "substance abuse ministry." She described it as "pretty much a lifestyle, a part of your life" and valued the benefits to her and others: "Makes you feel strong. It's enlightening to others. Gives them a sense of direction. . . . I do some mentoring and stuff like that."

Other women found meetings a valuable reminder of the downsides of drug use. Tasha, after six years, continued to find going to meetings help-ful "because it still lets you know that, okay, you go through problems and different changes and stuff in life, but you still don't have to use drugs over them." She went to meetings "when I need to get reminded that ain't nothing changed and that it's gonna always be here waiting on me. . . . Just because I've been clean for x amount of years or whatever that it's so easy to go back and just give everything up, just like that." Similarly, Edie, who did not go to meet-ings often, found the reminder useful when she did: "Sometimes when you go to those, like, if you go to the in-house meetings at different programs, you'll see how the people look. And it's, it's a deterrent for me to see how they. . . . Some of them haven't been clean two days, five days out of detox, things like that. And they look terrible, actually. Face sunk in, and you know, sores from heroin, using. I mean, it's a deterrent for me, because that, that could be you again, you know." Women make similar arguments about the value of seeing the effects of addiction. They may see this through a twelve-step meeting, at their jobs, or in their neighborhoods.

The women who regularly went to meetings used different standards to decide which meetings to go to. Some got involved with meetings at their housing site (Mercy Home or later supportive-housing programs). These women appreciated the familiarity of a known group of people. Others sought out meetings that were further away or which did not include coresidents. As Danielle explained, "I go to meetings where none of the women here [Refuge Apartments] go, so then I can really talk about things that bother me and I ain't gotta worry about hearing it again." Others went to a variety of meetings because they liked meeting new people.

Some of the women lost interest in being active twelve-step participants over time. Several of the women said they had outgrown the meetings. Edie, who had been at the Mercy Home a few years earlier and had been living in her own apartment for a year, explained her reduced involvement in Narcotics Anonymous meetings. "I go to meetings occasionally. I don't go like I used to, because, you know, sometimes it's the same rigmarole. Same people, you know, same problems. And, you know, once you heard fifteen hundred of them, you pretty much heard 'em all. It's basically the same scenarios." Lisa D, who had lived at the Mercy Home six years prior, said, "Meetings are like this apartment. You outgrow them.... One day a light bulb comes on and you need to go above that level that you are, sitting in those rooms listening to the same stories over and over again." Lauren consistently went to meetings for her first five years out of prison; since then she went more sporadically and was more flexible in her approach.

Lauren: Sometimes me and the girls get together and we make our meeting together.... I have such a wonderful network of people in recovery that I can get with and have a meeting at a moment's notice that I really don't have to go out and support any particular group. You know, in the beginning that's good. You get out, you meet people, you know, you learn about the steps and you understand how other people through their struggles and how it relates to you.... There are some people that dutifully make the same meetings every week and they probably will go they grave doing that. I'm just not one of them people. I'm real diverse as far as getting what I need out of recovery and utilizing the people that are in recovery. I'm not making the same meeting every week.... On my calendar every week? No. My life is too, it's too full for that.

Some women disliked meetings because of the drama, both in terms of the glorification of drug use and interpersonal dynamics. Mary, for example, found meetings unhelpful because they reminded her of the enjoyable aspects of drug use.

MARY: Because to me, the meetings just wasn't working for me. I just, you know, like I told you before, I have my meetings with God, so that's, that's what works for me. . . . 'Cause they would always be talking about what they used to do and how they used to do it and the fun and you know, and so that would having me sitting there reminiscing about when I used to get high, so I was like, there's something wrong with this. So, I just, I just stopped going. Though when I was in the Mercy Home, we used to have meetings every day and then we would have to make outside meetings too, and then we had [outpatient treatment] where we would have to go four days a week. I was just about meeting'd out anyway [laughs].

Mary began scaling back her meeting attendance once she began working, while still living at the Mercy Home At the time she moved out, she was attending only the in-house meetings, and she stopped altogether when she moved into her own apartment. Although Lauren said, "I would never feel that meetings are not necessary," she also felt "probably half that shit that they be saying in the meeting probably would disgust me and I probably would leave. 'Cause you know, recovery is tricky. It really is and some people are in there just to showboat and that kind of stuff just rubs me the wrong way. It really do."

Common complaints were that there was often gossip and emphasis in some meetings on impressing one another, particularly potential romantic partners. Delilah stopped going because "they just go there to meet each other and to have men and to have sex and, you know, and do things like that." Marie similarly disliked meetings and attended rarely. She said she went "I'll say twice out of the year. I don't like them to be honest. Because a lot of, sometimes a lot of chaos and drama and there's a lot of, you know, real, you know, people talk." Marie also complained about "just the gossip, and I'm like, I'm kinda like a private person. I don't like telling everybody my business, so I prefer not to even go to meetings. If I feel I need to talk to somebody, I talk to the [executive director] or my coworkers, Lisa D, somebody like that."

Most of the women who had disengaged from twelve-step groups found alternatives to serve similar functions. While twelve-step programs no longer (or never) worked for them, they found alternative sources of support. Church involvement, personal support networks, and individual reflection often satisfied the women's desire for understanding and camaraderie. Delilah occasionally went to meetings at the Mercy Home or women's groups and was actively involved in her church. For her, this served the positive purposes without the distractions and drama of twelve-step groups. Carolyn also found "camaraderie . . . an outlet for your problems" through her church. Lauren also felt she could get the positive benefits of twelve-step groups through her work as a drug treatment counselor, along with the personal support networks she had developed over the years.

CONCLUSION

Looking at some of the key changes the women faced during their reentry, we begin to see how their narratives play out, and how their sense of self emerges over time in interaction with other individuals, institutions, and messages (Abbott 2001; Giordano, Schroeder, and Cernkovich 2007; Mead 1934). We see how their narratives change across interviews as a result of changing circumstances and as they experience the limitations of the twelve-step narrative in relation to their own lives. Many of the women, like Erica, feel a sense of accomplishment at having a job but immense frustration over their lack of a continued sense of progress and accomplishment. They go from a goal of establishing a "normal" life to the reality of the drudgery of that life to acceptance of that life. We can also see the emergence of a sense of generativity in Dee Dee, but also the temporary loss of it in Erica. The twelve-step framework gives them a language with which to frame their desire to desist, but they also begin to experience its limitations and develop alternatives.

The importance of social context and social networks also is apparent. The women interact with coworkers, potential employers, twelve-step participants, and friends and relatives. All of these interactions shape their sense of self and their understandings of their world. In the next several chapters, I explicitly discuss these relationships and how these shaped their reentry and desistance efforts.

PART II

*The Social
Context of Reentry*

CHAPTER 4

Family Dynamics in
Reentry and Desistance

THE WOMEN IN THIS STUDY are actively working to re-create their social identities. This includes not only their identity as an ex-offender, prisoner, or drug user, but also their identities as a mother, sister, daughter, girlfriend or wife, and friend. Importantly, these identities often come into conflict with their sense of self as defined through the twelve-step and other self-help messages they learned at the Mercy Home. The majority of the women in this study are from low-income African American communities, in which motherhood and family are highly valued. Most of the women have children, and regaining custody of some or all of them is often a primary goal (Brown and Bloom 2009; Enos 2001; Richie 2001). All of the women with children aspired to strengthening their relationships with their children; about two-thirds said it was important but not difficult, and the remaining women expressed some level of difficulty in reestablishing or improving these relationships. In addition, many of the women have extensive histories of abuse, often at the hands of family members and romantic partners. In spite of these histories, many of these women remained loyal to their parents and other relatives, and strengthening relationships with families was important to them, during, and after their incarceration.

For these women, the people, places, and things related to their offending and drug use often included family members. Thus, removing themselves from relationships with connections to their past offending may be financially, socially, and emotionally difficult, and doing so comes with significant costs (Maruna and Roy 2007). Sharon described what she saw as the most important factors in the lives of her and women in her position.

SHARON: Maybe about the difficulties adapting, you know, after coming home from prison. You know, how difficult that has been. The steps that they took to get, you know, to the next level. Relationships with their children—well, you asked me that, but I think that's a real good one. I believe that's a lot of things that a lot of us struggle with. Although I wasn't in prison for a long period of time, I had been in and out of my children's life. Relationships with other family members. Because when you start changing, then they change, you know, and they used to you being one way and then you change, you know. It's hard for them to really deal with the new you, 'cause I experienced that a lot with my family, so you know I kind of stay distant. . . . It's a difficult transition, coming from prison and back out here to get into the swing of things.

The women's offending, drug use, past incarcerations, and drug relapses had long-lasting effects on their families of origin and their relationships. Still, they rarely led to a termination of the relationships. Family members returning from prison or desisting from offending and drug use led to shifting family dynamics and a need to redefine relationships. These redefinitions were influenced not only by offending or drug use but also by gendered expectations of family roles. This chapter details these shifting dynamics, including how the women attempted to reconcile twelve-step messages with their family demands.

CHILDREN AND MOTHERHOOD

Motherhood is one of the most common themes in both the research literature on female prisoners and in these women's narratives. All of the women with children had at least one of their children before going to prison the first time. Many had children before becoming involved with drug use or offending, and many gave birth to children throughout their period of active offending and drug use. So, for these women, giving birth to children did not lead to desistance from drug use or offending (Huebner, DeJong, and Cobbina 2010). However, children were central to their mothers' narratives of desistance (Enos 2001; Giordano, Cernkovich, and Rudolph 2002). They were commonly mentioned as a motivating factor for "going straight," and the women wanted to do right by their children, even where they failed in the past. Regardless of whether the women were custodial parents, children were central to their sense of self.

Children and Addiction

Dee Dee's history illustrates the complicated interplay between drug use, offending, and motherhood. Dee Dee had her first child as a teenager, and although she drank and smoked marijuana in her teens, she first began using cocaine when she was twenty-one. "I had just broke up with . . . my second son's father. And I was real caught up with him. I was with him for three years, but [it] was very depressing when I broke up with him. You know, as a outlet, I just wanted to dull the pain." Her oldest child was approximately five years old when Dee Dee first developed a drug addiction and she first became involved with the Department of Children and Family Services (DCFS). She explained, "I think it was one time I left 'em [children] and I think someone had called in on me. People came and again, my son, he opens the door. And when I got there they were gone. Of course I was high and tired as hell, living on the street. All they left was a card. I didn't know what to do. I tried to hide from my family. I did not call them. I remained invisible. I just was not gonna let them know that they took my kids. That was the ultimate thing. I was really ashamed. . . . And I never forget, October of '86, that's when they took them from me. I don't know what happened or even how they found out." DCFS mandated drug treatment, but "I knew I had no intentions on coming. And each time I would come, I was getting high. So, eventually, I just stopped going, period." Much of her offending history was related to getting the money to support her addiction.[1] Her history also included significant violence, committed both by and against her. Dee Dee's main motivation in offending was "quick, fast money. . . . You know, you gotta fend for yourself."

A little more than two years after her children were taken away, she went to prison for the first time for an armed robbery conviction. She described this as, "Baby, look, after three weeks, I started talking committing suicide and stuff. I, you know, I just, I cried. I blew my daddy's phones up. I ain't never been in jail in all my life. It was a wake-up. Trust me. It was a wake-up call. I think after the three weeks, it finally dawned on me, you fucked up big time." Her first incarceration also led to her seeing herself as an addict. She said it was "when I first began to learn that I had a problem. . . . So that's when I first started getting my most help. . . . And I started being real honest."

Once she was released, she tried to go straight and found a job at a fast-food restaurant. She was fired from her job a few months later when her drawer was short of cash (which she believed her manager was responsible for), and her drug use escalated. She said, "I was already happy about me getting the job by me being honest and being out of prison for armed robbery and what not and I got the job. . . . Anyway, they fired me and I was very disappointed because I liked it so much and I started back using again. And I had already been kind of using anyway, but when that happened I just stopped the excuses and went full-fledged with it." She now described this incident as a scapegoat; she used her disappointment over being fired to justify her escalating drug use. She continued to use drugs until she was arrested and charged with forgery, possession, and felony theft.

Over the next decade, Dee Dee went to prison several more times and eventually began using heroin as well. "The heroin, I didn't really get into that until like, in the last part of my addiction. . . . And that was just, you know, most of my friends were, you know, cross-addicted and they were always offering and I would always accept. You know, so eventually, you know, I got to

liking it, starting buying it for myself, you know. So that's how that happened."
She also had three more children and suffered two miscarriages, which she
described as homicides and attributed to her drug use. Then she was incarcerated for a third time.

DEE DEE: In '99, I caught a felony theft. I was in possession of credit cards and
   I was also pregnant with my twins. That's when I said God was willing to
   do for me what I wouldn't for myself. I didn't know I was pregnant and
   I had a shooting [heroin] habit. But anyway, I got caught up when the
   police were looking for someone else, the person I was with. . . . It was
   also the first time I was ever pregnant and locked up and had somebody
   [a boyfriend] at home, you know, totally waiting on me. Even though I
   was gone for a short time, the relationship was low; it was down and out.
   I was determined to be different once I got home. Unfortunately, when I
   got home, I got high with those twins.

There are several significant aspects to Dee Dee's story that occurred
commonly among these women. Much of her offending began once a drug
addiction had escalated and she needed the money to support it and her
household. By then, she had several young children at home, who were left
unsupervised while she went to the street. She tried to keep this a secret: "I did
not want my family to know [about the drug use and illegal activity]. . . . It was
like I was two people. I didn't want my neighbors or anybody—even though
I socialized a whole lot with my neighbors and things." Keeping her drug use
a secret was important to her, but keeping her failures as a mother secret was
even more significant. The shame she felt kept her from seeking her family's
help, in spite of their demonstrated concern. Similar feelings, along with the
"selfishness" that often accompanied addiction, led most of the women to
distance themselves from family during their addictions. Dee Dee spoke of
her failings as a mother in harsh terms. In spite of having two of her children
taken away and in spite of the "wake-up call" of her first incarceration, Dee
Dee's addiction and offending continued for an extended period of time. Her
first incarceration and attempt to go straight came over a decade before she
achieved a period of sustained desistance. This too is common among offenders and prisoners. While she, like many returning prisoners, had good intentions when she was released from prison the first time, she was not able to
sustain them through setbacks and disappointments.

Some of the women took some pride in their continued ability to provide for their children even during periods of active addiction. For Sheila, this
meant giving her mother control of her public aid money. At first, she was
able to maintain a fairly conventional lifestyle, "'Cause I was in my addiction
for, like, twenty-five years, you can say. Basically I started doing real crazy

stuff, like after fifteen years I was into my addiction. Because I had a job and my boyfriend too was selling drugs and stuff, so I didn't have to go out, you know, basically to do things to have them. They was there already for me if I wanted them."

SHEILA: My aunts and my mother got together and stuff, tried to take my kids away from me several times. DCFS came out to see me out seven times, and every time they came, my kids always been clean, my house was clean, you know. Actually, if you ever came in the house, you never would think I was heavy into drugs the way I was, the way I kept my kids up and stuff like that. Because, basically, you know, then I started to take public aid and stuff, you know, for my kids' stuff, and . . . I put my mother over that, controlled all that. Because I knew that I was weak and what I would do. . . . I bought groceries and stuff . . . I would take care of my business, but the rest of it I would spend up in drugs. I was going to be broke until I got that check again. So, basically, I prefer take the public aid and put her all over that.

Sheila regretted her drug addiction, but she also took practical steps to ensure that her children were cared for, at least materially. For some of the women, an addiction was one more thing to support in their lives, along with their own needs and those of their children. Illegal activities like theft, prostitution, and drug selling were common ways to do so. Sharon described the reasons she began selling drugs and engaging in prostitution: "Ways and means to get money, to use drugs, to support my family. You know, because my children always have been in my custody. Helping family members."

Dee Dee speaks of her experiences using the self-help terms of taking responsibility and giving herself over to God. Lisa D went through a similar process of accepting responsibility for her life and her children: "For the first time [in prison] I dealt with the situation that my children were caught up in because of those things: my addiction, alcoholism. . . . I stopped blaming everybody else for where I was and started holding myself accountable for the choices I was making. . . . I had lost so much. I had lost my children. Three of my children had been caught up in the system, because of what? You know, so it was a lot of stuff and a lot of that I kept to myself." Bennie also attributed her arrests—two of which occurred just before the births of her first two children—and incarcerations to God helping her. She said, "But the weirdness of those incarcerations was that it wasn't so much becoming arrested, but being rescued. Because in each event, you know, I was brought into the world and I wasn't living nothing. My life was just torment and turmoil. So, I summed up both the arrests to a rescue. You know, God did for me what I couldn't do for myself. So, once again, my family stepped in and got my child, my newly born child, and raised him. They both beautiful, beautiful human beings." These narratives are shaped by their experiences at the Mercy Home, though they are often exposed to this language during incarcerations and previous experiences with drug treatment, such as when Dee Dee first started "getting honest" with herself. In addition, many of the women, including Bennie, described themselves as spiritual people independent of their involvement with twelve-step programs.

The women's relationships with both their parents and children were central to their narratives about their desires to go straight. For example, Dee Dee's children and the ongoing support of her father (who had his own history with addiction earlier in his life) were not enough to prevent her offending or drug use, but she did credit them with motivating her to change. The timing of addiction and offending in Dee Dee's life course, relapse and recidivism in spite of an initial desire to change, and narratives of desistance coming through a combination of tiredness, age, giving oneself over to God, and a desire to be a better mother, daughter, and person were paralleled in many of the women's stories.

Impacts on Children of Addiction and Incarceration

The women's children were affected not only by their mother's incarcerations but also by the chaotic life and limited parenting during their addictions. Given the nature of many of the women's lifestyles prior to their incarcerations and their absences while incarcerated, it is not surprising that relationships with children often were, or had been, strained. Age, gender, and temperament influenced the ways in which children reacted to their mother's problems and their willingness or ability to move beyond their troubled pasts. Alicia, Adena's daughter, knew that her mother was "doing something wrong, but I didn't know the consequences." She described her childhood: "Things didn't get, like, really shaken up bad until I was a teenager. So, it was okay, and when I became a teenager I moved here with my grandmother. And I didn't like it, but I had to deal with it. And being new to this kind of world, and then it was kind of rough because I was just finding out my mother did drugs, you know, as a teenager. And, uh, and it, uh, it took a long time to accept it and to deal with it, because you know kids will tease you and, you know, torment you, and say things and, you know, they just try to hurt you. But other than that, I had a nice childhood with my grandparents." Alicia framed her mother's incarceration in both good and bad terms. She missed her mother and was embarrassed by the teasing she endured from her peers. At the same time, she felt her mother was safer in prison than on the street. "But I didn't feel bad about it 'cause I'd rather her go to jail, you know, than to be out here doing other things to get high, like some of 'em do, so I guess if I had—it was a give and take situation. I'd rather her, you know, feel than be out here belittling herself for men, doing Lord knows what for drugs, so it really didn't really bother me at first, like maybe after the third, fourth time. And then it seems like every time she go to jail, it'll be my birthday. It was always my birthday. I don't know. Even, yeah. But, it's just like I just got used to it. It was like it wasn't no new news."

Alicia's response highlights some of the complexities in the women's relationships with their children. Alicia was critical of the criminal justice system, calling her mother's arrests and incarcerations "bogus," yet grateful the system prevented her mother from engaging in more dangerous behaviors to support her addiction. Her childhood and her life were disrupted, both by her physical displacement to her grandparents' house and the emotional turmoil of her mother's addiction and incarceration. Although she downplayed the effects, her equation of her mother's arrests and her birthday suggests a strong and lasting emotional impact. In spite of this, Alicia remained close to her mother, valued many of the life lessons she imparted, and separated Adena's addiction from her role as a mother.

Alicia's experience with her mother and father's drug use shaped her own decisions. While she smoked marijuana regularly and drank alcohol occasionally, she did not use other drugs. She said, "I would never do that because I see what it do to my mother and my father and my family and everybody. No heroin. I never did anything but marijuana [laughs]. That's it. Of course, that's bad too, but that's the one thing I done. But, I don't—no crack, no rock, none of that." As a teenager, Alicia got in fights with other girls, "I would call myself a little gang member at the time, so you know, just being young and dumb, I guess. Hang, like I said, hang with the wrong crowd, doing the wrong things, you know. Fighting girls out in the street, acting crazy." Alicia never sold drugs, because "I couldn't accept the consequences. I never been in jail. . . . I believe the stories they told."

While Alicia and her mother are close, Alicia attributes much of her family's problems to her mother's drug addiction.

ALICIA: If she wasn't on drugs, she would be a different person, you know. She wouldn't be, you know, like she is or my life probably wouldn't be like it is. You know, everything. I just feel like everything probably would be different, you know. Completely different.

AL: How do you think it would be different?

ALICIA: I think we probably still be in our house down there. I think I may have would've finished school, went to school. My sister's the one, she wouldn't be going through what she going through. . . . I'd say from like when she was sixth grade on up, it was like she said they ruined her life because, you know, they weren't there for her like they were there for us, 'cause we was older. You know, I think the way, you know, things, she blames them for the way her life is and the outcome of her life. And see, she's not strong as me and my older sister. We learned to accept it. You know, her, you know, she's accepted it, but it's, you know, messed her up too. She has a different, different, she had a nervous breakdown. So, you know, I think she wouldn't be the way she is.

Alicia attributes these different reactions among her and her sisters both to their ages when their parent's drug use began affecting their lives and to their different personalities. While they have varying reactions, all were deeply affected.

As in Adena's family, other children had varying responses to their chaotic childhoods. Many were in college or were working and succeeding within conventional society, while others struggled with drug addiction, offending, and incarceration. Often, both occurred in the same family. Three of Lisa D's six children had been involved with the criminal justice system at one time or another. Several were in college or working. Delilah described her three sons:

DELILAH: The baby is twenty-eight. He's incarcerated. I have one in Milwaukee. And I've got one—he's the one that's never jaywalked, never smoked a cigarette. He's a maintenance man, a supervisor in one of those high-rise buildings downtown. That's the eldest. My life is so messed up because I never raised any of my children. I was lucky enough to have the two oldest boys' grandmother—she's eighty-eight next week—took them and my aunt took the two youngest boys. You know, because I was always on drugs, you know. And I couldn't have provided for them. They would have been up and down the street looking from pillar to post, probably be doing all kinds of stuff. But none of them are what you could call degenerate in society. The one that's incarcerated, he sold a little drugs. He made a bad mistake, but he's not a bad kid.

As Delilah illustrates, the women generally had the same attitude toward their children that many of the women's parents had about them: some may have done bad things, but the women loved them and saw them as fundamentally good people. The more successful children were great sources of pride.

Sheila's children had similarly divergent reactions to her past. She described talking to them about her past:

SHEILA: We had one [counseling/self-help] group—we were talking about that, and I said I want to talk to my kids. I feel as though they should have some kind of anger toward me for all those years being in my addiction and everything. So, I talked to my kids and I asked them, and I told them I want them to tell me exactly how they feel about the situation. This is what my [twenty-four-year-old] daughter told me: that she's not mad at me or nothing she just want to forget my past and strive on what I'm doing now. But my [eighteen-year-old] son did say he was mad at me, so I asked can we talk about it, but he didn't want to talk about it. He also told me that he proud of me, what I'm doing now, but he do got some anger in him, I guess. You know, at different points I was not there.

While Sheila's son expressed more anger toward her, she was more confident in his current path than she was her daughter's. Sheila believed that her son would be a good father to his new baby: "I think he will because of his child experience that he went through by me being out there in the streets and my daughter had to raise him and stuff. . . . He doing the right thing and he talking the right things. . . . He's none of that gangbanging and he tell me, I've never had to worry about him being on drugs 'cause he seen what it did to his mom and dad." At the time of the last interview, her son was in a GED class, "he's going to school everyday, he's trying to accomplish something." He also helped care for his nephews. Sheila said, "My son gets up and takes his nephews to school every day and they get out of school . . and he picks them up." She approved of her son's girlfriend and the mother of his child, who she described as "pretty smart, so I hope she's thinking about going on to college. . . . I like the young lady; she's real nice."

In contrast, her daughter was "hanging out all night" and not working. Sheila disapproved of her daughter's romantic partners. Her daughter's husband and father of three of her children was incarcerated, and the father of her oldest child was "on his way to be locked up," according to Sheila. Sheila's history of addiction was one source of tension in these relationships. "We didn't get along, especially during my addiction, and he [her son-in-law] wanted—he tried to keep my daughter away from me and my grandkids and stuff. He didn't want me around 'cause I'm using drugs, you know, and all this and stuff." Now that he was incarcerated, she gave him advice and tried to help him maintain relationships with his children, because "I've been there and I know you feel good when you get somebody to visit you from home, you know, or get a letter or something, but my daughter is not doing none of that." While she worried about both of her children, she was concerned that her daughter was following in her footsteps. In our third interview, Sheila described changes in her daughter: "I really try not to let things worry me. But right now, my daughter, my daughter, 'cause she's like she's breaking wild or something out there in the street, you know. Her husband incarcerated now [laughs] and I don't know, she didn't have a childhood, because she had her first child at fourteen and then plus when I got my drug addiction out there, you know, she really raised my son and stuff too, you know. So, now that I'm here at home, you know, she just like, take it upon herself. . . . See, I'm gonna stay at home and babysit. I really just wanna capture her attention, get her attention."

Sheila expressed a common fear, particularly about daughters: that she was following in her mother's path. Sheila said her daughter was not using drugs but had quit her job and was just "hanging out." Erica discussed similar concerns for her oldest teenage daughter: "It's like a cycle. And my mom had me when she was thirteen. I had her when I was sixteen, even though I got pregnant when I was fifteen. And I realize now that it's like a cycle. Even though I've stopped getting high and it's like, I see so many of my behaviors when I was that age in her. To where it's in—I be trying to see if it's too late. I just worry. That's all, I just worry. That's just a mother. I just worry. . . . Not that she's doing anything or—'cause she really communicates with me too." Many of these concerns are typical of parenting a teenager. Those with younger children worried about what would happen to them as they grew up, particularly as they entered their teen years. Erica, Sheila, and others had the added burden of knowing the struggles they faced and the shared burdens that their children experienced. They also were conscious of the ways in which their concerns for their children may influence their own recovery and desistance attempts, and they discussed these concerns in twelve-step terms as well. Sheila tried to "let go and let God" for her daughter's struggles as well as her own. In each interview, her greatest worries were for her children and grandchildren, but "all I can do is just pray on it, you know, I give it to the Lord because I can't concentrate on it, you know? That's something that can make me fall back into my addiction."

The women worried when their adult children were involved in drug use, street life, or illegal activity. They also were particularly concerned when they perceived their children failing in their roles as parents. For example, EJ fought for several months to visit her son while he was incarcerated. After he was released, their relationship became "touch and go. I don't like what he's doing as far as his son's concerned [his lack of involvement]. . . . He knows he hurt me, and he don't know how to come to me." EJ's description of her son and his behavior parallels the way many of the women described their own periods of drug use, the shame associated with it, and the related inadequate parenting. In the fourth interview, Sheila's worries about her daughter continued. She said, "She worries me a little bit because she's not doing what she's supposed to do as far as a mother-wise, but I ain't gonna let that bother me anymore either, Andrea. I'm just going to leave it alone, leave it in God's hands. . . . She's doing the same thing that I did too, that's what I told her."

Shifting Narratives of Motherhood

Although becoming a mother did not lead Dee Dee, Sheila, Bennie, or the others to desist, their children were central to their narratives of desistance. This was true for women with children, regardless of the children's ages and whether or not the women were, or planned to be, custodial parents. The time when Dee Dee first lost custody of her older children, shortly after her addiction began, to her final release from prison spanned sixteen years and included several attempts at drug rehabilitation. Her final prison sentence was for a parole violation, after she was put out of a drug rehab program for non-compliance and then went on the run. This time, she again felt she was ready to change, in part because of her children and her father.

DEE DEE: I had already made up my mind. I had already told God, "Keep me safe. Keep me alive and I'll go back to jail because I can't do this no more." . . . Every time he [her parole officer] came he'd have my kid. . . . That stuff started to get to me, and I started thinking about the love that my father—man, I just couldn't get over that love. So I had made up my mind that when I got caught, I was done . . . I just started connecting with that Man upstairs and allow the change that was going to come over me come over me, because I couldn't do it no more. I just started thinking, I told God that if I could just get clean just for a minute, just long enough to get my head on right one more time, I could make it this time.

Once Dee Dee started to get her life together, she gave her children and family members much of the credit for motivating her.

The women recognized the disrupted and unstable childhoods their children had, in many cases, and regretted the hurt done to their children. At the same time, they needed to move beyond their past, and being good mothers in the present and future was one important way to do so. At the time of her first incarceration, Lisa D's youngest child was approximately twelve. When I met her, her children ranged in age from nineteen to twenty-nine. Her children clearly played an important role in her redefinition of her life and her goals, and she regretted the impact of her choices on her children's lives and on her own life. She said of her children, "There's a part of their lives that even when they were living with me I still missed, you know, because I realize that I wasn't mother of the year even then because of the drugs and because of the alcohol. So I'm at the point in my life where I value those relationships and that time, even if it's just a phone call to say, 'Hey. How you doing?' . . . And I got one son that's still sort of dealing with those sorts of issues that were going on in my life at that time. So I pray that that will get better." Few of the women considered incarceration itself as the source of their problems with their children or the difficult lives their children led. This is consistent with the women's learned narratives of taking responsibility for their choices and actions.

In my first interview with Sunshine, she illustrated the ways in which children were central to her sense of self and how the narrative shifted depending on the circumstances. Sunshine was then in her early forties and had three children, who were living with relatives in New York. She had been involved in drug trafficking since her mid-twenties and served one prison sentence. In describing this, she highlighted both the benefits of her offending to her children and the costs of her incarceration. "It wasn't anything easy; you have to work. And I got to take my kids places and do things with them. I got to have a good time with them. I was always with them. We was always doing something. And I was figuring if I was working I couldn't do none of this. But I didn't have to work; I was doing that." While Sunshine regretted the years she lost with her children because of her incarceration, she also highlighted the ways she believed her criminal activity allowed her to spend more time with her family than most jobs. Sunshine was one of the few who made an argument that her offending allowed her to be a better mother. More typically, the women characterized their children as a collateral consequence of their mother's addiction and offending. Still, incarceration was a strong blow to Sunshine's family. She went on to describe this period:

SUNSHINE: I lost track of the years there. They used to be so young and now they're grown. My son is eighteen. My two girls are fifteen and twelve. And if I would have made it at home I would have had a chance to talk to my youngest daughter. Because she's twelve, she's at that age where she's curious and she's asking questions. She's in junior high school and they're talking about human biology and all that. She's asking me questions over the phone, which I would like to talk to her face to face and talk to her about it myself. I didn't have an opportunity to talk about it with my other daughter because she was already going on ten [when I went to prison] and she was with her father and he told her. But I thought I could do that with mine, at least with [my younger daughter]. She was asking. I have to tell her something about it over the phone but she couldn't go into detail and with her on the phone everybody's around listening. So I told her to go to her aunt. But she said, "I want to know from you, ask you." "I'll tell you pretty much the same thing. Ask her and she'll tell you." And that hurt. That hurt a lot.

Sunshine's daughters were then living with their fathers and her son was living with her parents, all in New York. After her stay at the Mercy Home, she was still on parole in Illinois. She said, "I did a pretty good job with them before I left, but they're doing real well. They still love me and miss me very much . . . and they're doing real good in school." Sunshine retained custody of her children, and said about this, "Thank goodness. I would have died." Her children were central to her life narrative, even while they were physically separated, and her legally recognized parental rights were central to her sense of self.

In talking about her incarceration, Sunshine again talked about how her children and her role as their mother influenced her time in prison.

SUNSHINE: I think that's the reason why I didn't get in trouble or go to segregation, because I would think of my children, because I would lose time. They would take time from me and give me more time. They kept me going. You know, "Just bite your tongue. Don't say nothing. Let it go." If I didn't have kids I would have been in trouble many times. I would have just kept going back and forth. I wouldn't have cared. But it was my children that had me, "Don't say nothing. Leave it alone. Walk away. Let it go." Because if you go to seg they're going to take your time from you and give you more time on top of that. I wouldn't be sitting here now. I would have been sitting over there in Dwight [Correctional Center] for a couple more months. So thinking of the children, that helped.

Like Dee Dee and most of the women, having children did not prevent Sunshine from getting involved in drug trafficking. She did, however, credit them with her good behavior while in prison and as a motivating factor for her future plans and goals, which included going to school, getting a job, and finding her own place to live.

Postincarceration Family Configurations

At the time of the interviews, the women had complex familial configurations and arrangements. Some of the women's children were grown and living on their own, occasionally caring for younger siblings. Several of the women had permanently or temporarily lost or given up legal custody of some of their children. It also was common for children to be split up, living with multiple relatives, or for the women to retain legal custody of one or more. Even when they did not have legal or physical custody of their children, many hoped to regain custody of some or all of their children. This was complicated by the supportive housing programs available to them. A minority of women lived in subsidized housing programs that would allow them to live with their children. Two women, Sharon and Iris, were placed in larger apartments in subsidized buildings immediately from the Mercy Home so that they could live with their children. Andrea and Erica moved into apartments big enough for their children, with three years' support through a program providing rent assistance for women enrolled in school. Gertrude moved into a Section 8 apartment with her children after spending several years in a single-room-occupancy building. Most commonly, the women had to choose between housing programs and living with their children.

For the most part, the women were grateful for the child care provided by their families, and they sometimes planned to leave their children in the custody of their current caregivers. Dee Dee's father adopted her three younger children. Dee Dee's two oldest children were young adults and were the only ones who knew that Dee Dee was their mother. She said of her father, "He has always been taught that if, that if a family member is having difficulty, you look after that family member. And that's just how he is." Her father's attitude about caring for those who needed care was common among the women and their families, though the caregiving was more common among female family members (Collins 2000; Sarkisian and Gerstel 2004). Dee Dee said that although she had a close relationship with her children and her father, she did not plan to try to regain custody of them. "My father has had my daughter since she was two days old. And . . . my boys, they were in a foster home for a few months, but eventually my father got them. Because of the bond that's there, I wouldn't do that. It's not necessary." Dee Dee saw this as doing what was best for her children, in the interests of maintaining a stable life for them, and therefore making the best decision as their mother.

DEE DEE: That's [her relationship with her children] been good. I went to church with 'em last week. . . . We've never, you know, me and my parents we haven't sat down and actually let them know of the relationship that I share with them. My daughter . . . knows that I'm not her auntie. She knows that I'm not just a friend. You know, and then I have to just trust that, you know, that's just a mother/child thing. You know, that they know some kinda connection with me 'cause my twins, you know, they, "We don't want you to go. How come you can't come with us?" And, you know, and it makes me feel good . . .

AL: So, none of them know that you [are their mother]?

DEE DEE: I really don't—unless my parents told them. I don't even worry about it. You know, because I don't have to go through no system to see them or anything. You know, anytime I feel the need I might wanna talk to 'em . . . I talk to 'em.

Dee Dee's case illustrates the ways in which many of their family arrangements took place outside of the legal or child welfare systems. Allison, the mother of two young adult daughters and a younger son, said, "Well, I have custody of him. In our culture we don't go through that a lot. When I was incarcerated, I was like, 'Can you come with him and keep him until I get my shit together?' I thank God I never lost custody of none of my children." Arrangements were made and remade informally among family members, regardless of who had legal custody. Still, sometimes this led to permanent and legal arrangements. The friend who had cared for Sugar's older son for years had recently adopted him. She said, "I haven't really been there since he was two. And also the woman that has him, I finally let her adopt him. So technically he's not mine anymore. I still think he is, but." Even in cases where the child was well cared for, being able to take on the mothering role again was important to many of the women and they felt significant conflict when they were not able to do so. Although Sugar relinquished legal custody, she strove to maintain a relationship with her son and traveled to visit him several times.

Other women had equally complex family configurations and arrangements. In several cases, the women regained, or hoped to regain, custody of some, but not all, of their children. These decisions also were typically framed as being in the best interests of the children. Linette's extended family, including her aunt and her children's fathers' families, was taking care of her five children, who ranged in age from a toddler to teenagers. She talked to all of them "every chance I get" and saw several of them regularly. She said, "The oldest one and the third oldest, those are the ones I see the least. The second oldest lives in Chicago [with the child's father's family], so I can see her anytime. And the youngest two, I get to see them anytime. Because my auntie—I gave her custody of [the second youngest] and the two-year-old I gave her guardianship." Linette retained legal custody only of her youngest child, whose father was her fiancé. While she wanted to regain custody of the older children, "that would take a miracle because of the situation of them being fully adopted. But if they were willing to give me my kids, I would take them." The hardest thing she was dealing with was "being away from my [youngest] daughter. Because I don't want to upset my family members. I mean, it's what they want and I know that once I go and get her I'm going to have a lot of work on my hands. I know it. Because she's got to get used to being around me and being around the other side of her family, her father's side of the family. But I'm willing to go through it."

Similarly, Marie had been living with her older daughter, who was then a teenager, in the studio apartment she had been living in since leaving the Mercy Home. Her son was living with her mother, who had custody of both children, because "once I was released I never did go through the procedures to get it changed and all that." It was only in our fourth interview that she revealed that she had two other children as well. In talking about her previous attempts at drug treatment, she told me about being placed in a mandated methadone program. In explaining this incident, she revealed the existence of her two younger children, whom she had not previously mentioned to me.

AL: And what led you to getting treatment that time?

MARIE: I had, I got four kids—did I tell you that?

AL: I don't think so.

MARIE: And two of them were taken away, so they end up putting, making me go through treatment and all that.

AL: So, DCFS made you get into a methadone program? . . . But only two [kids] were taken away? . . . How come?

MARIE: Because my son was with my mother and my daughter was down South with my grandmother.

AL: So you only had two with you at that time then?

MARIE: Mmm hmm, that was the younger two. . . . The younger two, they were adopted. So, I'm close with the family . . .

AL: So you're still in touch with the [younger two]?

MARIE: Yeah, as a matter of fact, I just went to his graduation in June. He graduated from eighth grade. . . . 'Cause we take the—, they live in [a suburb], so [my older son] is the one that mostly goes. [Her oldest daughter is] now at the phase where she likes to hang out with her girlfriends, whatever, so she hasn't been in a while.

Marie, like all of the women with children, felt regret for the ways in which their drug use and incarcerations affected her children. The women all also took pride in their children and emphasized what they had done right, or what could have gone more wrong. Those who had not lost legal custody emphasized this. Those who remained close with their children, regardless of custody status, emphasized it. And regardless of where their children were living or who formally had custody, the women's role as their mother remained important.

Decisions about custody reflect the intersection of the women's drug addiction, offending, and incarceration histories, when they had children, the current ages of their children, and family arrangements. Children born in the thick of an addiction may have little experience living with their mothers, and some women voluntarily gave up custody of their children during these periods. Children born prior to the onset of a serious addiction may have suffered significantly during an addiction and may or may not be willing or able to move past these experiences. Some women were able to maintain a stable enough front or had sufficient family support to retain custody through an addiction. Consequences of their addictions and incarcerations included complex family arrangements involving lost custody, informal arrangements, and children dispersed among multiple relatives and foster homes. In spite of these complicated family structures, the women strongly valued motherhood and their role as mothers.

Evolving Relationships with Children

In addition to the strains of their children growing up in similar environments and exhibiting behaviors similar to that of their mothers, the women also had to adjust to new relationships with their children after incarceration and while in recovery. Danielle frequently talked about her pride in and love for her children, but the transition to being actively involved in their lives again was a challenge.

DANIELLE: Well, how do you get back with your family? Where do you begin? And then, how do you keep it up? You know, 'cause I'm not used to being around my kids, you know what I'm saying? It came to that point being at the Mercy Home, 'cause I was going to visit them every weekend, but integrating with them again, that was hard! That was hard, because they were getting on my nerves, you know, 'cause I wasn't used to being around them anymore. And I would get frustrated, you know, and agitated . . . I was like, well okay, they have to learn to accept me too. . . . So now, they're learning me all over again. It's not just me, you know, it's them learning me too. I used to be just bitchy, screamin' and hollerin' and they look at me now, and are, like, "Are you okay?" And I'm like yeah. "Ma, no, something's wrong." No, I'm fine, really. "Then why you so quiet?" Because, I'm quiet, you know, and they're not used to that. They're not used to me being who I am now, you know. Like I was trying tell you, I had discovered that I am a quiet person, just like my mother. Something that I always hated in her, my mom was always quiet, and I used to hate her for that. And I've come to realize that I'm quiet just like my mother. It's them getting used to me too, 'cause they ain't used to me being quiet.

As Danielle adjusted to a new drug-free life, she and her daughters had to get to know one another again and adjust to their personalities and the ways in which they had changed. In addition, Danielle was learning about herself and her past. She was redefining her own understanding of her mother, their relationship, and what it meant in her own development. The ways in which she viewed herself and her relationships and the ways in which she behaved in her relationships with her children were all evolving, and everyone had to adjust.

This adjustment period was most challenging for the few women who regained custody of their children. Those with teenagers often experienced rebellion and misbehavior, and they struggled to reestablish authority in their household. Gertrude had stayed at the Mercy Home about five years prior, then stayed at another transitional housing program until moving into a Section 8 apartment with her four children, who ranged in age from seven to seventeen. When I met her, she was "trying to adjust to having them back. . . . I don't have any opportunity to be a stay-at-home mom and that's hard, extremely hard on me." Gertrude was struggling with her own mental health and adjustment issues, along with managing her household. She said, "My kids have gotten so spoiled and rotten that we have to go through this thing of yelling and screaming instead of talking that I get so stressed out. If I don't do something and make my life better, it's not going to be good for any of us. . . . My kids really get on my nerves and my boyfriend knows I can't really separate myself from that situation." Three of her children were teenagers, and they were rebelling and resisting her authority. During one of our interviews, she got a call that her daughter had been in a fight in school and was being suspended. She relied on her boyfriend for both financial support and help in running the house. This was in spite of his drug relapses and her children's desire to have him out of the house. Her daughter implored her, "Mom, in our new place you need a new life." While it seems likely that her boyfriend's presence in the home exacerbated the tension, she did not feel capable of taking care of herself or her children on her own.

Gertrude was experiencing a high level of difficulty relative to the other women I interviewed, especially for those who had been out of the Mercy Home for longer. However, she also was one of the few women who was living with her children at that time and whose children were at prime age for rebellion. Sharon, a thirty-four-year-old mother of four, was one of the few women who moved with her children into a supportive-housing program immediately upon leaving the Mercy Home. While she was still at the Mercy Home, she was beginning to reconnect with her children, but she said, "I have difficulty sometimes with my children to get them to understand what it is I really need to do. And why I'm here and they are over there [with her cousin]. Especially my teenager; it's really hard to establish a deep relationship with her." She was most concerned about her fifteen-year-old daughter, who "just want to be grown. She has her own way that she prefer doing things, she don't like to follow rules." Over their first few months of living together, Sharon said that "we've came to some agreements on some things and have been able to talk more than we had been," but her daughter remained a source of worry and she continued to rebel.

Sharon emphasized that she was much more patient than she had been, partly because of coping skills she learned at the Mercy Home. She was "learning their different personalities" and adjusting to living together with her children again. She said, "There's a lot of planning when you got, you know, kids." Her youngest child was in day care near her job; the three oldest were in school and after-school programming. Her oldest daughter made sure they got home from school, and by then Sharon would be home from work. She tried to incorporate her children into family decision making: "I tried to involve them with the planning as far as the arrangement of the household. Asked them all for their input for whenever we had, we sit down and we'd have little family-time meetings to talk and I tried to get they input on a lot of things, especially when it comes down to me doing meetings. That's why on the certain days that I go and certain days I don't go 'cause I want them to have free days also where they don't have to come straight here and, you know, or they can go outside. So, I created a balance, so to say."

Sharon tried to maintain a balance between caring for and providing for her children and maintaining an active involvement in twelve-step programs. After she left the Mercy Home, she regularly attended three to five meetings a week, and chaired one of them. Being involved in this way was important to her "because I'm able to be in an environment around people that working on the same things that I'm working on. That understand, you know, what I'm going through." The meetings also allowed her to give back; "I go out and speak for other people, you know. It's part of service work." She maintained her involvement even when she experienced resistance from her family, though she tried to get them to understand their value to her and include them in her planning. In addition, she brought them to work with her, so they could better understand the other demands on her time and energy. "And let everybody really see what I do all day, and on the way home they was all knocked out before we even got home. So they understand now that I be real tired 'cause of the type of work I do, I work with mentally challenged people and . . . it requires a lot of attention, you know."

It is not surprising that the women would experience tension and resistance when they tried to reestablish their authority in the family and their role as mother. In most cases, a return to their families meant not only a consistent presence in their lives but also significant changes in the nature of their relationships and the way they parented. In all of these examples, it also was apparent how the lessons the women learned at the Mercy Home and through twelve-step programs affected these evolving relationships. Sharon took an active role in twelve-step programs. This also meant asserting her role as an individual who existed in important ways beyond her role of mother. This was somewhat at odds with their families' expectations of them, which centered on resuming their role of caregiver within their families.

Despite these strains, the women spoke with pride and affection about their children. Danielle said that although she did not like much about her life at that point, she was proud of her children. "Each have a little bit of me; I get to live through them. The things I've always wanted to do I can see through them. I always wanted to be a doctor, and my baby girl [who was then in college] wants to go to medical school." Danielle especially identified with her middle daughter, who "needs me more. She reminds me of me, I'm trying to protect her . . . she had a baby at fourteen. The others don't need me as much; they are more independent." Most of the women, like Danielle, strongly identified as mothers. Their children, and their failings as mothers, were a source of regret and a motivation to desist, but they also often conflicted with twelve-step goals of avoiding worry and avoiding people tied to their offending.

FAMILIES OF ORIGIN

Although children were dominant themes in the women's desistance narratives, they were not the only family members through whose relationships the women defined themselves or their narratives of desistance. Many of the women distanced themselves from family during periods of active offending and drug use. As Bennie said about her own experience, "I didn't involve myself with my family. When I was in crime, I was in crime, I wasn't in a family. I wasn't involved with anything but crime." Even when the women's family members were implicated, directly and indirectly, in their offending histories and they had attenuated family ties prior to incarceration, these ties were rarely completely severed. As Winifred said, "My family . . . you know they got angry when I continued to act like I was a teenager. [But] it never was a strain to the point where no one's talking to no one." The women's relationships with families of origin—especially their mothers, but also fathers, siblings, and cousins—were prominent in their narratives and among the key relationships they hoped to strengthen. This was true even among those women who had abusive relationships or offending histories that were closely intertwined with family members. As such, these relationships formed a key point of tension and resistance to self-help messages to avoid people, places, and things related to their offending.

Families as Child Care

The most common and ongoing family support was child care during the women's addictions, incarcerations, and reentry. The majority of children lived with their mother's parents, siblings, or other relatives, sometimes beginning before the women's incarceration. A few of the children lived with their fathers, fathers' families, or in nonfamily homes. Frequently, temporary child custody arrangements continued after incarceration, as the women were not allowed to live with their children at the Mercy Home or in most of the other supportive-housing programs to which they transitioned. As described in the previous section, Dee Dee, Bennie, and many of the other women relied on family members to care for their children while incarcerated. Sharon's four children lived with her cousin while she was incarcerated and then living at the Mercy Home; "She been willing to give me the opportunity to get myself together. She been provided for my children and she really don't have to. She really in my corner."

In addition to full-time care, family members also often provided child care while the women worked, went to school, and attended twelve-step meetings. This gave the women the flexibility to work on their own recovery and desistance efforts without needing to worry about providing full-time private child care. This was a tremendous value, in terms of both their financial needs and their perceived cognitive change needs. Many relied on public transportation and often worked far from home. Children in their custody ranged in age from babies to teenagers and often needed care outside of school. The women also were taught the importance of focusing on themselves and their own needs, which required significant support for those with young children. This allowed them to maintain their identities as mothers while developing an identity as a desisting former offender or recovering drug user.

Tensions did emerge when the women wanted to regain custody of their children or have more access to them, or disagreed with parenting decisions made by caregivers. For example, Bennie, a forty-eight-year-old mother of three adult children, was friendly, but not close, with the sisters who raised her children. While she said they raised them into "beautiful human beings," she failed in her earlier attempts to regain custody. She said, "Like my two sisters, they raised my, one raised my son 'cause I was incarcerated. And one of them raised my daughter. And I never could get them back. I went through the courts and the whole gamut, you know, for years. . . . I would always entertain the thought of how can you profess to love my child when you don't even love her mama?" Bennie had stayed at the Mercy Home in the mid-1990s and had a stable life at the time of the interviews. Her children were grown, and she was close with them. So, although the custody battles had been a struggle at the time they took place, she went on to observe that "whatever life deal you, man, you just have to deal with it and work through it. You know, put some perspective with it."

In Bennie's case, the custody-related tensions were no longer salient to her present life. For women with younger children, these tensions were current and were often tied both to parenting decisions made by the caregivers and to the financial arrangements involved. Edie faced both issues with her sister, who had guardianship over her ten-year-old son and was living downstate. Her son had been with her sister since he was two, but after a recent visit, she was concerned. Edie said, "The time we spent together, I realized that, you know, she's not doing all she can in order to enable him to be in a better position in life, actually. . . . She's allowing him to be pushed through school and I don't think that, you know, that was fair. They shoulda, she shoulda had him in a learning program, actually." Edie expected her sister would resist letting her son return to Chicago to live with Edie, "because basically he is a provider for the house with my money and his. It kinda takes care of her home, so. But, yeah, some things have to be moving on." Edie's son received Supplemental Security Income support and she contributed court-ordered child support. She suspected that this money went toward general household expenses, and that her son's needs were not being met.

Sunshine, whose three children were then teenagers, experienced many of the same struggles as Bennie had years before. Sunshine had been arrested, incarcerated, and paroled in Illinois, though her family was in New York. This added to the logistical difficulties of seeing her children, and she had not seen them since she was arrested nearly six years before. Her son, Michael, was staying with her parents, and her two daughters, Ruby and Jackie, were staying with their fathers' families. In each interview, we discussed her plans for reuniting with her children, and each time those plans shifted between bringing one or more of them to Chicago or her moving back to New York. In the first interview, she said, "I want them here with me. I want them all here with me. But my son's got his own life. He's eighteen. Ruby's fifteen; she's got her own thing going. So the only one that would actually want to come up would be Jackie. The other two'll probably come on holidays. But that's not what I want; I want to just go back and be there with them." Sunshine also worried about being able to find housing and a job that would allow her to support her children in New York. In Chicago, she had the resources and connections of the Mercy Home. Many of her relatives also had criminal records, making it more difficult for her to stay with them while she served her three years on parole.

Sunshine clashed with Jackie's caregivers on several occasions. Jackie first lived with Sunshine's brother and his wife. Sunshine explained why this arrangement, which had initially been Jackie's preference, ended.

AL: What made you so angry with your brother and his wife?

SUNSHINE: Because, umm, they had my daughter . . . and ummm, I don't know what happened exactly, 'cause I haven't heard both sides in the same room. I heard her side and I heard their side . . . and she had hit my daughter. And that made me angry because you don't hit my daughter. My daughter ran away, my daughter umm, when she got out of school, she was in school that morning when she came out of school she didn't go straight home, she went to a park, and then stayed at the park from about quarter to three to like two in the morning by herself. For my daughter to do that, she must be going through, she must be going through some stuff with this person, these people, this lady, going through some things to make her run away, go sit in a park till two in the morning. And she wasn't even twelve years old yet, she was only eleven, and that hurt me. I just wanted to get, just escape prison, 'cause I still had about another year and a half to go, I just wanted to get out and kill this woman, and I kept saying as soon as I'm paroled I'm going straight over there, that's all I kept saying. Even when I got here, the first thing I wanted to do, I just wanted to hurry up, get paroled to New York and go over there and just kick this woman's ass. . . .

AL: So is your daughter still staying with them?

SUNSHINE: No. My daughter, she's with her father's family. She's with them, and she's doing good. She'll be coming to live with me by next year, hopefully by June of next year she'll be with me. . . . I still need time for myself to get financially stable, so before I know I can take care of her when she does come. And I still need help 'cause I've only been out four months, and I'm still trying to save, work and get things together. So I'll give myself another year.

Sunshine's daughter then went to stay with her friend and daughter's father's cousin (Barbara). By our last interview, Sunshine was planning on having Jackie return to her brother's, because she disapproved of how her friend was treating her.

SUNSHINE: Because, um, she's, Jackie's getting tired of staying with Barbara 'cause Barbara has her kind of like a slave. 'Cause every time I call her, she's washing clothes, she's washing dishes, she's babysitting, she's giving the kids a bath. She is taking Barbara's two young kids to the park. Every time I turn around she's doing something, scrubbing the bathroom. Okay, it's understandable where you treat this young lady, who's responsible and who's cleaning and cooking. But ... I mean, she cooks, she cleans, she does laundry, she babysits. I'm like, wait a minute. She's only thirteen years old. When does she have time to go—and they don't even let her go outside. They won't even let her go out. If she goes out, she can't go by herself. And I know at thirteen years old, you want to go outside and be with your friends for a little while. Let her go and play. Just give her time. Know where she's going, who she's going to be with. If she has friends and you don't know the parents, get to know the parents. ... Give her a curfew.

Sunshine wanted to parent her children, but was trying to do so from across the country and through the intermediaries she had caring for them. When she perceived mistreatment, or decisions that differed from decisions she would make, she resented it and was frustrated by the difficulties of arranging to be with her children. In the intervening months, Sunshine decided that she would move back to New York rather than have her youngest daughter come to Chicago to live with her. Both Edie and Sunshine faced the added problem of being physically far removed from their children. Many of the women's children remained in the Chicago area, so contact was easier. But the tensions and resentments between mothers and caregivers was common, especially when the mother wanted to reexert control.

Independence and Evolving Family Relationships

Few families of origin had financial resources to offer the women, and equally rarely did the women express interest in receiving financial support from their families.[2] Beyond child care, the families primarily provided emotional and social support. When the women talked about their future plans, and when family members described them, most emphasized their self-reliance and their efforts to achieve independence. EJ's brother Robert described what he liked most about her: "She stand on her own. She stand on her own. In order to survive, she's trying hard to work things out doing her own little things, you know, like finding a job, taking care of herself, being responsible. That's what I like about her more. She's got an understanding about responsibility. Now she's got more understanding about it."

Later, when I asked Robert what he had done to help EJ, he said, "The only thing I did try to do is influence her, just try to talk to her. That's the only thing I can do. I can't make her do anything; the only thing I can do is just talk to her. That's the best I could do. I talk to her a lot. It seems like I talk to her, but she's got her head on straight. She already knows what she wants to do. She don't want to go back to that place anymore." Robert supported EJ, but for him that meant emotional support and encouraging her independence. When EJ described why she felt close with her mother and brothers, she also emphasized the social supports. About her mother, she said, "She's been in my corner regardless of whether I was right or wrong." Of her brothers, she said. "They call, we get together, stop by." With both her siblings and her mother, she said, "Whatever I need I can call them." With all relationships she discussed, she emphasized the emotional and social support, not financial or other tangible, practical supports. She neither expected nor desired the latter type of support.

This desire for independence was fostered at the Mercy Home, and it motivated some of women to go to the Mercy Home. This was a way to establish their own footing, without needing to rely on their families, who had often suffered as a result of the women's addictions and offending. Dee Dee described her decision to go straight: "It was really important that I didn't do it with my family, because I felt like I wore out my welcome with my family. I didn't want to ask them for no help. It was important that I showed that I meant it this time. . . . Like, my dad don't even have to say it. I can just look in his eyes and see the pride. He's proud of me. He's always been proud of me, but he's even more proud of me now." The decision to go to the Mercy Home was one step in demonstrating to their families that they were serious about their efforts to change. Much of the emphasis once there was on the need to establish independence, especially from men and romantic partners, and to take responsibility for and control of their futures. For most of the women, this was an important goal.

The changes that the women were going through as they adjusted to their post-prison lives and attempted to desist from offending and drug use meant changing family relationships and dynamics. While their senses of self changed, so too did their understandings of their relationships with families of origin, as their perspective on past dynamics and events evolved and as they experienced new things. Bennie stressed the need to let go of past resentments and blame toward her siblings and her parents. She did "not consider my life to have been their [her now deceased parents'] fault." Similarly, Dee Dee discussed problems with her mother: "See my mother was tight. When we grew up, she wasn't affectionate, you know? She did what she was taught, you know. My grandma hollered and fussed with them, so she hollered and fussed at us. . . . I don't want, that baggage I carry, the resentments I carry. Miss B and my outpatient counselor down the street, they help me get rid of resentment for my mother. . . . At any point, I'm gonna fight this. This negative feelings, the devil, however you wanna put it. . . . Because I love my mother. You know, that's my girl."

The desistance and recovery efforts that the women were going through helped to strengthen their relationships with family and their understandings of their family members. The mere fact of the women going to the half-way house and what that represented gave family members hope for change, and the women's efforts to desist contributed to their redefinitions of family relationships. For example, Danielle characterized her relationship with her mother as "growing. . . . Because throughout my addiction I didn't, we just did not see eye to eye. I thought my mom didn't love me and I realize now that she does. And it's growing, ya know. It's coming back together." Danielle credited her sister with bringing her back into her family. "She's been clean about thirteen years. Because my family didn't, nobody else used or have used, she had to break down and understand that she was an addict too, you know? So how could she turn her back on me? So she came around before anybody came around, you know, and put her hand there for me, you know. She was a bridge to my family coming back together again." Danielle's experience illustrates the evolving nature and meanings of relationships with families of origin. Many of the women, and their family members, experienced emotional shifts in the meaning of their relationships as their circumstances changed and as their postincarceration lives became increasingly stable and positive (Giordano, Schroeder, and Cernkovich 2007). Many of the women were attempting to "let go of past resentments." Regardless of their stage of reentry, their identity within their family of origin and the resulting responsibilities remained central to their sense of self.

In many ways, family relationships are central to navigating twelve-step programs. They are often key relationships involving people with whom one in recovery must make amends. Occasionally, family members were co-offenders or living similar lifestyles. Sunshine, for example, was part of a smuggling network, and her involvement was initiated by her father. More commonly, Tasha and her cousin Sarah were both involved in offending and alcohol and drug use at the same time. Shorty D knew of her sister's offending and EJ knew of her brother's. Often, family ties were attenuated during periods of addiction, active offending, and incarceration, and improving these relationships was of central importance to the women. This is key to making amends and changing the way they relate to others, and family ties are often the only category of relationship the women cared to rectify.

Conflicting Sources of Identity: Desisting Former Prisoners and Family Caregivers

Although the women typically did not rely on their families for tangible needs, they did expect to provide support and care to members of their families. Many of the women eventually moved back to family homes, either from the Mercy Home or after time in other supportive-housing programs. The women typically framed these decisions as a need to provide support to family members, especially their mothers. For example, Lisa S, a forty-seven-year-old, moved into her mother's house after approximately two years at the halfway house and a single-room-occupancy (SRO) building. "I was working two jobs at the time. I had another job and my mother was getting sick and I needed to be there with her more. My other job was paying me pretty good money, actually. It broke my heart to leave [her job at the halfway house]. But the other job was paying more money. It was closer, it was flexible. I was able to come home and check on my mom, things of that nature." She felt that she had "outgrown" the SRO, but she also needed to be closer to her ailing mother. While she was sorry about the job she gave up, she was matter-of-fact and accepting of her decisions and her role as a caretaker of her mother and siblings. Now, the home remained a "family building. Family oriented, you know. My mother passed three years ago and this will just always be the family house. Always. All she said to me and my brother was just please never let any of her kids be out in the street."

When the women failed to live up to their caregiving responsibilities, they often experienced resentment from family members. For example, Sharon's brother Samuel was incarcerated when Sharon was the Mercy Home, and Sharon was "trying to get him some positive things that he can do upon leaving prison." Sharon's approach with her brother clearly reflected her heavy involvement in twelve-step programs. Helping her brother was a way both to provide restitution to those she had hurt, by positively changing her relationships with family members, and to carry the message forward, by giving him a positive opportunity for change. When he was released from prison, Samuel helped Sharon care for her children while he looked for a job. Caring for the children gave Samuel something positive—an important role in Sharon's family. At the same time, it provided Sharon with the time and flexibility to work and participate actively in the recovery community.

Although mutually beneficial, this arrangement also led to some tensions. Samuel said, "She's self-centered with her recovery. She always makes statements about 'me and my recovery.' Without help it wouldn't be possible. She doesn't look at what I do for the kids." From Samuel's perspective, Sharon was focusing on her own recovery to the detriment of her family responsibilities and without giving him due credit. Sharon, in contrast, emphasized her struggle to balance her needs with those of her family. In our first interview, she said that she was gaining independence at the Mercy Home. She said, "I became much more independent, in terms of doing things that I thought I couldn't do that I can do. I just landed a job, a couple of months ago. I'm just giving myself a chance . . . I actually have the opportunity to share and talk to people and give them advice, organize some things, get speakers to come in, you know. I never really took the time to involve myself in anything like that. But it is very effective, because it helps me just as much as it helps them." Sharon's greatest worry was finding the balance between her needs and her family's needs, and getting them to understand it. Along with her children, Samuel struggled with understanding why Sharon prioritized things outside her family. While he supported her recovery, Samuel also resented Sharon's new lifestyle to the extent it took her out of her home and her family caregiving roles. Sharon, Samuel, and her children expected Sharon to maintain her family roles, even when these obligations came in direct conflict with her recovery and desistance attempts.

A need to prioritize family relationships was important even among those with difficult relationships with their mothers or other relatives. For example, Tasha, her mother, Ms. Lewis, and her cousin Sarah all discussed the contentious relationship between Tasha and her mother, dating back to her childhood and continuing to the present. Tasha, who was thirty-two years old at the time of the interviews, and Sarah attributed their initiation into drug use and offending to dysfunctional and abusive home lives, and Tasha accused her mother of emotional abuse. In spite of these ongoing tensions, Tasha stated, "I actually came back here really to take care of my mom. . . . I wish that I would have stayed in Chicago, because I had built up a network there. . . . Yeah, I came back here to take care of my mom, 'cause my mom, she is not really used to Chicago life." Tasha repeatedly stressed the benefits she gained through her recovery networks in Chicago and her fears of being back in the community in which she had offended. During the interview period, she and her mother moved out of a shared apartment to separate apartments, though both remained in the same area. Despite ongoing conflict between them, Tasha felt a responsibility to take care of her mother and made significant personal sacrifices related to her desistance efforts to do so.

A sense of responsibility to parents, especially mothers, and siblings was a consistent theme among the women. A few of the women did distance themselves from their parents or other relatives, but this often took the form of less frequent contact, not no contact. Most maintained relationships and a sense of responsibility, obligation, and loyalty. These examples highlight the ways in which these women's sense of identity was tied to their ability to be what they saw as a good mother, daughter, and sister, and how this aspect of their identity often came into conflict with their identity as a desisting former prisoner or probationer. They often made significant sacrifices in their desistance efforts in order to care for ailing mothers, to support siblings and parents, and to maintain ties with and obligations to families of origin. For these women, the messages that they should avoid people, places, and things related to their offending and drug use came into direct conflict with their perceived family obligations. Rarely did they express resentment or regret about these decisions, though they did express tension over balancing their own recovery and desistance needs with the needs of other family members.

This tension was especially pronounced when the women were newly desisting, or when there were significant other changes in the relationship or circumstances. For example, Lisa S's family relationships and her own desistance efforts had been fairly stable since the death of her mother several years before. In contrast, both Sharon and her brother had both been released from prison during or immediately prior to the interview period. She was actively developing a new sense of self in recovery and asserting these new aspects of herself, which resulted in some pushback from Samuel and her children when they felt she was not fulfilling her family obligations. In Tasha's case, she had been at the halfway house several years earlier, but recently moved back to her hometown to care for her mother. Their circumstances and relationship changed significantly during the period of the interviews; the resulting tension was evident in interviews with both women.

Cycles of Relapse, Recovery, and Reoffending

An important source of shifts in the nature of relationships among family members is the ongoing processes of desistance and relapse/reoffending. At the same time the women were struggling with recovery from drug addiction and attempting to desist from offending, many members of their families of origin were in similar situations. As drug use and offending ebbed and flowed, family members renegotiated relationships to fit current circumstances. Being involved in drug use or offending led to mistrust and a sense of betrayal, and desisting or going into recovery led to hope and renewed closeness, though this often was clouded by memories of previous relapses. Through these periods, the women's relationships with families of origin remained important to them and shaped how they responded to their own setbacks.

To illustrate these family negotiations, I focus on cousins Adena and Sheila. Despite the fact they both had self-described good and stable childhoods and equally long histories of drug use and criminal activity, Sheila was seen by her family as rehabilitated, while Adena was seen as having more deeply rooted problems. Both Adena and her family members talked about the impact of her drug use on their relationships. Adena said, "When my parents found out I was using they cut me off, financially and stuff. I was determined to show them I didn't need them and I really just made things worse, you know. You know, we got what we needed to get but we're not the same as before." Adena described her mother as "too judgmental" and said, "I love my mother and everything but sometimes she just gets on my last nerve. She comes in here and has no respect." In spite of these tensions, they spent significant amounts of time with one another.

When I first interviewed Adena's adult daughter Alicia, her mother, Ms. Banks, and her cousin Joanne, all were skeptical of Adena's ability to "go straight." When I asked Alicia the likelihood of her mother's staying out of prison and drug-free, she was skeptical. "Less than 30 percent. I don't see it happening. She say she wants to get it together, but it's on her to change. I hope she won't do anything to go back [to prison]. . . . She's not drug-free now. . . . She's a good person, she knows God. She was doing good, she was clean. She went around people, places and things. She has to get tired . . . I hope she do." Alicia thought her mother was a good person but did not trust her to avoid drugs. Similarly, Ms. Banks characterized her relationship with Adena as "not too good. I don't believe her, because of the drugs. Overall, she talks, she say one thing and do another. . . . When she came home, she was doing beautiful. Then she hang out with the wrong crowd. She was good for about three months." When I asked her the likelihood of Adena staying out of prison, she said, "Unless she leave that stuff alone, I wonder. She has to make up her mind, change peoples, look at life differently. She can't do wrong and get away with it. She talks good. She has a smart head, but she do the opposite." Alicia and Ms. Banks framed Adena's drug use and relapses in the language of twelve-step programs, though neither of them had experienced addiction. Adena's cousin Joanne gave her "a year, maybe not even" before she would go back to prison, because "she's got a lot of problems."

In contrast, Ms. Banks, Alicia, and Joanne perceived Sheila to be on the right track. Sheila entered the halfway house after Adena, in part because "[Adena] gave me the strength to do the right thing." Now, according to Ms. Banks, Sheila was "a totally different person. She's doing really good, she's working." Joanne said Sheila "has ways opening up for her. She sees things differently, she's tired." Sheila "had a drug problem, but without that, she's sweet." In contrast, Joanne said Adena was "lying. She's in denial. She's okay straight, but the next thing she's off again." Adena was aware of, and frustrated by, her family's mistrust of her. During an interview with Alicia, Adena joined the conversation from the next room.

AL: Ok. Do you think [Adena's] changed since getting out of prison?

ALICIA: No.

ADENA: You don't think I've changed?

ALICIA: I mean, what's changed about you? You still cuss, talk crazy and act crazy [laughs]. I mean, you ain't changed. You think you changed?

ADENA: Yeah.

ALICIA: See, 'cause, that's 'cause you're in denial. You haven't changed.

ADENA: Am I a good grandmother?

ALICIA: I mean, she didn't ask me that. She asked me have you changed.

ADENA: Wait a minute. Am I good grandmother?

ALICIA: Yeah, you tend to your kids. Yeah, you look out for your grandkids, but that don't have anything to do with you, who you are.

In spite of Alicia's lack of confidence in Adena's ability to stay away from drugs, she considered their relationship a close one and described her as a good person, because of "the things she taught me regardless of her, you know, what she did wrong in her life. She still tried to teach me better and raise me, you know, to be open-minded."

In this case, Adena, Alicia, and Ms. Banks adopted slightly different interpretations of the relationship between Adena's drug use and her role within her family. Adena looked to her successful fulfillment of family obligations as proof she had changed; that she was a good grandmother meant that she had changed. In contrast, Alicia separated Adena's family roles of mother, grandmother, and daughter from her drug use, allowing her to be both a good mother and grandmother and a drug addict likely to use again. Ms. Banks reflected on the ways in which Adena's offending and drug use affected their relationship and her family. For her, Adena's drug use limited her ability to be a good daughter.

Ms. Banks, Alicia, and Joanne all believed that Sheila had more potential for change and to sustain these changes. Although there were differences in their personalities and in their relationships to one another, their assessments were likely also shaped by timing. Ms. Banks was much more positive about Adena's chances when she first got out of the halfway house. Her perspective changed after more time had passed and after Adena had experienced problems, like a drug relapse and the police coming to her parents' house to serve an old warrant. During the interview period, she went back to prison for several months after violating house arrest. About this, Sheila said, "I hope this one will do the trick for her, I really do. You know, life is too short. I just don't understand. I thought she the one that gave me the strength to do the right thing, you know." However, Adena also had more time than Sheila to struggle and relapse. Sheila was released from prison later and so was earlier in her reentry and desistance processes. During the interview year, Sheila was living first at the halfway house and then in a subsidized apartment. She was in no serious trouble during the year, so had not recently "proven" herself untrustworthy. If Sheila relapsed, it is likely that their confidence in her also would falter. The lack of confidence in Adena was understandable from family members who had been directly affected by her offending and relapses, but it also added to the frustrations that Adena felt in continuing attempts to remain crime- and drug-free. Like Sheila, Adena also was more optimistic when she was first released. In this early period, Adena inspired Sheila to follow her to the halfway house, and her parents and other relatives also were encouraged by her desistance attempts. As time went on, and Adena returned to her old neighborhood and her family, she began to struggle, which shaped how her family saw her.

This cycle of hope, mistrust, and cynicism also was evident in other families in which a woman relapsed. For example, EJ had recently been released from her first incarceration after a long-standing drug addiction. At the first interview with her mother and brother, both were confident in her ability to "go straight." Her mother described her as "so sweet. She's a beautiful person. She loves God; she goes to church every Sunday. She loves her grandchildren. She's different all the way around. I just love her." EJ was, for the first time since her addiction began, satisfying expectations of being a good daughter, by going to church with her mother, and being a good mother, by spending time with her grandchildren. Her brother, Robert, said he was confident in her ability to stay away from drugs and street life.

ROBERT: Well, because she knows she hurt me. She hurt me real bad when she went [to prison]. She gave me her word and this time I believe her. I actually believe her this time.

AL: Has she given you her word before?

ROBERT: No, she never did. She never did. The last time she told me she'd try; this time she gave me her word and so far she's stuck to it.

When she did relapse a few months later, their confidence was shaken, but they stressed their ongoing support. Her mother said, "She hurt me real bad. Two people told me [about the relapse] and I asked her. She needs me more than ever. I had so much confidence. . . . I'm trying to get over the hurt." Her brother said, "She disappointed me, but she's still my sister. I love her regardless."

One of EJ's primary concerns after relapsing was the effect it would have on her mother and their newly improved relationship. Her mother and brother continued to support her efforts, in part because she spent time in inpatient drug treatment and continued her involvement with a supportive-housing program, thereby demonstrating a commitment to ongoing desistance. In spite of their continued support, their initial confidence and optimism in her changed life and in their changed relationships was significantly dampened. EJ's fears of the impact her relapse would have on her mother and brothers and their relationships made her fearful of asking for help, but it also gave her an added incentive to go back into treatment.

The women themselves were not the only ones in danger of experiencing relapses. Many of the women had relatives with significant histories of drug use and offending, and the women had to learn to negotiate these relationships while maintaining their own desistance efforts. Sometimes they took the initiative to distance themselves, temporarily, from family members who were using drugs. At other times this was not necessary, as the family members distanced themselves. Lisa S described one brother with whom she was not close. "It's only because he won't allow us to be close to him. He's actively using. He's living a different lifestyle from us. So he stays away from us. It hurts us, but I understand it because it only happens when you're ready." Again, this rarely terminated a familial relationship; rather, it created distance in it until a new period of recovery or desistance began.

When Sharon's brother was reincarcerated during the interview period, they continued to write to one another, as they had during his previous incarcerations, but he was no longer a daily presence in her home. Other relatives, including her mother, continued to use drugs. With them, Sharon "just set boundaries and [kept] my distance." For Sharon, this meant talking to her mother on the phone and seeing her every few weeks. Others also talked about suspected drug use of siblings, and the resulting distance. When Sheila's brother started using drugs again, she responded, "I don't care for that. I really don't want to see him." Likewise her younger brother, who also had a history of drug use, was showing signs of using again. He denied it, but she believed she could recognize the signs. Although this led to tension and distance in the relationships, most often the women maintained some contact with their relatives, and these relationships remained an important part of their sense of self. They did not "knife themselves off" from family members, but rather renegotiated the relationships and redefined what they meant to them (Giordano, Schroeder, and Cernkovich 2007; Maruna and Roy 2007).

While the women maintained some distance from family members who were using drugs, they also maintained a sense of responsibility for them, as their relatives did for them. As with EJ's mother and brother, the women with relatives who used drugs or offended often felt a sense of betrayal and disappointment when a relative relapsed. The closeness of the relationship ebbed and flowed with the behavior of all parties, and although there was often a cumulative growth in mistrust and lack of confidence as the number of incarcerations or relapses increased, the family members were typically hopeful for changed behavior. In addition, as evidenced by Alicia's complex view of her relationship with her mother, drug use and offending were not enough to sever ties with families of origin and were not the sole defining characteristics in familial relationships. To Alicia, Adena was simultaneously a good person who taught her well, had close relationships with her children and grandchildren, and was likely to use drugs again. For the women, maintaining these ties to families of origin was as important to their sense of self as were their desistance efforts, even when one potentially threatened the other.

CONCLUSION

In their experience at the Mercy Home and in twelve-step programs, the women developed a common language and a common framework through which to understand their relationships. They learned that they are supposed to avoid people, places, and things related to their offending and drug use, which for these women includes not only partners in crime and associates but also in many cases family members. The dynamics of these relationships were in constant negotiation, shaped by perceptions of the sincerity and likely success of desistance efforts, feelings about their children's development and care, and long-standing resentments stemming from past drug use, offending, and mistreatment.

In spite of past and present tensions, family relationships were central to the women's identities, and it was in these relationships that they experienced the greatest conflict with the desistance messages they had learned. Narratives about the importance of children and family abounded, yet these relationships were complicated by long histories of abuse and neglect by multiple parties. Families were deeply implicated in offending behaviors and often represented "triggers" they were told to avoid. Yet it also was important for their sense of self for the women to be the good mothers, daughters, and sisters that they had failed to be in the past, even when this came into conflict with their desistance understandings and attempts. Maintaining boundaries still typically meant regular contact, and they often relied on relatives to provide child care. Their desire to strengthen family relationships included reestablishing and improving relationships with their children as well as taking care of their own mothers and siblings, even in cases of troubled or abusive histories with those family members and even when they worried that a decision to care for a relative would weaken their desistance supports.

CHAPTER 5

Women's Chosen Relationships and Their Role in Self-Redefinition

RATES OF MARRIAGE ARE LOW in the low-income African American communities from which most of the women in this study came, and marriage is less central to the expectations and sense of self of many (Collins 2000; 2005; Edin and Kefalas 2005). This was evident among these women as well. Marriage was a stated goal of only a few of the women, and many avoided or minimized romantic relationships. Some would have liked to be in a romantic relationship or marriage, but saw this as a distant goal to achieve after they accomplished their goals of self-sufficiency, careers, and family. Romantic relationships and friends were both also implicated in twelve-step messages to avoid people, places, and things related to their offending. Unlike their approach to family relationships, many of the women learned and embraced the goal of "knifing oneself off" from past romantic partners and friends. Although they sometimes struggled with these decisions, they were typically more willing to follow these recommendations and expectations with romantic partners and friends than with family. In addition, incarceration, the time at the Mercy Home, and changed lifestyles were natural disruptions to relationships that were often less permanent.

At the same time, some women did continue long-term romantic relationships or develop new relationships with friends and romantic partners. Many of the people in these new relationships had similar histories. At the Mercy Home, the women were introduced to other women with whom they had shared experiences. Others they were exposed to, through participation in self-help programs, housing programs, neighborhoods, and jobs, most often included large numbers of people with backgrounds of criminal involvement, incarceration, and drug use. They were taught, and experienced, the value of peer support, and these networks provided both support and potential for relapse.

ROMANTIC PARTNERS

Like family, romantic partners are strongly implicated in women's pathways to offending, their desistance and reentry efforts, and their sense of self.

Over a quarter (29 percent) of the women directly attributed their current or former drug use, relapse, or offending to relationships with romantic partners. Approximately half of the women in this study reported being in abusive relationships with romantic partners at some point (see also Richie 1996). Several of the women described these relationships as "kill or be killed." The father of one of Danielle's children abused Danielle, and later served a long-term prison sentence for beating another woman. Sheila suffered from "broken nose, broken bones, ankles, and stuff" at the hands of her common-law husband of twenty-six years. She went to the hospital repeatedly, though she lied about how she got hurt. She described her history with him: "It's been so many times it's uncountable. Because people used to even tell me if I killed him I don't think I woulda even went to jail, you know. . . . He said he would kill me first before he'd let me be with somebody else. But, actually we got into drugs. The drugs gave him more courage or what, but actually, ten or twelve years I lived in fear of him." The "one time [she] had the courage," she poured boiling water on him. Still, she never thought of leaving him. EJ said she was abused by her husband "whenever he felt like it," until she finally left him. "I had been leaving off and on. On Thanksgiving 1997, I got up from the table, went to my mom's, and never went back." Abra and her girlfriends physically assaulted each other. Shorty D said that while she never endured abusive situations for long, they "come with getting high." Mary had several abusive relationships during her addiction, but she also said, "I did a whole lot of being abusive myself. I used to like to fight." The abuse the women endured ranged from single incidents to long-term physical and emotional abuse. Many of the women stayed in these relationships, which were often with the fathers of their children, for long periods.

Both the Mercy Home and twelve-step programs strongly discourage romantic relationships, particularly in the early stages of recovery. "No sex" was one of the halfway house rules, and administrative staff saw romantic relationships as the biggest cause of relapse and reoffending among women. Staff discouraged "fraternizing" between men and women, though socializing was common when the women went to outpatient drug treatment, school, and work. Romantic relationships between women at the Mercy Home could lead to one or both of the women being asked to leave, though 12 percent of the women I interviewed had been involved in romantic relationships with coresidents. In most cases these relationships did not begin, or were kept sufficiently under wraps, until one or both had moved out.

Nearly two-thirds of the women in this study had never been married, and less than 10 percent were currently married; 10 percent self-identified as lesbians. Over a quarter had relationships with both men and women and typically resisted labels of their sexual orientation. For example, Vivian said, "I like both, but I prefer more womans than men." Another 20 percent had engaged in physical relationships with women, but for utilitarian reasons, often during their addiction or incarceration. Of this latter group, Dee Dee said, "In my addiction I did [have physical relationships with women]; when I got straight, I left all that alone. These things go hand in hand. . . . When I was using, I was drawn to women when it wasn't going good with men. . . . They served a purpose, but were unnatural." While Dee Dee remained friends with a long-term female partner, she described the physical aspect of their relationship as "the devil's work." Bennie described relationships she had with women as "it's just a means to an end. . . . It was just being manipulative, you know, just, you know, survival stuff. . . . It's just a form of jailing. . . . It's just like any other hustling." The remaining women had only had heterosexual relationships.

Developing a Sense of Self in Romantic Relationships

The women's evolving sense of self was reflected in their approach to romantic relationships. Several of the women cut ties with previous romantic partners in order to foster their own recovery. Caprice, for example, said that she ended an eleven-year relationship while at the Mercy Home because "it was time to move on." The women sometimes held on to relationships in their early days at the Mercy Home but later decided that they could not move forward in their own lives while the men continued to use drugs and/or offend. This reflects their growing acceptance of the messages they learned about avoiding romantic relationships and developing their own independence. Melvina was ambivalent throughout the year about her on-again, off-again boyfriend of seventeen years, who was also struggling with drug addiction. In the first interview, she said she was single and not in a romantic relationship, but she went on to talk about how she had changed since she had been at the Mercy Home.

MELVINA: I don't go to the old places, because I've been here for like ten months and for maybe like eight of those months I was still going around the same stuff and I haven't been there in about a month. I've met quite a few people that's sober.

AL: What made you stop going over to the old places?

MELVINA: Because I kept feeling stuck; I wasn't moving nowhere. Now I go to school. I have a lot of homework so I don't want to stay focused on that no more.

AL: And where are the old places?

MELVINA: I used to go up to my boyfriend's house . . .

AL: And he's not still your boyfriend or he is?

MELVINA: Oh, he probably is but I'm not with him right now because he's still using.

The second time I interviewed Melvina, she was back together with her boy-friend, though not living with him. He had been clean for six months, after his mother moved and could no longer take care of him. She said then, "It's the first time I've been with him sober. I see the difference; he's nicer, gentler. I like it." The last time I met with her, the two of them had relapsed together. She said, "We do good till we get high; then it always ends in an argument." Melvina's relationship with her boyfriend parallels family relationships in that their closeness ebbs and flows with the drug use of one or both partners. She felt much less of a sense of obligation or commitment to him than she did to her children and siblings, however.

Sugar experienced a similar evolution in her attitude toward relationships. She was in an on-and-off relationship for several years when she first arrived at the Mercy Home. She became pregnant shortly after her release from prison, then broke up with her boyfriend.

SUGAR: Just for now, that's just the thing that I've been wanting to do. . . . It could just be something I'm going through, I don't know . . . I mean, I knew before I found out I was pregnant, I kinda knew that something wasn't right, but it was just so comfortable 'cause we've been together for such a long time, and he been there through a lot with me. It was com-fortable, it was security, you know. . . . It's just, I've changed and he hasn't, and I think he wants the relationship to be the same as it was before, which it's not gonna be 'cause I'm not that same person. So all of that wrapped up together, and the fact that I've been locked up for so long, and it seems like I'm always in a relationship or . . . , you know what I mean? I've never been out independently, on my own, and I'm thirty years old. I know it's kinda bad timing. I really, that's what I want to do.

Over her first few months at the Mercy Home, Sugar attempted to foster her own independence, both from men and from government aid. Her pregnancy complicated these goals: "I don't want to be a welfare mom, you know. . . . I just got out of prison and was a dope addict, and you know, I'm in a recov-ery home and I'm pregnant. . . . It just doesn't look good. I don't want to be the statistic." Sugar then entered into a new relationship with a fellow Mercy Home resident, Sasha. This was Sugar's first serious relationship with a woman, while Sasha had always considered herself a lesbian. Both characterized their relationship with each other as the most significant and meaningful of their lives. Eventually, Sugar, Sasha, and the father of Sugar's child moved downstate. The three of them lived together, with their newborn baby.

The relationships the women entered reflect their approach and attitude toward their recovery from addiction and their desire for a "normal" life. As their attitude and experience changed, so did the types of relationships. Some women realized that whether the relationships were new or old, they were based in the old behaviors that they were trying to shed. Dee Dee avoided relationships when she was living at the Mercy Home but allowed herself to "venture out a little bit" once she moved into a supportive-housing building. "I've got a friend. And that's all he is. . . . So I basically have me a friend come over sometimes and limit that because I'm real comfortable with my space you know, and I don't like to share it often. With my family it's different, you know. There's no limit, I can never get tired of my family. But outside of that, my limitations, my patience is very short, you know. But as far as relationships, I don't think I'm ready for that." By the next interview, Dee Dee had ended this relationship, which she described as a "fling" that she entered into out of a desire for companionship. She wanted occasional companionship, not a committed relationship or one that involved too much time or effort. Other women similarly described relationships with "friends," sometimes people they had met recently and sometimes long-lasting on-and-off relationships. These relationships provided companionship, but "no expectations." Dee Dee also made a clear distinction between her familial relationships and her romantic relationships, seeing the former as much more important.

In discussing this first relationship, Dee Dee said, "You can't keep doing the same thing, expecting different results. That's insane." Over the next few months, Dee Dee entered a relationship with another man, though she said "I don't love him to the extent he love me." Dee Dee said she entered this relationship because "I'm just trying to step out of the familiarity of the stuff that used to get me in trouble. You know, dealing with people because of how they look or what they got, you know. I kinda went a little deep, I try to see what would be compatible." She decided that she was ready for a relationship and tried to approach it differently than she had in the past. This man was in the same housing program that she was in and was also in recovery. Although she appreciated his affectionate nature, she complained about his jealousy, possessiveness, and resentment when she expressed independence. "If he's miserable, he wants everyone to be miserable. He wants submissive women; I'm not submissive."

That relationship lasted approximately eight months. She continued to rethink her choices in relationships and how they affected the rest of her life.

DEE DEE: I just don't want to be bothered, because I been pretty peaceful since I left the Mercy Home and I'm not gonna have, if I'm not gonna upset my peace with my crazy stuff, I'm not gonna let nobody else do it. . . . I'm just lookin' at a lot of stuff, comparing a lot of stuff, type of men I dealt with when I was in my addiction. The kinda stuff I would allow myself to endure, you know, just to keep a relationship. I'm finding a lot of similarities and I'm not gonna subject myself to that because you know I'm sober, there's no excuse for my bad judgment calls, you know what I'm saying. I'm sober minded, I don't have to, I don't need anybody to validate my worth today, you know, I can do that myself. I can look in the mirror today and be proud of what I see.

Other women reflected similarly on their changing understandings of themselves, their relationships, and the role of romantic relationships in their lives. Even when entering relationships, they strove to maintain their independence and self-reliance and to change their interactions within relationships. This reflects the messages they learned at the Mercy Home of independence, not relying on any men, but especially not on "bad" men, and not engaging in the same behaviors and expecting different results.

Choices in Partners

Almost all of the women's current and former romantic partners have a history, sometimes ongoing, of drug use and offending. They met new romantic partners in housing programs, in drug treatment, at twelve-step meetings, at work, and in their neighborhoods. In all of these settings, many of those they came into contact with also were in recovery and had criminal histories. About a third of the women were romantically involved with people who had a history of addiction but were not using drugs at the time. Given the social circles and neighborhoods in which the women lived, there were few opportunities to meet others, especially men, without this background. These relationships began with a common bond and experience. They evolved—and sometimes ended—as the women's sense of self evolved and their confidence grew. In some cases, they floundered when one or both partners relapsed, but sometimes they developed into mutually supportive long-term relationships.

There is a shared understanding and empathy among partners with similar histories. Mary described her boyfriend, whom she met through a previous job. "He's kind of nerve-wracking sometimes, you know. But he's clean and sober too. Both of us trying to struggle with this thing. You know, it can be kind of hard sometimes, you know, the emotions some days. But sometimes I have cravings. Sometimes he can just say something and it'll get on my nerves, because I used to have a problem with my anger and I still have a problem with it, but it's not as bad as it used to be." She said they were close, because of their similar backgrounds: "We're both trying to go through the same thing now so that makes us feel close." She described this relationship, which had lasted for about two years at our last interview, as the most significant she had experienced. In each interview, she said they were getting closer. In the last, she said "We seem to get along better now, you know. We laugh a lot now, 'cause we used to didn't, but it seems like we getting involved with each other now." The slow development of the relationship was common; several women talked about slowly letting their defenses down and slowly letting other casual relationships fall by the wayside.

Allison and Mark similarly had a shared experience in recovery programs. They met at the restaurant where he worked. He described their meeting as "love at first sight." Mark explained his approach to relationships:

MARK: We had to come open and clean with one another. That's basically me. When I meet a girl, you know, a woman, we sit down and talk and conversate. It's not like trying to jump in bed with her. She trying to jump in bed with me, I wanna get to know you first and it's not gonna be based on sex. If we just based on sex, to me, it'll run me away. You know, I wanna get to know your past, know your whereabouts, what's going on with you . . . Okay, I'm Mark, I got one daughter, I got a nice family. I did this in my past, you know. I drunk and I used. So, if you're gonna accept me, who I am, and I accept you, who you is, and maybe that way it can work.

Allison's past did not bother Mark. He said, "I didn't dislike her for what she been in the penitentiary for, what she did in the past or nothing like that. What matters to me is what you doing in your future now." Allison described their relationship; "We learn to trust each other a lot more. But it ain't all peaches and cream. He's gotta work too. Work through things." Mark similarly emphasized their developing trust: "We real close. She's my friend, you know. I can count on her on a lot of stuff. We do a lot of things together. We see eye-to-eye on a lot of stuff, you know. We have our disagreements, you know, sometimes it be bad, moments that I disagree with. But, we work through. And our relationship is really based on our principles and God, you know. Doing the right thing. And being honest."

Allison said she was "learn[ing] to let him see the bad as well as the good. And he tells me that all the time." Two sources of tension between Allison and Mark were the frequency of their attendance at AA meetings, and Allison's related jealousy. Mark described this tension: "Sometimes I want to go out, like, you know, I go to AA meetings. You know, being honest with you. I might like to go to a meeting tonight and she might say, 'I'm tired.' And I'll be like, I'm going to the meeting because this what keep me clean, going to meetings. . . . See, her say, 'Well, you probably went to the meeting to see a girl or you probably went somewhere else.'" This was compounded because Allison was working, but Mark was not and so had more unstructured time. He said, "I can't be in the house all day while you at work. I like to get out into the world, you know what I mean?" He had been working at a major retailer unloading trucks, in a seasonal position, but "when I got an interview for the permanent job, they pulled some stuff on me. My background, and then, like, laid me off. So, I can reapply again in three months."

Still, their shared experiences allowed them to be empathetic and supportive of one another. Mark described these supports. "We go to meetings and I push her a lot. Like, let's go to meetings. We do a lot of talking. We read the Bible a lot. We stay in the positive attitude. We go to church, praise God. We have made a lot of errors. . . . She keeps me focused on a lot of stuff and tell me it's gonna be all right. Keep your head down about it, you know. God, one door get closed, God open two or three more doors for you. Stay positive. Continue doing what you been doing. You didn't get this far to let yourself down." Both emphasized God and twelve-step narratives in their approach to their current lives. Allison said trusting God was one of the most important aspects of her life. She said, "Learning how to live sober and clean. And that's the second thing I would say 'cause the first thing is trusting and believing in God, that He can take care of me. And just taking life one day at a time." Twelve-step narratives and belief in God were closely intertwined for them, as for many of the women. Allison and Mark highlighted the importance of both in their lives, and reinforced them through their relationship.

Relapses of either partner were a possibility in relationships between two people with histories of drug use and addiction. Sometimes, the relationships survived, or were reignited later. Often, however, a relapse led to the end of the relationship. Jeannette described tensions in her relationship with her boyfriend, who was also in recovery, "I still have dope tendencies; he [her boyfriend] doesn't understand." Sunshine became involved with Vivian; in the second interview, Sunshine described the start of their relationship. "We were good friends when I came here. We became really close and we was always hanging out, we got along real well. And when she moved out she said, hey, if you wanna hang out on the weekends, I could go hang out with her. So, I went over there and we hung out. . . . And I had kinda never felt like that toward a woman before, 'cause it's my first, my first female relationship. But I found myself attracted to her, and I really did like her, so . . . I was just curious, and it turned out to be something more." Vivian was more circumspect about her relationship with Sunshine and never told me the name or gender of her romantic partner. She did discuss the relationship, and the difficulties she was having with it, in our second interview.

VIVIAN: The hardest thing I'm doing now? You know, my relationship, that is the hardest thing I'm dealing with, because I wasn't ready, but it happened and I'm dealing with no matter what. Sometimes I get so frustrated, sometimes I want to quit. I'm confused, so I don't know where that's going. It's like I wasn't expecting it to happen, I don't know. Love is strong. Jealousy come in, not trusting, you know, all that stuff make me go crazy. I'm not used to begin to trust somebody. It's hard for me to trust people, especially a relationship. I've got a problem with that. I'm learning though, but I still got problems.

In spite of her struggles with the relationship, Vivian described her "loved one" as the person she was closest to. She said, "That person has been a lot of good, you know, for me, good advice, you know. Tell me about, that I can make it. Always telling me good stuff and motivate me, you know. And I guess, love me and be there with me."

Vivian and Sunshine ended their relationship shortly after this interview. Sunshine described this decision. "We broke up because she was too jealous and overprotective. . . . If you're gonna be in a relationship, there's got to be some trust and if you don't trust, what's the sense of being in a relationship? There's got to be some trust. I trusted her fully, 100 percent, but she didn't trust me, not one bit, because she's been hurt so many times and she just swore up and down I was gonna, you know, cheat on her. I just couldn't do it anymore." After their relationship ended, Vivian said, "They are confused. They don't know what they want [laughs]. They don't know that by doing that it can hurt other people's feelings, you know, and that's not right." Vivian relapsed after her breakup with Sunshine and tried to persuade Sunshine to get back together with her, to "save" Vivian. In our fourth interview, Sunshine described Vivian's relapse.

SUNSHINE: I saw her messed up. . . . They gave her till the end of the month to give up her apartment and move out. She admitted it to me. We called and she told me, ever since we broke up, like, a month after we broke, she's been miserable . . . tried to blame it on me. And she also told me that she would be better and stop if I took her back. She tried to make me guilty and blackmail me into taking her back. 'Cause I knew what was going on and when she called me and we had a long conversation and we talked for a long time, and I asked her if it was true. . . . I said, you can't blame that on me, blame that on yourself. You have to go on. She goes, that she can't. She knows she'll do better, go into a program, and get cleaned up if I took her back. And I told her that I'm sorry. I'll be your friend, I'll be there for you to talk to you when you need me, but I won't do it. I'm not gonna go back. I don't go back. I go forward. And, I said, I wasn't happy when with you. I was miserable. 'Cause you're too jealous, too obsessed. You had me cheating with everybody that you can think of and I wasn't doing anything.

Although Sunshine was concerned for Vivian, she did not believe she could save her; rather, Vivian would have to go back into recovery herself. Sunshine's response to this was also influenced by her experience in twelve-step programs. "She wanted me to feel sorry for her, feel guilty, and blackmail me into taking her back. But that, she wasn't going to do that to me. Because I was told anyone who relapse, don't. If someone blames you for their relapse, don't ever feel guilty about it, because no one put a gun to their head. They, they control their own emotions, their feelings. They need, they need to learn to deal with it. Especially if they've been in recovery for more than a year. . . . That's all I heard." Sunshine did not have a personal history of addiction, but she did participate in twelve-step programs and drug treatment, as a condition of her parole and for living at the Mercy Home. While she first went to AA and NA meetings because they were parole requirements, she later said they provided a valuable perspective, "I'm learning from, it's helpful and it kind of hurts because I see what these people are going through and I was part of that. I brought it, you know, and I helped the people sell it to them. And you hear their stories and I was part of that. And that's sad and it hurts, because they tell some stories and I'll just be like, wow! What they've been through, what they've done." Through these experiences, and her relationships with others at the Mercy Home, she learned what to expect, which shaped how she responded to drug addicts in her life.

By the third interview, Sunshine was in a relationship with a new boyfriend, whom she met through Starr, another friend from the Mercy Home. "He's her best male, but I'm her best female, buddy." By our fourth interview, that relationship had also ended, because he also relapsed. She said, "I know he relapsed. I was waiting for him to admit it to me, so I kept going, giving him hints. He finally admitted it and I was really happy, 'cause I really care about him and I didn't want him to go down the drain." When he did not go into a rehabilitation program, as promised, she ended the relationship. She then met another man on the bus, but "he smothered me too much. I couldn't do it. . . . I said, You know, you're welcome to drop by once in a while. I didn't say every day, all day. And then he was just popping up, just popping up. I said, Oh, no, you gotta go. I need some freedom, honey." At the time of our last interview, Sunshine was single and planning to remain so, at least for the time being.

Shorty D experienced both destructive and supportive relationships with men with histories of drug addiction. Her first boyfriend, whom she met in recovery meetings, began using again and brought drugs around her. She also then relapsed. She said that while she might have relapsed anyway, it would not have happened when it did without his influence. Her second relationship was with Greg, whom she met at a Laundromat. Greg also had a history of drug use. He said the day he realized he was an addict was "the day I wanted to quit. It was the worst thing I ever fought in my life." He thought it was very likely that Shorty D would stay off drugs in the future, because "she's got me. She's not satisfied with that type of lifestyle; she's been through it already." When asked what he would do if she did relapse, he said, "I'd snap. I wouldn't want it to be around. I am dead against it myself."

In each of these cases, the partners' pasts were an important dimension in their relationships, both as a place of empathy and conflict. They had a shared history, often ongoing, of participation in twelve-step programs and other drug treatment. They faced similar challenges in finding and keeping jobs and resisting the temptation to use drugs or return to the streets. The dynamics in relationships also were a dramatic shift from the relationships they had while actively using drugs. Many women talked about violent and destructive relationships they had during their addictions and emphasized the need to learn to trust, and the difficulty in doing so.

Long-Term Relationships

While many of their early relationships were fleeting, sometimes they developed into longer-term relationships. In some instances, both the woman and her partner went into recovery and desisted from offending, and their relationship continued. While according to much conventional wisdom and the messages they heard in recovery settings the women should have ended these relationships, over time some developed into strong, supportive, and conventional relationships. The couple redefined themselves, both independently and together, as law abiding and in recovery.

Some of their relationships began before their current attempt to desist. Linette met her fiancé, Chad, when she was in a work release program during the second of her three incarcerations. During the interviews, which began shortly after she left the Mercy Home, they had been together for four years and were living together in his mother's house. She described him as "a big help. He's always trying to understand what's going on. He's a caretaker." Chad said, "I've been into stuff myself. We both had done bad things. . . . I'm getting too old; I woke up and realized it ain't a place to be. Now, I go to work and I come home. If I go out, we both go." He described Linette as "a beautiful person, she's kind and honest. She's never told me a lie, as far as I know." In talking to each of them, and watching them interact with each other, they did seem to have a strong and positive relationship. Their shared experiences with drug use and offending provided a sense of empathy, support, and equality in their relationship. In my second interview with Chad, he said their relationship had gotten stronger, in part because Linette was now off parole. "When you on parole, you think about a lot of stuff. Tension, tension be there."

Linette and Chad met late in their offending and drug use careers. A few women continued relationships with partners they had been involved with in the heart of their offending. One example of this is Bennie and Joe. They had been married for twenty-five years, with eleven children between the two of them (two together) and most recently had been living together for six and a half years. They stayed together through two incarcerations each and two attempts at recovery. Their latest period of desistance and recovery had lasted close to ten years, and both were confident it would continue. Bennie said,

"God and my husband, those are where my loyalties lie" and described Joe as "he wants to be the right side of my brain. He wants to finish my sentences and my thoughts. I need to put him in a box and sell him—he's a genius. . . . We're closer than close." Bennie attributed her incarcerations, and subsequent sobriety, to "God doing for me what I couldn't do for myself." Their last relapse was a reaction, according to both of them, to the death of her mother. Since then, they had endured the death of Joe's brother without relapse.

Bennie had long been involved in drug use and offending when she met Joe. She said, "And then I met Joe. And I liked him. . . . I was curious. I became curious because I didn't have a companion. I was just doing my own thing." Joe also had a long history of drug use when they met. Joe describes how he met Bennie, and the inauspicious start to their relationship.

JOE: I was having, I was in a situation with two other women. My wife, and another lady. . . . So, I got five kids with my wife, and three kids by her. And I was living in two houses: a situation. And I didn't know Bennie. And, one of the girls called my father and told her that, uh, she needed him to come get me one night. I was high, I was using, I was getting high, and the girl had stopped getting high. She was trying to straighten her life up, and so he came by, picked me up. . . . I think I was thirty-five years old at the time. . . . I was using at the time, right. So I went out, I had some money and whatever, and I went to this place to shoot some dope. And I had no place to get high, I bought some dope, now I got no place to get off. So, they was telling me where to go. So I went around this place on 47th and Michigan, and they told me to go in there, so I'm hearing on the third floor there's a shooting gallery. . . . And that's how we started going together. And it was hers, come to find out, the place was hers . . . I stayed. What happened is, I sort of stayed right there. I didn't go back to where I lived. I had two places where I was living, but I was like, I had sort of messed that up, being in a situation with women, or whatever. . . . And later on she got pregnant by me. I think it was during that same summer. So, we had our first child about nine months later, something. So, that was how we got together, and then we sort of stuck together pretty good.

Once their relationship began, Bennie and Joe were incarcerated several times with overlapping sentences. Joe said, "So, it's all a game until you wake up one day and you're thirty-seven, thirty-eight. Like, when I woke up in '84, I was what, thirty-eight? Somewhere around there. Almost thirty-nine years old. Still ain't got a grammar school diploma, you know what I mean? Sitting in, sitting locked up for a month, people call you Pops. . . . Start doing the things that's positive in the jail instead of playing games, you know?" Joe emphasized that he and Bennie were not charged on the same cases: "They wasn't together. It was two separate cases. . . . I just, it just happened like that. We were not in the streets together, get caught up. You know, it wasn't like that." After both simultaneous incarcerations, they both went into recovery.

JOE: We changed two times. We fell off once. . . . We talking about two different times, okay? And two different recoveries. They different. Okay? One recovery is based on spiritual Christianity. Period. The first one. The second one is based on the twelve-step program and spirituality. And, I mean, Christianity and spirituality. Okay? Now, what's the difference? It's a difference in them, okay? One is supported by God and the church, that's the first one we talking to, okay. Go to church and God, say prayers, this and that. The second recovery is covered by, recovered by giving of oneself and allowing other people to sponsor you and help you to see how you need to go in order to make this thing work. In other, the AA program, the NA program, you got another type of support. Okay? You got people that's been there, done that. Telling you they story. Then, you know, what's, you know, how to work, how to work if you worked it. On the other hand, the first recovery, you out there just don't wanna get high, just don't wanna use. Just wanna, you know, don't be a part of getting high and all that. Just live, you know. . . . Not no meetings or nothing, just straight soul work. That didn't work. It worked for seven, eight years. I think we went back out there in '90 and '91, then we stayed out for about four years and then we came back in on the next bid.

After her third incarceration, Bennie went to the Mercy Home and then moved into the apartment she and Joe ultimately shared. Joe went to an affiliated halfway house after his second incarceration, followed by a year and a half in another housing program.

Joe thought the time apart during their incarcerations and halfway house stays may have helped their relationship. While their lives and experiences paralleled each other, both made independent decisions and steps to stop using drugs and stop offending. Their shared background led to additional understanding and empathy, and their relationship was on an equal playing field. Joe described their relationship as a success because of "my maturity, basically being humble, allowing her ideas to come in without resentment." While Joe also attributed their success to God and the church, he considered himself an inspiration for Bennie. According to him, she "did a copy of what I did. What I do, I relate it to her, she do the same thing," and they supported each other in transforming their lives. At the same time, he saw her as an independent, strong, and intelligent woman who had her "own mind" and survival skills. Joe said that he helped Bennie by "staying clean myself. I am not doing it for her, but it may help her. It's an individual situation. It's on you, not me." Bennie's

loyalties were with "God and my husband." While the origins of their relationship do not sound conducive to a lasting and desisting lifestyle together,
they were both desisting from drug use and offending and were supportive of
each others' recovery.

That desistance from offending and recovery from drug addiction are
processes that often include setbacks and relapses affected these long-term
relationships. Bennie and Joe went through one relapse together, and their
relationship survived. Angela was struggling with her husband's relapse and
reincarceration. She described her husband: "Well, this is my partner in crime.
I've know Kevin twenty years. We entered the addiction together. Even though
this was my second incarceration, I went back after my first one. On the first
one, we got convicted off the same case. The second one, we were partners
in the same crime. We got convicted of the same crime. So that's what happened with that." At the time of the interviews, they had been married for
just under two years. Over the summer, he was jailed on charges of driving
without a license while visiting friends in their hometown. In addition, he had
used drugs. When she found this out, she would not let him come home. She
was frustrated and angry, because she "thought we were working toward the
same goals." She was doing well, working and getting involved in her church
and school and did not want to jeopardize her own successes. She did not
know whether she should stick by him or leave him. In addition to demonstrating the challenges of being in a relationship with an addict or recovering
addict, especially one with whom you have a shared history of addiction, these
examples also illustrate how these relationships change over the course of several months or years. The relationships reflect the inherent instability of the
desistance process and the ongoing process of redefining self.

Relationship Avoidance

Some of the women, especially those newer in their recovery, embraced
the messages about avoiding relationships. Their time at the Mercy Home, and
often beyond, was a period to focus on themselves and their needs and goals.
At the time of the interviews, 41 percent of the women were not in a relationship, and another 10 percent were "just friends" with someone and did not
want a serious relationship.[1] Some women saw this as a permanent state, while
others saw it as temporary, until they were ready to form solid, long-term
relationships. For many of the women, this was clearly influenced by the self-
help messages of avoiding relationships. While a few of these women wanted
romantic relationships, most were consciously single. When I first interviewed
Sheila, a few weeks after she arrived at the Mercy Home, she was not in a
relationship and said she was "not planning on having one too soon either. . . .
Because right now, I've got more important things to do, working on myself,

to start getting involved with someone else. I've got to put myself first, better myself." Similarly, Lisa D was "in a romantic relationship with her books," referring to her need to focus on her schooling.

Many of the women desired sex and companionship, though they kept their relationships casual. Tasha, who balanced several relationships, attributed her lack of commitment to any of the men to having seen her mother abused when she was a child. She was also a rare woman among this sample who listed getting taken care of as her main priority in a relationship. She described two of the men she was involved with, the first of whom was married.

AL: If he ended up ever leaving his wife, would you want to have relationship with him?

TASHA: Yeah, yeah, I would, 'cause Bogart is a good provider. He's very good. He's a very good provider. He make sure the bills paid, you know what I'm saying? And I wouldn't really, I would have to worry about nothing, I wouldn't really look at the sexual perspective with him. I'd just more or less look at getting tooken care of, you know.

AL: So, what's the most important thing to you then about a relationship?

TASHA: Getting tooken care of. You know, being able to, you know, for your boyfriend to be able to provide for you in some fashion or other. That's the reason why I can't be with Michael, 'cause he got, he had been in prison so many times his record is so bad that he doesn't even try to even try to find a job. He just automatically assumes that his record is so bad nobody will hire him. So, that's the reason why he is not allowed, that's the reason why I won't allow him to stay with me or try to move in with me. Because I tell him I'm not gonna take care of you. I can't take care of you. You know, I got all these bills and stuff and what money that I do have left is gonna be for me to do what I wanna do for me. I'm not gonna be in here giving you my money and you sitting up in here all day long ain't doing nothing for yourself, you know. You a man. You know, you supposed to be out here, you know, providing for me. You know, at least be able to say, here, here's a couple dollars on the bill. You know, so basically, me and Michael's relationship is really sexual. We get together and just have sex and I drop him back off, you know.

Tasha was one of a few women who wanted a man to provide for her financially. Some of the other reasons she listed for not getting more involved with Bogart or Michael were more common. She enjoyed having sex with Michael, but resisted having to take care of a financially dependent man. This reflects the men who were in her social world, whom she described as "guys that I know that can't really offer me nothing," and the lack of "marriageable" men in disadvantaged urban communities (Wilson 1987). Still, her relationships with Bogart and Michael both lasted several years. During the year of inter-views, she also had a relationship with a twenty-two-year-old man but said, "I just let him go 'cause he was just too slow. He wasn't trying to do nothing for hisself and I was just like I ain't got the time for it. But it was just like, I was like being a mother to him, you know?"

Women often kept their relationships casual. They repeatedly emphasized their need for independence, and their romantic relationships did not typi-cally form a central aspect of their identity. For most, a long-term committed relationship was rarely a primary goal, especially in the short term. In part, this reflects their structural position as primarily low-income African American women, who tend to have lower rates of marriage and lower levels of support for marriage than white women (Edin and Kefalas 2005; Sarkisian and Ger-stel 2004). As with those who did have romantic relationships, these decisions reflect their particular stage of recovery and desistance. Because men were heavily implicated in many of their drug addictions and offending, the women felt the need to be by themselves, at least for a time, in order to establish a drug-free and independent life (Cherlin et al. 2004).[2] Lisa S, who would like to marry eventually, says, "I would like to [have a relationship], but there's no room now. I have to prioritize [work, school, and her youngest child at home]."

A lack of interest in romantic relationships also reflects the disruption of incarceration. Tammy's long period of incarceration led to many of the same insecurities that the other women had. Tammy said, "I just have to remind myself that I don't have to rush, you know, 'cause I can't bring back the four-teen years, the things I missed out on, in, what, six months." She was incarcer-ated at age nineteen, and "I never had a relationship before I got incarcerated. I was going to school and I just never had one." She did have several relation-ships with women during her incarceration; "It was serious, but I wouldn't say that it was so much. It was serious, but it was not a sexual relationship. It was just emotional, just a relationship, during the time, at that time, it was serious to me." She found relationships in prison to be easy, because "a lot of females was attracted to me. I guess they saw me as resembling, as looking like a boy. So, there was a lot of people attracted to me, so you know, but I didn't just go with anyone."

Outside, however, she found romantic relationships difficult to navi-gate. Her entire experience of romantic relationships took place in prison. Over the course of the interviews, she seemed to become more comfortable with the idea of continuing to have same-sex relationships. In our second interview, she described her goals for a family. "About relationships. I would like a husband, because I like the family thing and I would like my children to have a father, but I just have a fear with men—the abuse. That's the only thing I'm afraid of with that, so I wouldn't go there with that. I'd probably adopt. . . . I'm not really looking for a husband, it's just that I would like for my children—if I have them." Tammy described herself as a wallflower, though she wanted to be more outgoing. In the third interview, she stopped referring to men as potential partners, and talked about working up the courage to go out more, be more comfortable in social settings, and, specifically, to go to gay clubs.

TAMMY: I wanna go to a gay club, but I'm scared, I'm nervous. Can't do it.
AL: How come?
TAMMY: I've never been to one and I'm just, I don't know, real nervous. Like, if someone approach me, I just, I'm just nervous. Especially with people I haven't met. It's frightening. But, if I go with a group of my friends, and I've always been invited to the gay parade and never went. And a lot of people ask me, even Danielle said she was gonna go with me and she's not gay, but she said she would go with me. And she been before. Her and her sister always go, you know. And they say straight people go and all that, but I said, Danielle, are you sure you're gonna go with me, 'cause I do not wanna go by myself.

Still, she did not feel comfortable approaching anyone, partly because "I don't want to guess if they're, you know, what's their preference." In the fourth interview, she self-identified as a lesbian. Still, her primary interest was in developing friendships and in having children, not in a romantic relationship. She said, "My mind just hasn't been focused on it." Tammy struggled with developing her social life. She was shy, which made it a struggle for her, but spending her entire adult life in a prison setting also hampered her. Her interactions with potential partners were dramatically different in the highly constrained environment of prison. Getting to a point of feeling comfortable with a romantic relationship was a long-term process for her. In some ways, this paralleled the women who were attempting to learn to change their expectations and patterns from earlier relationships that often involved drug use and offending, along with violence and mistrust.

In all cases, the women were learning to reframe their expectations of others, while also setting new goals and expectations for their own lives and a growing sense of self-efficacy. Many of the women desired companionship and sex, though many resisted a more committed relationship. Many also reflected on the ways in which previous relationships were implicated in many of the behaviors they were now trying to avoid, which made them wary. While some of the women had a hard time moving past long-term relationships and aspired to having new relationships at some point, many viewed romantic relationships as much more disposable than those with their families.

FRIENDS AND ASSOCIATES

Like family members and romantic partners, friends and associates are closely tied to the women's histories of offending and drug use. Drug use and criminal activity were common among their social networks in childhood and adulthood. This became even more pronounced during periods of active drug use and offending. In contrast to family, however, the women had few qualms about cutting ties to "people, places, and things" related to their drug use when it came to friends and acquaintances. The women characterized their friends into three groups: associates, childhood or long-term friends, and friends from the Mercy Home or other recovery and desistance contexts. Relationships with associates were centered on drug use and offending and were often utilitarian. The women had little desire to resume these relationships. Ending them posed little conflict or difficulty for them; they had little in common outside of drug use, so neither person had an incentive to maintain ties. In some cases, the women were able to reestablish relationships with childhood friends. Typically, these friends were churchgoing people who had no criminal or drug histories or had established periods in recovery. Occasionally, the women maintained tentative ties with friends who were beginning to desist. Although they did not want to maintain close relationships with active drug-using associates, they also strove to treat these people with respect and equality, an attitude also influenced by Mercy Home and twelve-step messages. In addition, the women developed new networks, largely through their experience at the Mercy Home and in drug treatment. These friendships formed a valuable source of peer support, though these relationships, like those with romantic partners, were often challenged or terminated by periods of relapse.

Cutting Ties

When asked if they wanted to reestablish contact with old friends, most women quickly said no. Avoiding associates who remained involved in drug use or offending was a twelve-step message that the women embraced to a large degree. Sheila made distinctions among her old friends. She said, "I'm not trying to find none of my old friends because I know what they're all about, except a few. And I found one of them. I went to church with her yesterday as a matter of fact. The ones that's clean and sober, but the other ones I'm not trying to find out." Outside of a few childhood friends who were in recovery or who did not have a history of drug use, most made little attempt to reconnect with those who were their most recent social circles. Winifred missed some of her old friends, but she did not trust herself to reestablish contact with them. She said, "I'm scared to do that. I'm not that strong yet. I try to kind avoid them, but I do miss and want to talk to them."

In addition to being taught the value of avoiding people associated with their drug use, they also reflected on their behavior and attitude toward others while using drugs and offending. Shorty D described her former relationships, "I mean, really I wasn't close to anyone. I was just close to whoever had what I wanted, you know, money or drugs. I really had no friends, 'cause you know when you getting high, well, for me, it was like I trusted no one, respected no one, because I knew power, you know what I'm saying? I felt they was out to get what I got, and be up, so 'cause that's what I used to do. Be around people for what they got. When it was gone, I was gone." Dee Dee similarly reflected on her past, "I can remember when I used to do people like that. You know, they're trying to get their life together; in a blue moon they pop up, and I'm like, what's you doing around here? Take me to where the stuff at." This influenced her choice to maintain distance from most of her old friends. She compared herself to a friend in recovery who had recently relapsed: "I have no use for 'em [old friends], you know, because most of them are still in their addiction. I have one friend, he had like thirteen years clean and it seemed like when I got it together, then he fell off. And I actually used to go over out of concern. He actually tell me he didn't want me to come over no more. . . . He said, 'because you look good, and I've never seen you look this good or do this way. I just don't want you to lose it.'" Dee Dee was touched by this, and said, "I know that was love." She continued to talk to him on the phone, but kept her distance. The women recognized that drug addicts, including themselves, could be unreliable and untrustworthy, and they believed that too much contact was likely to trigger a relapse. Lisa S had a similar perspective on her old relationships, adding that the resulting distance was often mutually desirable. "Because they use drugs and I don't, I feel like we have nothing in common. . . . When you stop using drugs, users don't want to be friends. I love them from a distance."

Although it was generally easy for the women to avoid contact with old associates, they balanced their desire to avoid them with a need to be non-judgmental and supportive. Dee Dee described another friend of ten years who was currently incarcerated.

DEE DEE: I been being there for her, you know, as best as I know how. I never stopped loving her, even though I got straight. I just know I can't be around her, you know. And I let her know that, you know, I don't never think that I'm so above you all now that I can't come [to visit her in prison], you know. I don't have no problem if you call me, I talk to you. But, just to be visiting or things like that, I can't do that. If I wanna keep what I got, I can't do that. . . . And, like I told her, you got something I didn't have, you know. I had to kind of build all my new contacts and new friendships. But if you come out and you give yourself a chance, you got

me. . . . So, I'm hoping that, you know, I can be of some help to her. . . .
You know, and let her know she is not by herself. And that's what's important. That was what was important to me.

Dee Dee drew some boundaries with her friends, but she also strove to support them in ways that she was supported at the Mercy Home, consistent
with "carrying the message forward." In addition, she asserted that she did
not think she was better than her friends who were still using drugs. This balance of maintaining some distance but not putting themselves on a pedestal
was important to the women. They frequently asserted that they do not snub,
judge, or disrespect current drug users.

   In the preceding quotes, Dee Dee described her relationships with friends,
not associates, but the women have similar nonjudgmental attitudes toward
acquaintances. For example, Mary moved back to her old neighborhood and
continually saw former associates. She avoided spending too much time with
them but did talk to them in passing. She said, "Most people in the neighborhood I know around here I used to get high with them, you know, but I
tend to shy away. Well, you know, I can speak to them or something, because
you just don't do people like that. You know, because they got a problem, you
know, because I don't want nobody to do me like that if they was clean and I
was still getting high." The women did not see themselves as superior because
of their desistance, and they remembered when they were in the same place as
their friends and acquaintances then were.

   This attitude reflects their experiences of feeling judged and Mercy
Home messages of humility. In addition, it reflects twelve-step messages of
equality and mutuality, and an emphasis on the shared experience of addiction
(Archibald 2007; O'Halloran 2005). Women who violated this norm were
strongly criticized. Mary, for example, described one woman who was a cores-
ident at the Mercy Home: "There was this one girl and she would never see
her own problems, but she would say something about everybody else's like
she was special. And I couldn't figure out why she would feel that way, because
she wouldn't be there if she was. . . . You know how people will judge you for
what they done did." Any perceived sense of superiority or "specialness" caused
significant tension among residents, and between residents and staff, and there
was often a fine line between progressing in one's own desistance and recovery
and appearing judgmental of those newer to the experiences.

The "Sisterhood" of the Mercy Home

   In most cases, the women strove to establish new friendships and new support systems. Many women cited the camaraderie, support, and "sisterhood" of
the other women as a primary strength of the Mercy Home. While there was
a general sense of this supportiveness, they typically formed close friendships

with one or a few of the other women. Danielle described her friendships with Tammy and EJ, which continued from their stay at the Mercy Home to the Refuge Apartments. "I can talk to her [Tammy] and she does not judge. You know, she's just a friend. Not like any other friend that I thought I ever had, she's a true friend. . . . We three [Danielle, Tammy, and EJ] basically take care of each other, you know. Out of all of us that came here together, the three of us basically take care of each other." Similarly, Tammy and EJ both considered Danielle a close friend. Tammy described Danielle: "She's like a big older sister to me. I was incarcerated for a long time so there was places that I was not familiar with on the West Side and she would go with me. . . . She really do not mind at all, going out places with me, and I really appreciate that." EJ said, about Danielle, "we understand each other. . . . She is good support. If one of us is feeling down, the other is there. I have other friends, but I wouldn't confide in them."

Their shared experiences, in prison, at the Mercy Home, and with drug addiction, were central to the bonds the women shared with one another. This type of bond was central to the peer support model of the Mercy Home. These relationships were particularly close when they were living together, either at the Mercy Home or in other supportive housing, though they also extended beyond this. Adena described her relationship with Jeanette:

ADENA: What makes the two of us close now is, I think, the struggle that we both have with this addiction and trying to stay focused and trying to stay clean. You know, that's really, that's it. You know, trying to stay focused and help each other. And because we both been incarcerated, I think we understand that we can tell each other things that we can't tell other people that's not been locked up. For me, that's how I feel. You know, and she's a decent person. She's just like everybody, she just needs a chance. Oh she's pissed me off and I've pissed her off more than once. We piss each other off, but we be okay.

Because these relationships were typically new, they had similar experiences, but without the burden of having experienced the hurt and mistreatment that was common among family members and close loved ones during active periods of their addictions. In addition to forming bonds with fellow residents, many of the women cite staff members among their friends and confidants. Women commonly cited the program manager and director as important supportive relationships, which often continued past their Mercy Home stay. Former resident staff members often served as both friends and mentors. They had lengthier experiences desisting, and so served as role models. Adena described Lisa D: "That's my best friend. She's my case manager. . . . I love Lisa D so much. That's like my mentor. I mean she's someone that really helped me a whole lot." Many women cited Lisa D as a friend, important influence, and role model.

The importance of shared experience with drug addiction, recovery, and incarceration continued after the women left the Mercy Home. Lauren had been at the Mercy Home about eight years earlier. In our first interview, she described the sense of family she gained with her fellow residents.

LAUREN: Because at first I thought I was just coming here to make sure that I wouldn't go back to where I had always gone to, so that I wouldn't use drugs. But in coming here, I gained a sense of family. Not with staff, but with the women here. And with staff, I'm just saying more so with the women here, because the women that I came to the Mercy Home with, I still bond with those women. So, you know, we still network together, we still talk, we still go out together. So it was like gaining a sense of what family is about. You know, and as in other families, you got roles to play: the kid that wants to jump around all the time, you got the one that everybody tries to blame for everything, the one that whines about everything, and we find that out in our relationships as friends and we learn to accept each other for that. We call each other on each other's bullshit. So it was pretty much not what I expected, especially with a group of women. I don't know why they always say, "I can't be with women. I never hung out with women," then they find out they'd rather hang out with a bunch of women over a bunch of guys any day. But it's okay.

Lisa S also stayed at the Mercy Home nearly a decade before the interviews took place. Although only one of her current close friends had been at the Mercy Home with her, all were recovering addicts. She described her closest friend: "She'll call me on my stuff. That's what friends do; she don't worry about my feelings, she worry about what's right and what's wrong. . . . Because a lot of times, Andrea, we can think we're doing the right thing and in our heart, we might feel like that, but somebody else might have a different viewpoint. And they can present it to you and give you a chance to look at it in another way and dig down in your motives. So she would be that one." Lisa D described her friends in similar terms: "They're like sisters. We have had similar experiences and have overcome a lot. They understand what friends are. They don't make excuses, they don't sugar coat."

Women commonly described their contemporary friends as a combination of support, understanding, and "tough love." Likewise, their friends often cited the women as having these traits. Laura, for example, was a friend of April and a resident of the same single-room-occupancy building. She described what she liked about April: "Her personality. She's a good person, very outspoken. She'll help you with a problem, she's a good listener and she'll give you suggestions on what you should and should not do. She has a soft heart. She's the only one I would go to with my problems." While Tonya, April's coworker, described her as "sometimes a little emotional for me," she also described her as "honest" and said, "I know I can call her and say 'I need you' and she's there."

Strains in Friendships

Relapses into drug use were a source of tension and strain among friends, as in other relationships. Among the women who did relapse, there was a sense of sadness, shame, guilt, and regret when they talked about it, both in terms of their own relapses and those of the other women. After Danielle relapsed, her relationship with Tammy shifted. During our last interview, Danielle described her relationships with EJ and Tammy. She valued both EJ's and Tammy's sincerity, but characterized their dynamic differently. "EJ's like a sister to me. Tammy is . . . so naïve and she looks to me for guidance with things, you know. So it's like more like a sister relationship with EJ, more like a mother-daughter relationship with Tammy." Tammy had little experience, prior to the Mercy Home, with drug use or addiction, and the relapses of her friends at the Refuge Apartments hit her hard and had a significant effect on her relationships with them. After Danielle relapsed, Tammy started spending time with Sunshine, who also had recently experienced relapses of friends. She and Danielle remained "more distant, because a lot of times she bail out on me. We set dates to go places and she'll bail out, or won't even call to let me know. One thing is, do not bail out on me." Danielle's relapse highlighted and made salient the differences between their experiences, which created distance in their relationship. In contrast, EJ and Danielle shared this history, and they remained close during this period.

Even for those who did have a history of drug use, the relapses were a source of tension and often led to distance in these relationships. Much as the Mercy Home staff members represented success stories, and lives to which they could aspire, these relapses represented what else could easily happen to them. Sally, a friend of Shorty D's and another SRO resident, felt close to Shorty D because of their shared drug history. She was in treatment for the first time, and when she learned that Shorty D and others had relapsed, she talked about the impact of relapses on her. "A lot relapse. It doesn't bother me what the next person does. I know what I want and I don't want temptation to come up on me. When I see them, I speak, then I move on. It hurts. . . . It's my first time in recovery. I stay my distance. There are two women on my floor that I talk to on a regular basis." As with the women's other relationships with active users, Sally was careful to not judge the women who had relapsed. She was polite to them but maintained some distance to try to protect herself from possible temptation. That the women valued these relationships because of their shared experiences with both addiction and recovery made relapses among their friends particularly painful, as reminders of their own possible setbacks.

Not all of the women's friends and acquaintances had uniformly positive views of the women, and it is here where gendered attitudes toward offenders become most apparent. Delilah maintained a few long-term relationships, and in them, her gender and her role as a "bad" mother shaded their view of her. In one case, her friend Denise described Delilah's past: "Talk to the kids to get the true story of dope fiends. She was the best pick-pocket on the South Side. She was with my son's father at the time; he was a hustler. They made money that paid the rent. What can I say . . . Delilah's doing good, but where are Delilah's kids? I don't like no woman who walks off and leaves her kids. . . . I love her like a sister, but I don't like what she done with her kids." Delilah described Denise as "nice in her own way. She lives in her own little world." Delilah also maintained contact with Jeremy, whom she met about twenty years ago "partying," and his mother. Jeremy was a heroin addict who had been in treatment in the past, and Delilah was trying to help him get back in treatment. Jeremy said, "We're pretty good friends. She tell it like it is, she don't hold nothing back." Delilah saw Jeremy's mother, Ms. Jones, as a positive influence on both her and Jeremy. She said, "His mother has strong ties to the church. She's good to talk to." Ms. Jones also described Delilah as "a truthful person. She didn't try to be something different. . . . Now she's a normal person. I wasn't used to seeing a woman in that type of stuff." She went on to say "When I first saw her, it was something different. She was running around with the guys . . . she was totally out there, she had lost her mind." For both Denise and Ms. Jones, the fact that Delilah was a woman and a mother was what was most problematic about her past behavior. Neither of them condoned anyone's drug use or offending, but it was particularly bad in Delilah's case because women and mothers should not be on the streets.

A history of drug use also colored relationships with friends. Sometimes this resulted from firsthand experiences with the woman's behaviors while using drugs, and occasionally it reflected a more general distrust of drug users. Denise, for example, said that although drug addicts may stop using drugs, the behaviors, "selfishness, lying, conniving," did not go away. Meghan, who worked in the single-room-occupancy building where Lisa D lived, had a similar attitude. She mentioned that one of Lisa D's strengths was "her honesty. She's very clear about who she is and where she came from. Most people don't want people to know, because they haven't got honest with themselves." At the same time, Meghan was skeptical of what she saw as typical drug addict behaviors.

AL: What was your impression when you first met her?

MEGHAN: I think she's a very intelligent individual. However, she has some slick and devious behaviors. And I know for a fact, me being starting off in the substance abuse [field], that they gonna run the game. They know the game, they know every nook and cranny of how long you gonna be in jail, how long you can get recovery, they know the game. They're very very smart people. However, it comes a time that you must make that inside change, to me, you know. Because you done did that, and look at the price you had to pay. That's a big price, that's an awfully big price. So, I just look at the fact that at this point you have to stand on what you say, what comes out your mouth. You gotta really stand on it.

Lisa D's "slick and devious" behaviors included "she'll tell you some of the truth, but it's not all," and "she's trying to uphold an image." Another example was Lisa D's reluctance to move out of the SRO building where she had lived several years. This was a common issue, with many people staying as long as they could. Meaghan said, "That's just my thing. If I had been in a program five years, going on six years, and they had helped me tremendously, I'm gonna move out the way so someone else can get part of the program." Many of the women shared this sentiment of sharing the benefits, but at the same time, struggled to earn enough money to pay market rent. During our second interview, Lisa D had begun talking to me about moving out the SRO building, because she had "outgrown" the place (about a month before my conversation with Meghan quoted here). She did finally move about nine months later. It is hard to tell, based on these interviews, if Lisa D was really using "slick and devious" behaviors, or if she was responding in a reasonable way to highly constrained circumstances. She was both working and going to school at the time, and was a popular friend and mentor to other Mercy Home residents. It is unclear if she could have done anything to alleviate Meghan's mistrust of her.

CONCLUSION

In all relationships, the women carefully attempted to balance humility with "carrying the message forward" about the possibility of change and serving as a role model for others in similar situations. In addition, they tried to balance a goal of independence with changing the ways in which they relate to others and the desire for strong, positive connections. The women were more likely to cut ties with old friends and romantic partners than they were with family. Many avoided romantic relationships or only engaged in casual relationships, in order to focus better on themselves and their own recovery. Here is where they most clearly accepted the twelve-step messages, though many struggled with these decisions as well. Relationships with romantic partners and friends provided valuable support and companionship, especially as the majority of these relationships were with others who had a history of drug use and offending. The women provided and received "truth telling" and understanding through these relationships, though in many cases they were transient and ended with the relapse of one or both parties.

The main role of friends was to provide support and understanding of the women's circumstances and struggles. In some cases, the women maintained relationships with childhood friends, and in many cases, they depended on new ties to fellow Mercy Home residents or others they met in recovery. The "sisterhood" of the Mercy Home often continued, as women maintained relationships with some of their coresidents and as they developed additional friendships with women in recovery. These relationships were often less fraught than relationships with romantic partners, and they were less central to their sense of self than family relationships. At the same time, they were important sources of emotional support, "tough love," and "truth telling."

CHAPTER 6

Education, Employment, and a House of One's Own

CONVENTIONAL MARKERS OF SUCCESS

TWO OF THE MOST commonly discussed needs of ex-prisoners and pathways to successful desistance are employment and housing. The ideal is for ex-prisoners to find a good job and stable housing in a quiet neighborhood, both of which will contribute to a role in conventional society and a cessation of offending. Former prisoners have learned the same broad cultural narratives of success that permeate U.S. culture: education and hard work lead to employment and financial success. While they are acutely aware of the stigma and barriers associated with their criminal records, many also believe, or hope, that with education and effort, they will be able to secure a stable job and move to a market-rate apartment or house in a quiet neighborhood.

Much of the research in these areas focuses on objective measures of education, employment, housing, and neighborhood context, and the extent to which they are related to offending. I briefly touch on this literature to provide a context to these topics, though the bulk of the chapter addresses the women's experiences with and perspectives on education, employment, housing, and neighborhood. The focus is on the women's aspirations, how they define success, and their experiences with broader cultural messages surrounding these issues. The women attempted to reconcile competing narratives they learned from the Mercy Home and the broader culture about what they should be working toward with their own lived realities. While most accepted these goals, particularly in terms of employment, their lives often did not correspond to this ideal. Faced with the disparities between expectations and reality, the women often experienced extreme frustration, which sometimes led to setbacks in their desistance efforts.

EMPLOYMENT AND EDUCATION

Evidence suggests that employment fosters desistance for at least some offenders (Uggen 1999, 2000; Uggen and Thompson 2003). There are at least three desistance-related benefits to employment among former prisoners. First, economic marginalization is central to female offending and persistence in offending. Kristy Holtfreter and colleagues (2004), for example, found that poverty status accounted for over half of the explained variance in rearrest among a group of female ex-offenders. Employment provides for material needs, which may make offending a less appealing or necessary option. Second, employment provides important social bonds, which increase ties to conventional society and thereby also increase the costs of reoffending (Laub and Sampson 2003; Sampson and Laub 1993). Finally, meaningful employment can contribute to a redefinition of an offender's self-conception, leading to cognitive changes and a sense of a law-abiding, conventional self (Giordano, Cernkovich, and Rudolph 2002; Maruna 2001). All of these are dependent on the job's being stable and high quality (Hagan and Coleman 2001; Laub and Sampson 2003; Uggen 1999). Employees need to be sufficiently well compensated to meet material needs and they need to be invested in the job for it to serve as a hook for change.

The latter two processes also are influenced by gender and race. For example, Rebecca Katz (2000) suggested that white women might define themselves more in terms of motherhood, while nonwhite women may define themselves in terms of kinship, neighborhood, and work. If work is more closely tied to African American women's identities, it also is more likely to have a desistance effect on them, whether in terms of social control, cognitive changes, or both. Education does not directly create a financial disincentive to offending, but it can contribute to more rewarding and better-paid employment. It also may lead to changed self-conceptions and greater ties to conventional society. In addition, education, independent of its connection to employment opportunities, may decrease recidivism, particularly among female prisoners (Uggen and Kruttschnitt 1998).

While quality employment is touted as crucial for fostering desistance, both male and female prisoners often lack both work experience and education (Giordano, Cernkovich, and Rudolph 2002; Holtfreter, Reisig, and Morash 2004; Richie 2001).[1] The lack of work experience is exacerbated by time spent in prison and the stigma of a criminal record, resulting in lost wages, and difficulty securing employment after release (Holzer, Offner, and Sorensen 2005; Holzer, Raphael, and Stoll 2001; Pager 2005, 2007; Pager, Bonikowski, and Western 2009; Western 2002, 2006).[2] Incarcerated women are particularly disadvantaged in their employment and wage histories. Fewer women than men work full time prior to their arrest, more have extremely low wages, and more are welfare recipients.[3] Still, the effects of incarceration on labor market involvement may be different for female prisoners than male, with one study finding that some female prisoners experienced employment gains after incarceration (Cho and LaLonde 2008). This was, at least in part, a result of their overall low employment rates and low wages.

The Jobs and How They Got Them

Most of the women considered employment a key aspect of their personal identities and goals. Thirty of the women were employed at the time of our last interview, and eighteen had heard about their current jobs directly through their connection to the Mercy Home. All of the women, by virtue of their felony convictions, faced barriers in finding employment. However, the Mercy Home had ongoing relationships with some area employers that were willing to hire people with criminal records, making the women relatively advantaged. This was a mutually beneficial arrangement. Residents gained work experience and the employers hired women with additional supervision and support from the Mercy Home. This arrangement was particularly beneficial to women who had limited work experience. Especially among the women who were working "legitimate" jobs for the first time, or for the first time in years, there was often a sense of pride in having a job and in the work they did. As a result of these supports and structure, almost all Mercy Home residents were employed at the time they left the halfway house, most often through these standing connections.

One employer for whom several women took jobs was a telemarketing firm in the suburbs. None of the women working there liked the job, the pay was low ($6 an hour plus a possible commission), and they had a long commute (two and a half hours each way on public transit). Danielle described finding the job: "Oh, there was a guy who came here recruiting. And I didn't take the job at first, but it got to the point where I couldn't find one, so I just took it to have a job." From the start, she felt trapped in the job because of its limitations, "then the hours that I'm traveling, I don't have the time to go out and look for a job unless I take a day off from work. So it's kind of like I'm locked in." Others worked in low-wage jobs, at fast-food restaurants, thrift stores, and other service sector work. Some, again particularly those with little prior work experience, appreciated these jobs as a sign of positive progress in their lives, even if they hoped they would soon be on the way to a higher-paid or more meaningful job.

For those who had a work history, it was often from years earlier, prior to lengthy drug addictions or incarcerations. Sheila had worked for the same factory for over a decade, before she left it when her drug addiction deepened. She began working there when she was nineteen; "Man, those were the days. . . . So that was a good feeling back then, when I could go into a store and buy what I want and not have to contemplate on about stealing it or nothing like that because I had the money, I could afford it, I had the money to buy it."

She had been given the opportunity to relocate to Alabama, which she did for a few years before returning to Chicago.

SHEILA: Which I went down there [Alabama] and worked for about four years and I just left everything. New house, furniture, and everything and I came back here and started smoking [cocaine]. I called the job and took medical leave. I took everything I could to keep from going back to working. When I used up all my sick days and stuff I never did go back. If I would have stayed there, I'd probably be in the $25–30 an hour bracket. They had good benefits. So I feel that was a good job that I lost. I could have made life a lot easier for my kids if I would have kept that job.

Sheila lost her job in the mid-1980s and had not worked since. She described her work goals during the first interview. "I would like to see if I can get something in factory work, a machine operator, line runner. I'm really flexible. Really any kind of job I get would be no problem for me, provided I haven't worked in the last fifteen years. You know, so just getting a paycheck would make me feel good. Whatever, it wouldn't make no difference. Because I believe in making things easy for me. You can work hard or you can work smart. You can work hard or you can work smart, you know?" Sheila received a job through the Illinois Department of Human Services (IDHS) Earnfare program.[4] She was one of five Mercy Home women who were hired at a nonprofit that provided day services to nursing home residents. These began as temporary and part time, though several of the women, including Sheila, were hired permanently at the end of the six-month Earnfare period.

In addition to using the connections of the Mercy Home to get a first job, several of the women eventually worked at the Mercy Home. Typically, they were not eligible to work there until all of their coresidents had moved out. Lisa D was a well-liked house manager; several women named her as a close friend. She received her job at the Mercy Home when the program director made her a job offer. "I came in one day, and the receptionist said the program director wanted to see me. . . . You never know who's watching. I didn't know she knew [what I had been doing]. She offered me the position; it was one of the biggest honors." A few women, like Lisa D And Marie, were able to work there full time. Often they started as part-time or substitute house managers. Mary and Dee Dee both began working as part-time house managers during the course of our interviews. Their jobs were as fill-ins, which meant they worked there sporadically. Mary continued working at her fast-food job. Even those who worked there part time benefitted from the feeling that they were giving back and the continued safe space for growth it provided them.

Some women found jobs through word of mouth and social networks. For example, Lisa S was offered a job at a drug treatment facility after her neighbor, a supervisor at the agency, saw her interacting with neighborhood children and thought she would be a good fit for the position. She was pursuing a college degree and had been working in the drug treatment field, but, as with Lisa D and other Mercy Home employees, her personal connections were central to her hire.

LISA S: My supervisor lives across the street from me, coincidentally, you know. And, I was, every now and then just, you know, wave at him and sometimes when I park, you know, hold a conversation with him. And he knows the field that I am in, because actually I know some people—some other people that work at [her current employer] that knows him and da-da-da. And one day he stopped and he was like, "You know I would really like to have you on my team." He said, "I sit on the porch and I watch how you interact with the kids in the neighborhood," right. Because all the kids in the neighborhood call me Auntie Lisa. Don't ask where I got that name from, it just, I don't know, it just seemed like one day the whole neighborhood called me Ti Ti Lisa. . . . And all the time, I know my supervisor [at my former job] used to always tell me, "You never know who's watching you," you know. So all the time, he was watching me, and I mean, I never, I do my thing, I do what I do, you know. And he stopped me and told me he want me on the team because he know I'd be good for the kids. And he asked me could I come in for an interview, and basically that's how I got the job.

Lisa S was able to demonstrate relevant social skills to her neighbor through her daily interactions. The value of personal connections in securing employment extended to all types of jobs. Mary, for example, got a job at a fast-food restaurant because her son knew the manager. These connections, whether personal or through the Mercy Home, were extremely valuable for the women in securing employment and overcoming the stigma of their criminal histories. While many of the women scoured the newspaper for job ads, filled out applications, and went to job fairs, it was rare for them to find a job without some sort of connection.

Generativity Through Employment

The women often worked, or aspired to work, in social service fields, especially drug counseling or prisoner reentry. During the study period, about a third of the women were working in a social service field. In many of these jobs, they were "professional exes" in which their histories of offending, victimization, and drug addiction were valuable experiences to draw on to help others (J. D. Brown 1991; Maruna 2001). In one of the strongest examples of this, Victoria opened a halfway house in the Chicago suburbs, which she modeled on the Mercy Home. Several women were on boards of organizations that served incarcerated or formerly incarcerated women. Other jobs were less directly connected to their own histories but still provided satisfaction through being able to interact with, help, and give back to those in need. These also were among the relatively few careers, particularly at the lower levels of case management, that were open to them and that provided a sense of meaning and generativity (Erikson 1950; McAdams 2006).

Women who did not initially aspire to work in these fields often learned to appreciate them. For example, Sheila's job as a cook and group facilitator was far from her initial goal of factory work, but she enjoyed her work. She said, "I do get joy out of some of 'em [the clients]. We got just as many young ones that come into the nursing [home] as old, and I get a kick out of 'em everyday. Just being around 'em, you know . . . I love my job." Sheila also had a measure of autonomy in her work, which she valued. Several women at this organization hoped to continue to work in helping professions, often in the substance abuse treatment field, and considered their current jobs valuable experience. Tammy worked as a facilitator at the same day program as Sheila. She enjoyed her job because she enjoyed "working with the patients. It allows me to open up, 'cause I'm very shy, so it allows me to speak and to, you know, communicate with others on a daily basis. I enjoy that. I always wanted a job working with things or books, but now I really enjoy it because it helps me." Tammy personally benefitted from this work, much more than she anticipated. Over time, this developed into a longer-term career goal: she wanted to work with women and children who were victims of abuse. Given Tammy's background as the daughter of an abused mother, this is clearly an example of redefining her past as meaningful for her future career goals.

Still, while many of the women liked the generative aspects of interacting with clients, they also complained about the lack of organization, low wages, and lack of benefits at this organization and others like it. In addition, Shelly reported "90 percent" of the people working at the organization had a criminal justice background and "100 percent are recovering addicts." Shelly herself had been hired back after a relapse and reincarceration. Although this meant the employers were accepting of the women's own backgrounds, it also often led to chaotic work environments. For these reasons, the women looked or planned to look for second or new jobs.

Angela was one of few women working in an environment where her background was neither common among staff members nor relevant to the work they were doing. She decided at the Mercy Home that she wanted to work in an office. She was hired at a nonprofit as an "assistant conference coordinator" after the organization called the Mercy Home and said "they had some temporary positions and [asked] if they had any [women] that wanted

some exposure to working in an office. And it was a little intimidating at first."
She began as a temporary worker and was hired permanently ten months later.
She described the office: "It's like a family over there. They accept you. . . . As
a workplace it's been really, really great. People there help me find and set my
goals. They give me direction on the goals that I want to reach. I feel like that
even because of my background, I can make it, you know, make a difference."
Several times, she emphasized the value of the "diversity of coming from different backgrounds and still being able to see each other as equals, as human
beings." While Angela's job suffered from some of the same challenges as other
nonprofits the women worked in, such as a fear of budget cuts and layoffs,
her present work was cut off from her past—no one knew of her background
unless she chose to share it. This allowed her to move forward, though she also
struggled with the decision to share her personal struggles with coworkers
when her husband was reincarcerated.

Although many of the women enjoyed working in fields where they
could help and give back to others, this was not universal. Some preferred jobs
outside of social services or "professional ex" fields. For example, Abra wanted
to continue her career in the construction field and hoped to open her own
business. April worked in building maintenance and wanted to open a cleaning business. A few women wanted to work in a factory, usually because they
explicitly preferred less human interaction. Several women participated in a
hospitality training course and planned to pursue this field. The women who
chose jobs in which they were not "professional exes" still often gained a sense
of meaning and enjoyment out of their chosen fields and took pride in the
work they did. In addition, some experienced "professional ex" relationships
informally, such as with neighbors, family members, or acquaintances. Thus,
while generativity and "giving something back" were important to many of
the women, employment was not their only, and not necessarily a preferred,
means of doing so.

Job Turnover and Unemployment

Several of the women, particularly those most recently out of prison,
changed, left, or lost jobs or training programs during the period of the study.
Although most of the women wanted to work, for some the conditions became
too much to manage. For several women, this was because of ongoing and significant health problems. Sheila continued to work at the day program but left
a hospitality training program because of her many dental appointments at a
free clinic. Sheila had long had the goal of fixing her teeth. She said, "I would
like my appearance to look a little better. I'd like to get my teeth fixed, to get
into a dentist. I'm trying to get my medical card because I'm trying to get
my mouth fixed. Then I'll feel even better about myself. That makes me feel

better so that'd make me want to accomplish more." She planned to look for a new job eventually, but she wanted to take care of her "personal business" first.

A few of the women had significant physical and mental health issues that sometimes interfered with their ability to work. Jane described herself as a "mental health patient." After she left the Mercy Home, she moved into a nursing home. She said, "I get disability checks and I live off of it. And I don't think I'll be able to work a job. I've had three cancer operations and I can't lift nothing, you know. Let's see, I had three surgeries in 2002. I had three cancer operations within that year and I can't move this arm up." She hoped to go back to school and to work eventually, though she did not take any concrete steps to do so in the time I knew her.

Corrina was another woman who had significant physical and mental health problems. She had lived at the Mercy Home several years earlier, then moved into a supportive-housing program. When she first left the Mercy Home, she was working.

CORRINA: It's just that the job, you know, we didn't know what kind of a place it was. They would just hire anybody. They had temps there with no ID, no nothing and they would just let anybody work there. There was too many people drinking and using on the job, even the supervisors. One of the girls that was working there was stealing money on the computer because she knew she could make some money off the Mexicans who didn't have IDs. There was a lot of gang bangers there. It was scary. It's better off for me not to go there because I know what's going to happen. Maybe it was meant for that to happen because that job wasn't for us. . . . We didn't know. We were just happy about getting a job.

This was a type of work environment that many of the women complained about. For Corrina this was compounded by her struggle with her health and occasional drug use.[5] She took antiseizure medication, which caused numerous debilitating side effects: "Even when I take the Tegretol, it says it causes drowsiness. So, I'm supposed to take phenobarbs too and I'm supposed to get a job? Uh-uh [no]. I think the doctor wants to keep me on all these drugs. I'm going to write him up on all this. He can't force me to take all that. I don't need it." During the course of that interview, Corrina's energy level and mood dropped dramatically, which she attributed to this medication.

In other interviews, her mood also swung dramatically, and she talked about having had thoughts of suicide. In addition to antiseizure medication, she took methadone and medication for depression and anxiety. Balancing her physical and mental health symptoms, various medications, and their side effects was an ongoing struggle. Corrina occasionally engaged in illegal activity, such as prostitution and "copping" drugs for other tenants, in an attempt to make money. She said one of her doctors did not think she was ready to work. She said, "Because they said the recovery comes first. They're afraid if I go back to work like I went too fast back to work, what happens? You got money, triggers. You see, you know, when you go to work you're going to see people drink. You're going to see all that. But they, like, they teach you, you can't run from that. The stuff's all over." Few of the women had problems as debilitating as those of Jane and Corrina. More common were temporary health issues, like those of Sheila and EJ (see chapter 3), and ongoing, but manageable, problems with depression and bipolar disorder, both of which were common diagnoses among these women. The disruptions to work were typically occasional and temporary.

The work environment was a challenge for many. Most of the women were working for low wages and in jobs with limited long-term stability, and the benefits of working started to wane for some. Danielle worked off and on at the same suburban telemarketing firm as EJ. Both disliked the job from the start, and both worked there approximately six months. In the third interview, Danielle described her work environment:

DANIELLE: Lot of unprofessional. The supervisors scream and holler and curse at you. . . . Very very nonprofessional. They sell drugs there. I mean, very nonprofessional.

AL: They sell?

DANIELLE: Weed. What, and I guess, you know, blow. Actually, they sell everything else there too, you know, but I've only been approached with somebody selling weed there. I know they drink there, you know. Very, very nonprofessional.

Danielle was hired at another telemarketing firm that she liked more but was fired after four months. She said, "It was like a threat every day on the job. Every day they'd walk past, 'Oh, somebody's gonna get fired today.'" She went back to the first telemarketing firm but quit a month later. She said it was "too stressful. Drugs being sold, just very unprofessional. Sweetness works there, and she's fine with it. I just couldn't be there." While Sweetness did not complain about drugs at the job, she was also trying to leave as soon as she could find an alternative. Initially, the women were proud to be working and living a "straight" life, but for many, the perceived benefits of these jobs waned over time. They struggled to "take the long view" and see the jobs as stepping-stones but could not always withstand the numerous negatives of the jobs.

Some of the women also lost their first jobs because they were laid off or fired. Mary described the end of her job with a thrift store, which she first got through Mercy Home connections.

AL: Why did you leave that job?

MARY: Because my manager told me to do something and when it came back down she told me she didn't tell me to do it, so I got fired.

AL: What did she tell you to do?

MARY: She told me this girl that was working there, this employee, had bought this furniture—it turned out that she didn't—when she moved before. So they gave her in-store credit, which means that she can, you know, get something else. When it all came back down, the manager, she said, didn't give her in-store credit, that I just gave the girl the stuff. So that's what happened with that.

AL: And the other girl, she worked there as well?

MARY: Yes.

AL: Did anything happen to her? Did she get fired?

MARY: Yeah, she got fired under a dirty drop, but initially they were trying to get rid of her because she was always on the phone. But she didn't get fired for theft, which is what I got fired for. But I didn't take nothing, but I got fired for theft.

Mary then got a job at a fast-food restaurant. While she enjoyed the customer service aspect, drug use was also prevalent there, "and I don't like my job because everybody there gets high and drinks, you know, smoke weed and drinking. Now, they got some, they drinking at work and some get high, smell like reefer. You know, it's no big deal. Because the boss do it too, so it's really no big deal." Mary's story not only reveals her perception of an injustice but also speaks to common drug use among coworkers and a generally chaotic work environment. It also highlights the women's often-vulnerable positions on the job, in which they had little recourse from accusations or firings.

Education

The Mercy Home prepared the women to work in several ways. Helping them deal with issues of drug addiction and trauma was one step in getting them ready to be in a work environment. In addition, the women were taught, often indirectly, interpersonal and cultural skills that may be necessary in a workplace and to which not all women had been previously exposed (Kirschenman and Neckerman 1991; Neckerman and Kirschenman 1991). Women were expected to behave appropriately while in the Mercy Home and were admonished or punished if they did not follow house rules. Not following house rules included overt misbehavior (for example, missing curfew or using drugs) and inappropriate interactions with others. In addition, the Mercy Home encouraged residents to pursue additional education. Nearly two-thirds of the women said furthering their education was a future goal, and one-fifth were pursuing that goal during the study period.

The women set this goal in part because they saw education as a personal and social good. Getting a high school and college education was something they wanted to accomplish for themselves and to set an example for their children. Danielle said, "Since I didn't finish high school and things like that, I told my daughter we would graduate together. And I think she was graduating eighth grade, sixth grade, something like that, when I got my GED. And I said we would graduate from college together too, but I didn't do it. Maybe me and [my youngest daughter] will graduate from college together, you know. . . . I want a degree, you know, that's something I've always wanted."

While the women valued education for its own sake, they also saw it as a means of social mobility. They learned tangible skills and gained credentials, which they hoped would translate into conventional employment. Lisa D, who was then a Mercy Home house manager and a student in criminal justice at a community college, described her educational goals, and the ones she espoused to residents.

LISA D: One of the things that I push a lot at [the Mercy Home] is education. I had to find out how important it was. You know, I always knew, because I pushed it on my children. But when I came through [the Mercy Home], I was probably one of the oldest women [there] at the time, still didn't have a high school diploma, you know? And, I had to take a look at everything around me. What kind of job am I going to have? It's the difference between a job and a career. I had set up to be a cashier for the next twenty-five years. And there's nothing wrong with that, if that's what you want, that's all you want. Education will allow you to do a little bit more than that.

Lisa D hoped to continue working in a similar field once she finished her degree. She emphasized education because "it's needed for jobs, it's needed for life." Lisa D explained, "I've had women sit down and share with me, 'I was on the job, I knew how to do everything, but because I had not finished high school, and say somebody comes in and say they're a student in college—just a student—they would get the job and become my supervisor. And I would have to train them, because I knew stuff, but because they had the education I didn't get the position.' So, I always, you know, remind women of what can be done." Most women similarly related their pursuit of education directly to a desire for more stable, secure, and meaningful employment. The pursuit of education and job training was a way to gain the credentials that demonstrated that they were skilled and prepared for the workplace.

Typically, those who were in college or who hoped to pursue college in the future had concrete career goals in mind. Delilah had recently graduated from college. When she first went to the Mercy Home, "I told them about my dreams of going back to school. They gave me the first money you need to start the paperwork, my admission fee. [The director] helped me fill out my financial aid papers. And I got accepted at Chicago State [University]." Delilah had already earned a GED and college credits from three different universities while incarcerated. She said, "So I had acquired a lot of credits, but none of them were geared toward a particular major, you know, it was just scattered all about. And so then I said, well, I know I wanted to help people. I wanted to be in a field helping other people, trying to give back. So I told them I wanted to major in sociology. So, then they told me I needed 45 credit hours. Even though I had 103 credits when I stepped in the door and they accepted 99 of them, I still needed 45 credits in my major. So that held me down for three years."

Other women also typically chose majors and tailored their approach to education based on concrete career goals. Andrea hoped to work in case management: "That's why I'm still in school. I just, I really like, you know, just talking to women that have been homeless or struggling through drug addiction, anything like that. I just, I really like helping them." She was struggling, but wanted to earn a bachelor's degree, "just something I can have, something on my resume stating that I've gotten something, you know. I haven't wasted that, those whole years." Andrea and Erica were in the same program that provided rental assistance to women enrolled in college, though they were taking classes at different colleges. Erica's goals included "to actually get something out of school," and she noted that "school is not easy." She was majoring in social work and criminal justice, which she hoped would help her in a career in HIV counseling. Others pursued job training or professional degrees to further their career goals. Starr, for example, was interested in being a chef and enrolled in a culinary arts school. Angela enrolled in a community college to complete her associate's degree in business administration. Abra was a carpenter's apprentice and took a class on construction management. She wanted to take other classes in electrical, plumbing, heating, and air conditioning to further her goals of starting a business to rehab homes.

The Mercy Home also facilitated connections with several basic job skills programs geared toward a low-income population. This was valuable, particularly for those women facing fears of reentering society. Shorty D described the job training she was receiving:

SHORTY D: They're teaching you how to be professional. That's what the course is basically about, you know . . . your computer skills, you know, like I'm learning how to log in, log out. Make my own e-mail. Make my own résumé on the computer. . . . They really teach you a lot. . . . When you been out of school for so long, you know, you already got fears. You know, far as a felon, you know, so I have to pray a lot. . . . I have the courage and strength, you know, it's scary. You know, but at the same time, you know, it's something that I want to do, you know, and regardless if I pass or fail . . . I look at it like this here, you know, to ease my mind: only way you can fail if you don't try. That's failing. . . . You have to read up in this here class, you know, you have to listen. . . . . I been out of school for over twenty years. I, 1985. You know, I know nothing about computers, cause computers weren't out when I was in school. . . . I'm just grateful that I got a B+ on one of my assignments, so I guess that was pretty amazing, you know. I mean, he had us write, you know, write letters the proper way, you know. I remember doing things like that in school, but, God, you know, it's been so long and I haven't been doing any writing period, you know. I haven't been doing any reading, picking up a newspaper. Nothing, you know.

This program was Shorty D's second job training program. When she finished it, she said she was "100 percent satisfied" because of what she had learned, which included classes on self-image, communication, sanitation, computers, résumé writing, job searching. She frequently referred to the program as "facing her fears" about going back to school. For many who had long been out of an educational or work environment, this type of program provided a welcome and valuable introduction.

While the Mercy Home encouraged education and many women valued it, a few were not interested beyond the extent to which it was required. While Libra was encouraging her children to go to college, she was not interested in it for herself. She said, "I don't wanna do that. You know, I tend to sleep in classes. The groups is hard enough and the meetings. I don't want to do that anymore. . . . Now if by chance my job requires that I do go to school, I would be willing to do that. But, other than that, if it's not mandatory, I'm not going." Libra did have her high school diploma and had some college, but was not interested in pursuing it further.

The Limits of Education

Many women needed support as they began or transitioned back to working. For those women pursuing education after incarceration, it also served as a symbol of rehabilitation. It demonstrated to potential employers that they were taking steps to be a part of mainstream society. A few women, however, found the services available to be ill suited or inadequate to their needs. Carolyn, for example, described the employment programs available through the Mercy Home:

CAROLYN: All of them are pretty much the same. They find out, most of these job programs have a program that they wanna send you through, you know, to prepare you. Most, you know, it's just, it's not designed for, for me. I'm, I don't fit the category, you know. I don't, I don't need to be taught how to talk, how to interview. Or, I take that back. I do need help with interviewing because sometimes I do have a problem. I usually intimidate the interviewer or something, you know. Or my reactions to questions that might seem dumb or, so I have, I do need work with that. But, I know how to do most of the things that they so-called teach you. So, I don't, I don't need to go through their programs.

Carolyn felt multiply disadvantaged in her job searches. Because she was highly educated and had extensive professional experience prior to her incarceration, job training programs targeting former prisoners or low-income populations had little to offer her. At the same time, she faced the stigmas of having a criminal record, being overqualified for jobs that might hire someone with a record, and being in her fifties. She felt all of these factors disadvantaged her, making it unusually difficult for her to secure employment. She was highly skilled, yet her degrees and credentials, which predated her incarceration, did not demonstrate atonement for her crimes, as they did for women who pursued postincarceration education. Carolyn's experience was consistent with the experience of women who had an established work history or education. These women lost a lot through their criminal involvement and incarceration, so knew firsthand what they were missing. For those who began the reentry process never having experienced a "straight" or mainstream work life, a low-wage or low-skill job often felt like a significant accomplishment and contributed to a sense of progress and self-worth. For a woman like Carolyn, it felt like a failure.

Carolyn's primary goal was to find stable employment. She was fired from her last job when her employer found out she had a felony record. She said, "I was fired because a felon can't work [there]. . . . She [the person who hired her] thought she could get a waiver." Although she applied for low-wage/low-skill jobs, such as in housekeeping—and occasionally lied about her education and work experience, but not her criminal record—she did not have "the same goals and desires" as many of the other women. Carolyn aspired to work, but she wanted to work in a job that did more than meet her financial needs. "What's really happening in my life—I'm qualified and I can't get a job. The other people I know, they can but it's not soul satisfied. You know, it's like I want to be soul satisfied. I don't just want to, I spent my whole life just working and making money. I need that to survive but what satisfies your soul? I think we're missing that. You know, and we go in search of a bunch of other stuff that is really irrelevant." Carolyn clarified that "peace" and the "patience to be still" would satisfy her soul, yet her description of soul satisfaction also evokes the "quality" and generative jobs that others have argued are more likely to lead to desistance (Laub and Sampson 2003; Maruna 2001; Uggen 1999). Carolyn wanted these two goals—employment and "soul satisfaction"—to come from the same place, though she was forced to separate them and look for life meaning elsewhere.

Carolyn's professional background was an exception among these women. Still, she was not the only woman who received feedback that she was over-qualified for the positions to which she was applying. Mary also was told several times that she was overqualified. Mary's primary experience was work-ing in fast-food jobs, and she had risen to the level of assistant manager. She explained:

MARY: I've been to, I went to a hotel fair that they had out in Willowbrook, or something. I went down there. I got one interview, but they sent me a letter telling me that I wasn't what they was really looking for. What I couldn't understand was that I had all the, all the other skills that they was looking for, but they said I was overqualified.

AL: They said you were overqualified?

MARY: Mm-hmm.

AL: What was the job for?

MARY: For, for housekeeping. I guess they want somebody to teach they own ways, so, I don't know. But, it didn't seem like I had a problem with my background check or anything 'cause they went and, you know, called me in for a interview. So, I think it was just that, you know, 'cause I used to be assistant manager and stuff like that . . . so they said, "You should be in a manager's position somewhere and I wouldn't feel right paying you this amount of money," you know, and stuff like that. Then I went to the place that [the Mercy Home program director] had turned me to and she was like, I was overqualified. . . . Yeah, I went there and I was overqualified, but I'm still trying 'em.

It is impossible to know through Mary's interpretation the actual reasoning of the employer. She was aware of her criminal record as a possible barrier, but she also perceived other barriers, including her age and her professional experience. Mary continued to look for a new job, "Anything that I can make over $5.50, which is what I am making now." By our last interview, Mary was still working at the same restaurant and had recently been promoted to crew leader (with a raise to $6.25). She had been there for close to two years at that time and still hoped to leave if she could find a better job.

Other women began to see limitations in the value of education or col-lege degrees, as their criminal records often still trumped these credentials. At Delilah's first job, as an outreach worker at a social service agency, she was frustrated by administrative disorganization and what she perceived to be a jealousy of her education among her coworkers. She said, "They are jealous of my education. . . . I am the lowest-paid person with a degree. I didn't go to school to walk routes [do street outreach]." She had several conflicts with her coworkers and supervisor before being laid off (one of several at that agency to be laid off due to funding problems). In addition, the women's education usually had little connection to their job responsibilities. Andrea, who worked at an SRO building, complained about her (then current) job: "We all have basically the same position. Like, a lot of the women, they have degrees and stuff, but we still do the same thing." When she lost that job due to budget cuts, she was considered for a position at a drug treatment center—a job she thought she had a good chance of getting, in large part because her sister-in-law was a well-liked long-term employee there.

While the women were often frustrated by a lack of a clear connection between their educational accomplishments and their employment experiences and opportunities, occasionally they did think their education made a difference. A few months after Delilah was laid off from her outreach job, she received a new job offer at another social service agency that worked with incarcerated women. She said, "I got the job through doing a good deed for the Mercy Home, you know." In running an errand for the Mercy Home, she told someone at the new agency that she had been laid off, and she was invited to interview there. She competed with several other former Mercy Home residents for the job, including Angela and Erica, and believed that her college degree gave her an advantage over the other candidates. In this case, the women were competing with other women with criminal records and they all benefitted from their connection with the Mercy Home. Delilah said, "I just interviewed better . . . I talked a little about femininity and all, you know. She [Erica] was in school, I was already finished. So, I, you know, I was aware of some of the things they were looking for." Erica also believed that she did not get the job because Delilah already had her degree.

Employment and the Narratives of Employment

Using the narratives that women used to talk about work, it is clear that employment is central to their self-conceptions and their goals in reentry. This is connected not only to the emphasis on independence at the Mercy Home but also to broad cultural narratives in the contemporary United States of success through hard work and the importance of work in African American women's self-definitions. On the surface, this may seem to contradict existing research. Giordano and colleagues, for example, emphasized just how rare stable and quality employment is for contemporary criminal justice–involved populations (Giordano, Cernkovich, and Rudolph 2002). Melissa Thompson and Milena Petrovic (2009, 383) write, "Among women, however, economic factors appear less important as a means to promote desistance ... factors other than high income, job stability, or occupational prestige are the major hooks for change for women." The women in this study struggled to achieve financial independence. But although the jobs they had tended to be low paid and unstable, they carried important symbolic meaning for the women, especially in their early stages of recovery. Employment was a sign of normality and desistance. Many also interpreted the jobs they had as generative. They enjoyed working with clients or customers. Depending on the priority they placed on those relationships, they were more or less satisfied with the work they were doing, sometimes in spite of problematic work contexts of widespread drug use and disorganization. Women at the day program were generally satisfied with the work they were doing, in spite of near universal criticisms of the management of the organization. In contrast, the telemarketing job had little generative meaning to counteract a similarly chaotic environment, inconvenient location, and low wages.

At the beginning of their time at the Mercy Home, many of the women believed in education and hard work leading to employment success, but over time they began seeing the limitations of these narratives. Through their experiences, they began experiencing renewed doubt, frustration, and cynicism. Some women, like Carolyn, came to this point sooner than others, because of their backgrounds and their early postincarceration experiences. Those who had the most limited work experiences had further to go before reaching the glass ceiling of their likely employment trajectories or the benefits of their educational accomplishments. Even those who experienced the greatest satisfaction and meaning in their work often continued to experience limited job growth and financial difficulties and continued to rely on subsidized housing programs. The goals of employment as a source of financial independence were, in large part, distinct from the goals of employment as a source of social bonds and cognitive change. These women could experience the latter but had a much harder time with the former. This raises the question of whether the positive benefits of employment will be long-lasting for the women or if the bond and identity benefits wane over time in the absence of financial independence.

NEIGHBORHOODS AND HOUSING

Neighborhood change is an important self-described turning point for many desisting offenders (La Vigne, Visher, and Castro 2004; Laub and Sampson 2003). These turning points may "knife off" offenders from their immediate environment and offer them a new script for the future. The change in context provides an opportunity to redefine one's lifestyle, routine activities, and sense of self and to break away from unsatisfactory relationships, all of which are tied to desistance from offending (Giordano, Cernkovich, and

Rudolph 2002; Laub and Sampson 2003; Maruna and Roy 2007; Warr 1998). This need to avoid people, places, and things related to substance use is one of the most prevalent messages these women relay from twelve-step programs.

In addition to avoiding people, places, and things, many returning prisoners want to live in heterogeneous and safe, low-crime, neighborhoods. When asked where they would like to live, the women typically valued peaceful, convenient, and diverse neighborhoods with minimal crime, drug use, and street activity. In short, they strove to live in the same neighborhoods, for the same reasons, that most other people do (Charles 2000; Harris 1999; Taub, Taylor and Dunham 1984). Heidi, an African American woman who grew up in disadvantaged, segregated, and predominantly African American communities on the West Side of Chicago, described where she would like to live: "The North Side . . . it's clean. It ain't as much hanging out on corners. It's like, I think it's a good environment. Plus, it's like a majority of economic, you know, people from different races. You know, it's a mixture of people. It ain't all black or brown. On the West Side you see mostly black. You know, up North you'll see white people. You'll see African people. You'll see Chinese people. All types of people up there. My cousin lives there." Heidi, and many of the women, would like to live in racially and economically diverse neighborhoods where she would feel comfortable and safe and that would provide amenities like quality housing stock and programs for their children. Shelly similarly emphasized quiet and safety: "I would like to look for a neighborhood where people are working, going to schools, striving to do better. I wouldn't want to see a drug dealer on the corner, or gangbangers. I wouldn't want to see people hanging out on the corners."

Even when former prisoners want to move, they have limited options and often move to similarly disadvantaged communities (Huebner, DeJong, and Cobbina 2010; La Vigne, Visher, and Castro 2004; Leverentz 2010; Massoglia, Firebaugh, and Warner 2013). Returning prisoners are likely to have limited funds to pay for housing, especially immediately after their release, and often experience discrimination in private housing markets. In addition, formal restrictions often limit their ability to stay with family or in subsidized or public housing. These problems are more pronounced in major urban areas, and many former prisoners experience homelessness (Petersilia 2003; Travis 2005). Programs geared toward helping people out of homelessness or helping ex-offenders or drug addicts can provide some assistance. However, these programs often are time-limited and have extensive waiting lists and admission requirements (Travis 2005). In addition, many are single-room-occupancy buildings (SROs), limiting them to those not living with children or other family.

As with most criminological research, much of our attention to neighborhood dynamics and crime is focused on male offenders. Female prisoners are being drawn from the same neighborhoods as male prisoners, however, and are shaped by at least some of the same neighborhood dynamics. Crime, drug use, and violence are widespread in the neighborhoods from which female prisoners are drawn and to which they return. For women reentering the community after incarceration, these race, gender, and power dynamics continue to shape their negotiation of neighborhood life (O'Brien 2007). When female prisoners return to the community, they, like men, return primarily to disadvantaged neighborhoods.

Neighborhood and Housing Choices

The types of neighborhoods in which the women aspired to live were often in stark contrast to the neighborhoods in which they were able to live. In choosing where to live, they had to balance financial limitations, a desire or need to receive case management and rent subsidies, and family demands. As a result, about half the women in this study lived in those neighborhoods in Chicago with the greatest concentrations of ex-prisoners in the state, and nearly all lived in neighborhoods characterized by racial segregation and poverty. Living in supportive and subsidized housing was the most common first step after the Mercy Home. At the end of the study period, roughly a third (38 percent)[6] of the women lived in single-room-occupancy (SRO) buildings and an additional 10 percent lived in scattered-site subsidized studio apartments. Another 10 percent lived in either subsidized townhomes or scattered-site multiple-bedroom apartments. Most of these programs were in largely African American neighborhoods with high rates of crime and poverty, though several were in areas that had recently begun to experience gentrification and redevelopment efforts, and a few of the scattered-site apartments were in more racially and economically heterogeneous neighborhoods.

Many women viewed living in supportive-housing programs as a temporary arrangement. They appreciated the supports and the increased independence but aspired to live in market-rate housing. They viewed life in supportive housing as a stepping-stone toward something more permanent. This frustrated some women, as they wanted to feel more successful and more "normal" quickly. Winifred, who felt frustrated at the slow progress at the Mercy Home, felt a similar frustration while living at the Refuge Apartments. She described how she felt living there: "Wishy washy. I get stuck, I just get stuck in these apartments." Still, given their limited incomes and unstable employment, a need for rent support often continued for years after their release. For example, April, Lisa D, and Delilah had all lived at the Mercy Home more than five years before, and all continued to live in SRO buildings during the interview period.

For women who were trying to reunite with their children, choosing between a subsidized program and living with their children was often a significant source of stress. Sweetness and Marie had typical experiences in making compromises between housing and living with children. Sweetness chose to move into an SRO apartment in the Refuge Apartments when her request for a townhouse did not come through.

SWEETNESS: I had originally put in for the townhome, because I had wanted my baby daughter and my son to come stay with me, but they consider him as grown, because he was nineteen, and I don't really consider him grown till he is twenty-one. So anyway that was put on the back burner, so they offered me the SRO instead of a townhome, you know. So that's how it end up that I'm living in here. So I was like I'd stay here for a while, but I'd still want my daughter to come stay with me and my son. If I'm gonna end up getting an apartment just to get the space, you know, he can stay with me till he's twenty-one . . . and then, but I didn't want to turn it down or nothing because you know there's other people that need to get in the program [halfway house] you know . . . so I make room for someone else.

Sweetness's struggle to find an apartment for her two younger children, who were then staying with her oldest daughter, continued throughout the interview period. Her SRO unit was considered permanent housing, so she was denied housing through another program because she was not considered homeless. She hoped to get moved into one of the few townhouses in the Refuge Apartments. Similarly, six years earlier, Marie had moved from the halfway house to a rent-subsidized studio apartment on the South Side of Chicago. Once the temporary housing assistance ended a year later, she stayed in the apartment, assuming the entire cost of rent. Her teenage daughter moved in with her while her son remained with her mother. At the time of the interviews, she was looking into the possibility of moving into a one- or two-bedroom apartment but was not sure she would be able to afford to stay in the neighborhood.

The remaining women lived either in their own apartment or house or in a family home. This was much more common among the former residents, some of whom had transitioned from the Mercy Home to a subsidized program to private housing. A few women did move straight to private housing, however, typically either to live with family or in response to a conflict with the halfway house staff. Many who moved into their own apartment wanted, either immediately or in the near future, to live with their children, romantic partner, or other family members. Linette, for example, had recently moved from the Mercy Home to the basement of her fiancé's mother's house, where she lived with her fiancé. She said "My mother-in-law treats me like a daughter. . . . And she reminds me of my mother a lot. . . . I didn't want to go back to where I was living. I love my family from a distance." She hoped to move with her fiancé into their own apartment, and "establish" herself so that she could bring her youngest daughter to live with them. Adena moved into a building owned by her family and helped Jeanette, her boyfriend, and her mother move into another family-owned building. Starr, who was in a fairly unusual position of having family resources to draw on, moved into a market-rate apartment with her girlfriend and girlfriend's son, with the financial help of her father.

Albany was living at the Mercy Home when I met her. She stayed for six months and then lived in a series of motels.

ALBANY: When it was time for my apartment I didn't have a job. Then when I had found a job [the aftercare coordinator] didn't call the people back to tell them I had the job. She really wasn't helping me so I told them I could do better on my own. Then they got mad, [the director] got mad and told me I had a lot of resources and maybe I could put them to use for myself . . . so I just left when I was ready to leave and I never looked back. So, that was that. So the lady said she was gonna help me find a place but then I thought there's too many rules and regulations so I didn't even bother with them.

Albany resisted the restrictions on her behavior throughout her time at the Mercy Home and was dissatisfied with how she was treated and the level of effort she believed others were exerting on her behalf. When she saw a clear opportunity to free herself from these restrictions, she left.

Albany took the initiative to leave, but Sugar and Sasha were asked to leave by the staff, Sugar said, because they were involved in a romantic relationship with one another, which was a violation of house rules. They eventually moved to Sugar's hometown in downstate Illinois, where they lived with the father of Sugar's baby. She described why she moved back: "Well, because I have tried in Chicago, after, you know, they kicked me out of Mercy Home, and I went and I thought I would be able to get a good job and you know find an apartment in Chicago, but it was just too hard. I did get a job, but it didn't pay enough, and in Chicago the rent is a lot higher than here. And then I didn't have, I didn't have any furniture or anything, I woulda been starting out from scratch, and it was hard so I came back here." Sugar's experience also highlights the difficulties of reentering society on her own, as she struggled to earn enough money to pay market-rate rent in Chicago. Her experience demonstrates the value that the subsidized housing programs provide, particularly to those who are newly released. Few women were in a position to support themselves and few had families that could support them to that degree.

While these women lacked the case management supports that those in subsidized programs received, some were able to transition to stable lives on their own. Bennie, for example, was at the halfway house in the mid-1990s.

Because she "didn't see eye to eye" with the then-director, she chose to move out without receiving housing assistance. She found a market-rate apartment, where she still lived with her husband. Bennie had limited options in choosing an apartment and neighborhood but found one with affordable rent and no required security deposit. The following excerpt from my field notes describes her immediate neighborhood and apartment:

> I looked around and didn't see an address for the building I thought was hers. The building next door had an address, but no apartment names so I couldn't check to see if that was her building. . . . Several of the buildings around hers had boarded-up windows, but all looked occupied (at least partially). The neighborhood in general was run down, with older, moderately maintained buildings, and no green space. . . . There is a metal gate on her front door (of the apartment) that could be pulled closed and locked with a padlock. It was open, as was the gate on the [apartment door the] floor below. The front door of the building was left open for the mailman, she said. . . . We sat down in a small, cozy front room. Judging from the size of this room, the apartment is quite small but I didn't go beyond it.

While Bennie, and all of the women I interviewed, maintained her apartment well, hers was in a fairly typically neighborhood, particularly for those in private apartments. Boarded-up buildings were common, buildings were sometimes poorly maintained, and there was an active and visible street life. In spite of her constrained choices, she and her husband had lived in the apartment for several years and had fairly stable lives.

Some women worked their way over time to their own apartment or house. Blanche was one of the few women to own her own home. She was at the Mercy Home around the same time as Bennie, after her first incarceration. She then went back to her old neighborhood on the North Side of Chicago and was reincarcerated. Following her second incarceration, she went to another recovery home and then to an apartment on the West Side. At the time of the interviews, she was living in an "up-and-coming area" on the West Side in a multifamily home she had recently bought with her husband, who also was in recovery. She described this neighborhood: "It's not a bad neighborhood. We have a family block. You know, people over there, they've been owning their buildings like thirty, forty years. So I have a lot of older neighbors. It's a couple, you know, not so good. But, you can't expect for the whole block to, you know." Blanche said that the next block over was "rowdy," but she was "familiar" with her neighbors and felt safe when she came home late. She and her husband, whom she met in a support group, hoped to buy another building to turn into an independent-living recovery home.

The women's experience at the Mercy Home and other drug treatment programs strongly shaped the narrative frameworks they used to talk about their choices and experiences in neighborhoods. Avoiding "people, places, and things" was a significant theme in how they talked about their apartments and neighborhoods. However, while they all recited these messages, they translated them into several very different interpretations. Some women, particularly those newly in recovery, embraced the message of avoiding people, places, and things, and they aspired to do so. In contrast, many women appropriated the phrase but rejected the message. Instead, they embraced their old neighborhoods as a neutral or positive force. These women adopted three common frames: drugs were so widespread as to be unavoidable, so neighborhood did not matter; their old neighborhoods were comfortable and desirable because of their familiarity; and "bad" neighborhoods could be beneficial, as a reminder of their past selves and as an opportunity to give back. These appropriations and reframing of the message allowed them to reconcile their "bad" neighborhood with their "good" self-conception. Through this reconceptualization, they developed a sense of their own agency in the desistance process.

Avoiding People, Places, and Things

Several women embraced the message of avoiding people, places, and things. In doing so, they typically interpreted it to mean avoiding neighborhoods where they had used drugs or offended in the past. Making a move to get away from "people, places, and things" did not necessitate moving to a crime- or drug-free neighborhood, just avoiding areas and people known to them. For some, this included the entire city, or large portions or it, and for others, it was merely staying away from their former block, immediate neighborhood, or people with whom they had used drugs. Jeanette had grown up in K-town, an area with high rates of crime and poverty. She moved from the Mercy Home to an apartment in Austin, one of the neighborhoods in Chicago with the highest concentrations of ex-prisoners in the state, about a year prior to the interviews. While the neighborhood had been experiencing some redevelopment, it had high rates of unemployment, poverty, and crime.

AL: What made you choose this as a place to live?

JEANETTE: I wanted a new start, away from people, places, and things.

AL: What do you like about living in this neighborhood?

JEANETTE: I don't know nobody. The only one I know is my landlord. Everybody minds their business. They stick together. It's a community, there's no violence.

AL: What do you like least about living here?

JEANETTE: The drugs, you see all the traffic.

Although Austin had many of the same disadvantages as Jeanette's previous neighborhood, it was new to her, so she considered this to be consistent with her twelve-step goals. Jeanette was well aware of the social disorder, crime, and drug activity in the neighborhood. Yet because she was from K-town, an area with many of the same social problems as Austin and physically just a few miles away, she felt she was in a better area.

Attempting to avoid known places was especially common among women who were new to the Mercy Home or in recovery for the first time. Those who were more experienced with drug treatment or who had been out of prison for longer often learned the limitations of the admonition. This also was true of Jeanette's experience. In the second interview, Jeanette complained of her continued "dope fiend tendencies" and reported using drugs several times in the past few months. In my fieldnotes, I described our interaction: "Last time I talked to Jeanette she seemed pretty willing to talk. This time, she seemed more agitated and was much more terse. I got the sense that she really just wanted the money and wanted to get it as quickly as possible. She wasn't unfriendly and I didn't get the sense that she was editing herself. . . . She just didn't seem very interested in talking at length. The interview went very quickly. At one point, Jeanette seemed emotional, as though she might cry (I think talking about her fear of relapsing)." As I left, Jeanette walked me out and then ran to join a group of men down the street. Between this interview and when I attempted to reach her for the third interview, Adena told me Jeanette's fiancé had asked her and her mother to leave the apartment they had shared because Jeanette was again using drugs. Adena said Jeanette was living on the street and her mother was in a nursing home. While Jeanette knew few people in the neighborhood initially, she seemed to establish ties with those involved in street life. For her the geographic "knifing off" was insufficient, possibly because she formed new criminogenic ties or because she could still easily access her old neighborhood and her old ties (Maruna and Roy 2007).

Several of the women had similar experiences during attempts at recovery. Danielle, for example, initially believed she needed to avoid people, places, and things.

DANIELLE: It wasn't as hard as I thought it was going to be. Well, I've lived in that environment [recovery home] before but I was out in the suburbs and I was lonely out there. And I was also afraid to come here because it was in Chicago. And I know Chicago like the back of my hand, you know, at least all the bad areas. And I was scared to come here. And I conquered one of my fears. It wasn't like I thought it was going to be. You know, I think that if I would have went back out to the suburbs I would have messed up again. You know, because I would be out there and be lonely and it's like, okay, I keep running from it. You know, so I dealt with it, you know.

Danielle was initially wary to come to the Mercy Home, because she believed she needed to avoid familiar places, which for her included all of Chicago. However, when she had tried relocating to a new area, to her previous suburban recovery home, she felt socially and physically isolated. Several other women likewise stressed a desire to avoid the suburbs, which also reflected their experiences as poor urban women of color in an area where suburban most often meant "white," with limited public transportation. Given these experiences, Danielle began to reframe the desirable conditions of a neighborhood, beyond the messages she was taught. By facing her fear of being in the city, Danielle also began to emphasize her own agency as she learned to live in Chicago without using drugs or offending.

As the examples above illustrate, the women in this study quickly learned that avoiding people and places often did not protect them from relapsing or reoffending and may even contribute to it. The women who rejected this message continued to use the language of "people, places, and things" but reframed the messages they were taught so that they were consistent with their own living conditions and goals. In doing so, they stressed their control over the desistance process. The women used the rhetoric of self-help to emphasize their ability to thrive in spite of their constraints.

Drugs Are Everywhere

Staying away from "people, places, and things" was rarely easy or possible. In addition to their structural constraints, many of the women learned firsthand, in current and past attempts at recovery, that there often was not a straightforward relationship between place and drug use. If they wanted to use drugs, they had the skills and knowledge to find them, even in an unfamiliar neighborhood or city. Being in a new area might slow them down or add an additional step to the procurement of drugs but would not prevent them from finding them. These women still used the rhetoric of "people, places, and things" but reinterpreted its message as irrelevant or misguided. Abra described the events leading up to her arrival at the Mercy Home:

AL: What made you decide to come here [Mercy Home]?

ABRA: I left Cook County Jail and I went out to my mom's and you know, I love my mom and my family and everything but it's like a place where I used at, you know, so before I knew it I started using again. And I had been clean for a while. You know, I guess my family and stuff like that is a trigger for me. So, I got high for about thirteen or fourteen days, a bag here, a couple of bags there. . . . Being in Chicago, where I knew, this is the place where I knew where drugs is at everywhere. Every side of town, even in the suburbs. I have been over there. I have tried to do a geographical change, that's why I ended up in [a city in western Illinois]. You know, to stay away from the blows. Okay, well I stayed away from the blows because they didn't have none, but they had rocks. You know, so, that's like they say that in the book, that shit doesn't work. Excuse my expression, but it don't work that geographical thing. If you want to find it you're going to get it. I needed a support team in my life. Like a family, and that's what I get from [the Mercy Home].

Abra grew up in a disadvantaged predominantly African American neighborhood on Chicago's South Side and was familiar with the city and where and how to locate drugs. In an earlier attempt at recovery, she had tried to abide by the message of avoiding "people, places, and things" by moving to a new city, where she relapsed. She used that experience to reinterpret the message. At the time of the interview quoted here, Abra had been staying at the Mercy Home for approximately two months; both her decision to go there and her interpretation of its value were shaped by her evolving understanding of what it meant to avoid people, places, and things. She now believed that the presence of positive relationships, rather than avoiding negative people or places, was the most important aspect of her recovery. Avoiding drugs was both impossible and insufficient.

While many women argued that drugs were inescapable, they also stressed that the presence of drugs need not lead one to use drugs. Several women acknowledged the drug use around them but framed it as a mundane characteristic that was separate from their experience in the neighborhood. For example, Carrie, who was then living at the Mercy Home, emphasized the omnipresence of drugs.

CARRIE: Drug dealers [are] everywhere you go. It's the same old thing over there: people walking the streets selling drugs, selling clothes or whatever. Some people out there selling their bodies out on the street trying to get that drug. It's the same thing but I chose not to go that way. If I do I just have to choose to be strong. If somebody wants to talk to me I got to say, "I can't talk to you. I got somewhere to go" and just leave them where they at. Just tell them I don't have time. Some people'll say, "You think you all that 'cause you clean now." Then you like, "I don't think I'm all that." You know, it's just that I don't want to be bothered with it. That's not my lifestyle no more; that's what I choose not to do. I don't want to do that, drugs. I want to go shopping, go places, do things, stuff like that. I want to enjoy life.

AL: What do you like about living in this neighborhood here?

CARRIE: It's nice. It's what you make of it. It don't matter because everywhere you go they're going to sell drugs.

Carrie could "leave [drug dealers, users, and prostitutes] where they're at," but she could live her life while surrounded by drug users and sellers, because they were everywhere. In part this reflects the women's continued presence in neighborhoods that often had visible drug markets and street prostitution, contributing to the impression that all neighborhoods, or all neighborhoods in which they were likely to live, shared these characteristics. However, it also reflected their drug procurement skills and experiences and the relative ease of moving across neighborhoods in Chicago. Even when surrounded by drugs, Carrie could choose not to use them. Sheila made a similar argument that even though drugs are everywhere in her neighborhood, "It doesn't matter where you live; it's what you make of your home."

These two perspectives—"if you want it, you'll find it" and "just because it's there, doesn't mean you will use it"—share the idea that the presence of drugs and the use of drugs are two independent phenomena. From this perspective, the women believed that neighborhoods did not matter as much as individual agency and how one defines one's experience in a neighborhood (Gubrium and Holstein 2000; Maruna and Roy 2007). In addition, Abra argued that positive supports were more significant than negative factors and could counteract the influence of people, places, and things related to her drug use and offending (Vaillant 1988). Whether the women were in the same neighborhoods in which they had used drugs and offended or in equally disadvantaged and drug-infested neighborhoods, positive social supports, more than negative reminders or triggers, would influence their own behavior. In part, this framing may be a practical response to limited options. By framing their environment and negative influences as less important than their own agency, they retained a sense of control over their life chances (Maruna 2001).

Comfort in the Familiar

Moving to a new neighborhood allowed the women to stay away from drug-using associates and old locations, but they sometimes felt anxious and uncomfortable in new and unfamiliar areas, particularly predominantly white and/or suburban neighborhoods. Because of this anxiety, some women chose to move back to their old and familiar neighborhoods. This often was an affective decision; that is, they wanted to go back to neighborhoods that had meaning, history, and familiarity in their lives. These neighborhoods were most often where the women had grown up and were typically disadvantaged African American neighborhoods with a high crime rate and common and visible drug use. Moving back to childhood neighborhoods also was sometimes driven by a desire or need to be close to and care for family members. This was useful financially and allowed the women to fulfill caregiver responsibilities. By the last interview, close to 20 percent of the women lived in the same neighborhood in which they had grown up.

Mary was one example of someone who moved back to her old neighborhood because of its familiarity. She moved back to Englewood, an African American neighborhood with one of the highest concentrations of former prisoners in Chicago, after leaving the halfway house in 2001. Like Bennie's neighborhood, Mary's neighborhood was rife with boarded-up buildings, run-down houses and apartment buildings, and vacant lots. Mary recognized some of the disadvantages of her neighborhood, citing the crime and the "bad" youth. Yet, although Mary described her neighborhood in what sounds like undesirable terms, she liked living there.

AL: How would you describe this neighborhood?

MARY: This neighborhood, to me, is quiet. I guess since I live at home. It's all right. I've been around here so many years I guess I just adjusted.

AL: What do you like best about living here?

MARY: Mostly because I know people in the area. Because you know crime is real bad in Englewood. So when I leave home I don't have to worry about it being broken into because I know people all around the neighborhood. Somebody's going to see something.

AL: What do you like least about living here?

MARY: Least about it? Let me see. The kids is real bad around here.

AL: How so?

MARY: They're just bad. They like to tear up and destroy things.

Mary was well aware of crime in the area, but for her, this was minimized by the neighborhood's familiarity, which she perceived as providing a level of safety and security. In spite of the problems in the neighborhood, she liked living there and intended to stay there.

Many of the people Mary knew in the neighborhood used drugs, and she maintained a friendly, but distant, relationship with them. This parallels Carrie's response about "leaving people where they at." Mary said, "I would say, most people in the neighborhood I know around here I used to get high with them, you know, but I tend to shy away. Well, you know, I can speak to them or something, because you just don't do people like that. You know because they got a problem, you know, because I don't want nobody to do me like that if they was clean and I was still getting high." This attitude is consistent with the messages they received in self-help and drug-treatment programs. They were taught that they could not control others' behavior, could not force anyone to get help, and must avoid people who might contribute to their own relapse. Thus, they should avoid close contact with others who are using but attempt to avoid judgment. In addition, Mary valued the familiarity of her neighbors, even as she distanced herself from their behavior. This was a balancing act, as she strove to distance herself without being perceived as superior. Mary, like most of the women, defined herself as different because of her desisting behavior, but not better than active users and offenders.

A few women did not see their neighborhood or the people around them as part of what led to their offending. For example, Sunshine blamed her own stubbornness and the influence of her family, not the influence of her friends or neighborhood context, for her offending. For her, this meant that the idea of moving back to her old neighborhood had different implications than for many of the women. She wanted to go back to her old neighborhood because "my friends were the ones I was fighting with [who] were telling me to quit my shit and stop it. They were the ones that kept telling me, 'No, no, no.' I mean they were a good influence on me but I was hardheaded. I wouldn't listen. But, yeah, I'd go back over there. Over in my part there's no gangs and nobody selling drugs so it's not a problem." She did not see neighborhood influences as important in her own offending, so there was no need to avoid any places. Similar to Abra, she desired the positive influences of her friends. Although Sunshine may face stigma in her childhood neighborhood, the temptations of "people, places, and things" was less salient to her. As most women did have a history of drug use, this dismissal was unusual.

Moving to a childhood neighborhood was much more common among those who had been out of prison and the Mercy Home for longer periods of time. Only one woman who was a resident of the Mercy Home at the beginning of the interviews moved directly to her old neighborhood. Often, women transitioned from a stay at a single-room-occupancy building to their old neighborhoods. This time lapse gave them distance from their old neighborhood and networks early in their recovery, when it may be most necessary (Kirk 2012; Maruna and Roy 2007). At times, there was practical exigency in the decision to move back to an old neighborhood, as frequently the women moved into a family-owned home or moved to help a sick or elderly parent.

Finding comfort in familiar neighborhoods also reflects the women's race, class, and gender positions. Most of the women grew up in neighborhoods that were highly segregated by race and class, and they often had little experience outside these neighborhoods. As Danielle experienced in her previous drug treatment stay, they often felt socially and physically isolated in largely white suburbs with limited public transportation. The caregiving roles they adopted in their families was a gendered pathway for women and one that strengthened both their affective ties to the neighborhood and family and their perceived need to move back (S. Covington 2003; Leverentz 2011). Other women, even when they were unable to live in their old or childhood neighborhoods, maintained strong ties to the neighborhood, considering them "home." The vast majority (88 percent) of the women thought of the area in which they were raised as home. In contrast, only one woman identified her new, current neighborhood as home.

Part of the Solution, Not the Problem

Some of the women reframed their neighborhood context as beneficial, both personally and for the community. These women felt they did not need to avoid "people, places, and things" and thought being around them was a good thing, for them and the community. In their neighborhoods, they were reminded of the lifestyle to which they did not want to return. Angela, originally from western Illinois, described her current neighborhood of Auburn Gresham, an African American neighborhood on Chicago's South Side, as "not a destination, but a place on the way." While she said she would move to middle-class and racially diverse Hyde Park or another state if she could afford it, she also said that a benefit of her neighborhood was that "it keeps the addiction up front. I look out the window and see where I don't want to be." Although Angela disliked the view of drug dealers out her windows, she constantly was reminded of the effects on her life of her own long-term drug use. Her experience in the neighborhood was substantially different from her experiences when she was using drugs; she was working, going to church, and spending little time on the street. Her attitude was similar to Danielle's experience of facing her fears and learning how to live in high-crime neighborhoods with a strong drug presence. In many respects, the women were taught in drug treatment to fear Chicago (or at least its high-crime neighborhoods). Yet, being in a high-drug-use neighborhood "kept the addiction up front" and demonstrated Carrie's point noted earlier—that just because drugs were there did not mean they would use them. Learning this lesson was valuable to Angela, Danielle, and others, strengthening the women's sense of self-efficacy and accomplishment.

In addition, the women saw themselves as positive role models for others in the neighborhood. This contrasts with the common messages that ex-prisoners are a scourge in communities; many of these women saw themselves as living in a realm apart from the drug addicts, prostitutes, and others involved in the street life. Rather they took on the role of the "female old head," dispensing advice and providing social control (Anderson 1990). They saw themselves as uniquely situated to play such a role, as their position was distinct from the purely law-abiding individuals precisely because of their experience as part of street life. They could serve as role models and inspiration for other drug users, dealers, and offenders in the community and as a bridge between the criminal and law-abiding members of the community.

Bennie highlighted her changed role, saying, "I used to be part of the problem, now I am part of the solution." Women who took on this new identity had elevated themselves to a pro-social status. Bennie had lived in her current neighborhood of Englewood for about seven years. She described her experiences in both her current and former neighborhoods, both of which were predominantly African American and had high rates of drug use, crime, poverty, and other disadvantages.

AL: What was that neighborhood like?

BENNIE: Hell. This neighborhood is like hell too, but I'm not a part of the environment, you know, negative wise. . . . It's that I just wasn't into the nice part of it. This is a dope stroll, a ho stroll, everything else but I'm not a part of it so it doesn't affect me, you know, unless I be a neighborhood watch and you know and put a too noisy, disturbing the peace or something and put a cease and desist on it or something like that. But other than that. I was part of the problem. So it was different because at this point in my life I'm not a part of the problem; you know, I'm part of the solution. So it's different. . . .

AL: What do you like least about living in this neighborhood?

BENNIE: It needs to come up. There's some nice neighborhoods back east. They got block clubs and everything. It all depends on where you're at in this neighborhood, you know, if you're a homeowner or renting. The least thing about it is the prostitutes, the drug trafficking, stuff like that. But, you know, everybody got a part to play in society. You know, they got a place in life. That's their place in life at this time in their lives. So I don't bother them either. I don't knock them. You know, they don't bother me and I don't bother them. You know, because only by the grace of God there go I. You know, so I just thank God. Then the pastor, he owned this building. Even though he passed on, they got the church downstairs so I feel this is holy ground for me too. From where I was at, from where I came from to where I'm at.

While Bennie's current and former neighborhoods were comparable in many ways, her experience in them was vastly different. She recognized the similarities, yet saw the two neighborhoods in very different ways because of her role in each. While she had relapsed in the past, she had a long period of sobriety and spoke with confidence of being a role model and an asset to the neighborhood. She emphasized her efficacy and her ability to shape the neighborhood, either through a neighborhood watch or merely by not participating in the "dope stroll, ho stroll" and other street activities in the neighborhood. Bennie went on to talk about conversations she had with others in her building and neighborhood about her own experiences, stories that may serve as inspiration for others who were in positions similar to her own years before. Bennie also emphasized the possibility of change, both in herself and in others. The current drug users, prostitutes, and offenders in the neighborhood were in a certain place "at this time in their lives," a place she had known and moved beyond. She recognized "where I came from to where I'm at" and the possibility that others could make the same changes, and she strove to help them make those changes.

Lisa S took her new role further by actively engaging with neighborhood youth who were causing problems in the neighborhood and enforcing social control. Lisa S went to the Mercy Home because "I wanted more stability first before I went back to the neighborhood." Lisa S was then living with her teenage daughter in her family home "on the West Side—the only side I've ever lived on," in a predominantly African American area with high rates of poverty and crime. Her neighborhood had a lot of drug activity, including "disrespectful guys. They stand around on the corner and sell drugs; they do it right in your face." However, Lisa S brokered the relationship with the young drug dealers: "I talked to them. We're not used to this. Almost everyone has been here for twenty-five or thirty years. They don't live here; this block is our business. I went to them like they were somebody. We've always been able to maintain the neighborhood. Kids here respected their neighbors; we raised each other's kids. I asked them 'Is that fair to us?' They said no. They probably see how people treat me. It's been much better. Where they went, I don't know." Despite Lisa S's own half-dozen stays in jail and nine months in prison, she identified herself as someone who was a positive force in the neighborhood, helping raise neighborhood children. In addition, however, she could relate to the local drug dealers by treating them with respect and an absence of fear. Lisa S had a "passion to get everyone to feel what I felt. I never want to go back," and this was apparent in her interactions and attitudes toward her neighborhood and its residents.

These women identified themselves primarily with the law-abiding people in the neighborhood, while maintaining some connection and identification with those involved in street life. The women framed this position as uniquely advantageous, because they could relate to the drug dealers and users, prostitutes, and offenders in the neighborhood while contributing to the positive aspects of neighborhood life. In this sense, they took on the role of an informal "professional ex" in their daily lives; they redefined their past experiences as necessary for a meaningful future by helping others with problems similar to their own (J. D. Brown 1991; Ebaugh 1988; Maruna 2001). In doing so, Bennie, Lisa S, and others were also enacting the twelfth step of carrying the "spiritual awakening" to others. For these women, the neighborhood context was just one area in which they demonstrated the desire to give positive meaning to their offending past. Because of the women's firsthand experience in street life, they could interact with street youth with more authority than residents who did not have that experience. In doing so, they refined their role in the neighborhood as good and beneficial for themselves and the communities, not as a threat to their recovery and desistance. Like the other women who rejected the need or desirability of avoiding people, places, and things, they stressed their own efficacy and agency.

Among these women, the perspective that their neighborhood context was an asset developed over time. Both Lisa S and Bennie had been drug free and desisting from criminal activity for close to a decade and both were in their mid- to late forties. While many of those out of prison for shorter periods emphasized their own agency, they were more clearly in the midst of a process of understanding themselves and their lives as desisting ex-offenders. These women were unlikely to take an active role in neighborhood social control or express as much confidence in their ability to do so. Many first believed they needed to avoid their old neighborhoods, learned through experience that this was difficult and not necessarily beneficial, and then gained confidence in their ability to negotiate neighborhood life, as they did so successfully over time. Although this was not a perfectly linear process and not all long-time desisters took on an active role in neighborhood life, this general order reflects growing experience, stability, time, and confidence as desisting former offenders.

These women talked about the need to negotiate relationships with former co-offenders and drug using acquaintances, but the dominant theme was being careful to not act superior, rather than actively having to resist peer pressure to return to the street. Minding their own business, being friendly but somewhat disengaged, and playing an active role in monitoring the behavior of others in the neighborhood are all consistent with female gender norms of street behavior in urban black communities, particularly among adult women. Women like Bennie and Lisa S who took on a more active role in the community became like the female old head (Anderson 1990).

Narratives of Place

The ways in which these women viewed their neighborhood were strongly shaped by their experiences at the Mercy Home, in self-help programs, and by their positions as (predominantly) poor women of color. The women in this study used the language of twelve-step and self-help groups to reconcile a neighborhood context they have learned is "bad" with their desire to develop a coherent and "ex" prisoner identity. This reframing allows them to maintain a consistent life narrative, while acknowledging the ways in which it diverges from expectation. The stories they told made sense of their past relationship with their neighborhood and allowed them to continue living, in a very different way, in the same or similar neighborhood.

As with their relationships with their families, the ways in which the women talked about their neighborhoods demonstrate the ways in which they reframed twelve-step arguments so that they were consistent with their constrained circumstances. Over time and through experience, the women used the language of self-help to emphasize their own efficacy and control over their desistance (Giordano, Cernkovich, and Rudolph 2002; Maruna 2001). Race, class, and gender shape these processes through the ways in which these characteristics shape their roles in neighborhood life. Renegotiating the messages they received gave these women a vocabulary through which to emphasize their agency and independence. Most of the women in this study were from and continued to live in neighborhoods that were predominantly African American, poor, and high crime. This reflects segregation patterns of Chicago and the concentration of returning prisoners in a small number of inner-city neighborhoods. Living in high-crime, high-incarceration neighborhoods and often related and intimately tied to drug users and offenders, the women had little choice but to continue to interact with the people, places, and things related to their offending. At the same time, the new roles they adapted, as women who either avoided street involvement or behaved as "female old heads" enforcing neighborhood expectations, are more consistent with expected roles for women in disadvantaged neighborhoods of color.

CONCLUSION

With both employment and housing, the women struggled to meet the goals they had internalized, from both twelve-step messages and broader cultural narratives of success. Those that were most satisfied were able to reframe their own sense of success in ways that integrated aspects of these messages with their structural realities. These women were relatively privileged because of their connections to the Mercy Home. They received assistance finding a job, often through connections the Mercy Home had with employers. They also received assistance finding housing, particularly in supportive-housing programs. In spite of these privileges, the women faced many barriers in achieving their goals of financial independence, increased education, and a home of their own. They were working in often chaotic environments, often while balancing physical and mental health needs. Still, they appreciated the sense of accomplishment that having a "straight" job afforded them, at least in the short term. Over time their employment was also often a source of frustration and discouragement, as they faced the limitations of the "hard work and perseverance leads to success" message that they had internalized. The same was true of their experiences of education, which simultaneously fostered a sense of accomplishment and pride while making evident the ongoing limitations resulting from their criminal record and the jobs that were available to them.

Many of the women did persevere with employment, particularly when they could maintain a sense of accomplishment and meaning through the work, though these jobs rarely were stable or well paying enough to lead to financial independence. Similar to the ways in which women wrestled with the limitations of working hard, they also struggled to reconcile twelve-step messages to avoid people, places, and things related to their offending and drug use with their options of where to live. Those who were most able to reconcile their own "bad" neighborhoods with their desire to desist from offending again were those who found meaning and value in where they lived and in their role in the neighborhood.

Conclusion

THE EXPERIENCES OF THESE WOMEN embody desistance as a process. Through starts and stops, progress and setbacks, they actively worked to reconstruct their lives as desisting former offenders and prisoners. They worked to learn what it means to be a desisting offender and drug addict, and how to make this work in the context of their lives. They both learned and expressed this through narratives that integrated their social context and their interpretations of it (McAdams 2006). Their narratives were shaped by their race, gender, age, status as mothers, and how these factors influenced their expectations for themselves and the expectations that others held for them (Blumer 1969; Elder 1998; Goffman 1963). Expectations also were shaped by their histories of offending, drug use, and involvement in the criminal justice system. These various sources of identity sometimes came into conflict with one another, which led to frustration, recidivism, revised understandings of the path to desistance, and revised narrative identities. We begin to see how their narratives play out, and how their sense of self emerges in interaction with other individuals, institutions, and messages (Abbott 2001; Giordano, Schroeder, and Cernkovich 2007; Mead 1934). We not only get their retrospective accounts of what led them into and out of offending lifestyles but also see how their narratives changed across interviews as a result of changing circumstances.

The narratives of these women are historically contingent. In addition to personal characteristics and events, their experiences were shaped by current criminal justice policies, including mass incarceration, the War on Drugs, and approaches to drug treatment in prison and beyond. In many ways, the focus of this book is the effects of both incarceration and criminalized drug addiction on the people affected. Most of the women who participated in this project experienced both, and the line between the effects of the two can be a fine one. Even those who did not have a history of addiction were exposed to twelve-step programs and rhetoric through the Mercy Home, their fellow residents, and other supportive-housing programs. For many in our contemporary prison system, addiction and incarceration also often overlap, and the consequences of troubled home lives during periods of addiction, the separation resulting from incarceration, the adjustment to a prisoner's return, and adjustment to a non-drug-using lifestyle are all intertwined. In times and places outside that of the current system of mass incarceration and a War on

Drugs, these overlaps may be less significant. This is important to remember when comparing this research to other research on desistance and in planning future research.

Narratives are an important lens through which to look at desistance. Narratives allow us to see prisoner reentry and desistance through the eyes of those experiencing the processes, but they do not reflect an uncomplicated or unproblematic view of desistance or reentry. First, narrative identities and behavior are not always consistent. As evidenced by many of the stories of women in this study, a self-described turning point does not always lead to long-term change, at least not smoothly or quickly. Recall Dee Dee, who described her first incarceration sixteen years earlier as a "wakeup call." Eventually, she developed a generative narrative and sustained desistance, but not before she continued to use drugs, commit crimes, and go to prison for years after that first wakeup call.[1] In this sense, the idea of "making good" sounds like "psychological new-age optimism" (Laub and Sampson 2003, 299fn1). Narratives are revised and rewritten based on current views and circumstances, and the connections between key moments, behavior, and identity change are not always clear or stable in these narratives over time. Any of the other likely turning points—establishing a marriage or committed romantic relationship, having children, going to prison, getting a job, moving to a new neighborhood—function as such for some and not for others. Most people attempting to desist believe that this time will be different (Irwin 1970). Still, turning points are only ever evident in retrospect (Abbott 2001).

Second, the structuring characteristics of narratives are socially and culturally conditioned. For example, the love a good woman, a central turning point among the Glueck men (Laub, Nagin, and Sampson 1998; Laub and Sampson 2003; Sampson, Laub, and Wimer 2006), is also a narrative strongly influenced by one's structural position and historical context. The Glueck men came of age at a time and place in which expectations of masculinity and the structural opportunities for former delinquents or prisoners were different than they are today. Both of these shaped the narratives the men used to talk about their lives. In contrast, one could argue that a pro-social identity may be particularly necessary in the contemporary United States because structural social controls like marriage and employment are largely unavailable (Giordano, Cernkovich, and Rudolph 2002). In essence, former offenders or prisoners need to believe they can successfully desist, in spite of all structural evidence to the contrary (Maruna 2001). Believing is not enough to make it so, but it does provide encouragement and foster persistence in the face of structural barriers.

Other social and historical contingencies also shaped their experiences and narratives. Stable, well-paying jobs were extremely rare, though highly coveted by the women; work and education were important to their sense of accomplishment. Marriage rates were low, and rarely were romantic relation-ships a straightforward connection between a desisting former offender and a "pro-social" conventionalizing spouse. Spirituality and motherhood were both important aspects of many of the women's lives, identities, and narra-tives, but they did not serve as clear sources of social control. Often, addictions began after the women became mothers, and all who had children went to prison for the first time after the birth of their oldest child. Still, many saw motherhood, family, education, employment, spirituality, and the embodiment of the twelve steps as key to their ability to maintain their desistance.

GENDER AND DESISTANCE

This research highlights the importance of looking independently at the experiences of female offenders and prisoners, and taking seriously the ways in which gender shapes the experiences of people exiting prison. The women in this study had common pathways for women into delinquency, drug use, and offending (Bloom, Owen, and Covington 2004; Chesney-Lind 1997). These pathways into offending had important implications for their reentry and desistance experiences (S. Covington 2003; O'Brien 2001; Richie 2001). Many grew up in families in which drug use, abuse, and offending were com-mon. Many experienced horrific violence and abuse as children and young adults. Almost all of the women were in friendship circles and neighborhoods in which drug use was widespread and drugs were readily available. Thus, even those who described their childhoods as stable were exposed to drugs, and what began as casual experimentation developed into addiction, which then led to additional offending. Among these women, drug use, offending, and incarceration were all closely intertwined. This is also true of contemporary male prison populations, but is even more pronounced for women.

Regardless of whether we view desistance as a process that is driven by identity change, social bonds, or the interaction between the two, the experi-ences of women and men are strikingly different. Even when experiencing reentry and attempting desistance in the same social context, men and women also negotiate gender roles and expectations that shape their lives, their rela-tionships, and how others respond to them. Many women are expected by others, and expect themselves, to be caregivers within their families. In con-trast to many men who expect to receive support from family members when they are released (La Vigne, Visher, and Castro 2004; Martinez and Christian 2009), these women rarely expected such support but often did expect to take care of their relatives, especially their mothers and children. They were rarely the only family member who struggled with drug addiction and offending, but they were frequently held to different standards than the men in their family. Their offending, drug use, and involvement in street life were seen as particularly shocking and unexpected. The same is true of their expected roles within their neighborhood, where they could serve as (humble) role models and agents of social control, in spite of their background. In all of these cases, the women internalized these expectations and held themselves to similar standards.

The women's relationships with romantic partners, children, and family members were the most clearly gendered aspects of their narratives. The women's roles as mothers and as caregivers within their families were central to their identities, and sources of shame and guilt when they felt they fell short in either role, during their addictions and during their attempts at desistance. The shame Dee Dee felt when her children were initially taken away, the struggle of Alicia wrestling with her mother, Adena's, drug use and incarcerations, and the ongoing redefinition of family roles within Lauren and Shorty D's family illustrate the complexity, centrality, and evolving nature of these relationships. Most women aspired to independence from men and social services, while their roles as mother and daughter were central to their identities. Some women, like Bennie with her husband Joe, maintained long-standing relationships, but many others avoided getting seriously involved in romantic relationships. This resistance reflects their pathways to offending, messages in twelve-step narratives, and cultural understandings of "dependent" women (Haney 2010; McCorkel 2004).

TWELVE-STEP NARRATIVES AND DESISTANCE FROM CRIME

One of the prominent sources of the narratives the women used are twelve-step programs. The rhetoric of self-help has infused modern American culture (Haney 2010; Illouz 2008; Silva 2012; Wuthnow 1994). These approaches are popular, both because they fit individualistic and populist cultural narratives and because they are cost-effective (Archibald 2007; Wuthnow 1994). The twelve-step narrative as used by offenders and prisoners is an appealing one to the general public and to policy makers, as it emphasizes the offender or drug user taking responsibility for his or her behavior and offers a view of a drug user, offender, or prisoner as someone with a lifelong "sick" identity. The recovery is a process, never fully achieved or left in the past. The addiction must be kept up front; at the same time, most cannot move fully beyond being an "ex" offender or prisoner.

These narratives do not allow their adherents to "knife themselves off" from their pasts. Among the women in this study, twelve-step narratives were strongly woven into their descriptions of their past, present, and future lives. Although they did not always accept them at face value, and sometimes resisted or reframed them, they internalized the messages and incorporated them into their senses of self. They also modified the meaning, to better fit their goals, when the twelve-step narratives did not match the structural realities of their lives. The twelve-step framework gave the women a language with which to frame their desire to desist and their plans for doing so. They worked to make amends to their children and other family members and to reconstitute and strengthen the nature of these relationships. Many women talked about their spirituality and God helping them when they could not help themselves. Sharon learned to incorporate her children in family decision making, and Danielle and her children learned to relate to one another in different ways. Danielle, Shorty D, and Lauren, among others, also began to see their own mothers and their relationships in a new light (Giordano, Schroeder, and Cernkovich 2007). Many avoided old acquaintances and ended romantic relationships when they were tied to their offending or drug use, and developed new and supportive friendships and romantic partnerships. We see the emergence of a sense of generativity in many of the women, like Dee Dee, as she grew into her new role at the Mercy Home (Erikson 1950; Maruna 2001; McAdams 2006). Other women, like Bennie and Lisa S, developed a sense of generativity in their neighborhoods or in their relationships with family, outside the confines of their paid employment or major role transitions.

At the same time, the value of twelve-step ideals was limited in their applicability to the women's other roles and their structural positions. Many of the women, like Erica and Delilah, felt an initial sense of accomplishment at having a job, then immense frustration over their lack of continued progress and tangible accomplishments. The women struggled with the goal of establishing a "normal" life when faced with the reality of the drudgery of that life. Many struggled with messages to avoid people, places, and things related to their offending when those people, places, and things included loved ones, family members, and otherwise comfortable and familiar neighborhoods and places. A few women, like Carolyn, explicitly resented the lifetime invisible punishments they faced.

The use of twelve-step narratives by these women clearly highlights the interrelationship between individuals and their social context. Using a symbolic interactionist approach allows us to look at the structural realities of these women's lives, their own sense of their lives, and how they negotiated relationships and competing messages. We can not only see the narratives the women used but also understand how they developed within their particular social world and relationships and what they mean for the women. These women learned through interaction with prison programming, the Mercy Home, and the broader society what it means to desist from offending. In addition, they learned through interaction with families and communities what it means to be a woman, a mother, a daughter, and a community member. On an individual level, the women's involvement in twelve-step and self-help programs fostered a sense of self-efficacy and supportive relationships. It encouraged them to accept responsibility for their pasts, while allowing them to move forward and redefine their present and future selves. It also encouraged them to focus on the aspects of their lives that they could control and set aside worries about that which they could not control. For many, the twelve-step narrative was a meaningful part in their evolving sense of self, particularly when they were newly out of prison.

However, while twelve-step narratives promoted one way of viewing and approaching desistance, they ignored social and structural realities. A reliance on twelve-step programs and the strong emphasis on the women's pathologies discourage any recognition of the ways their lives and experiences are influenced by social context. These women, and other prisoners, do not live in the same world of the professional white male founders of Alcoholics Anonymous. The women were encouraged to believe that hard work and persistence would lead to success, in spite of the many structural barriers hindering such success for those with criminal histories. The unilateral emphasis on hard work shifts attention away from these structural barriers, the invisible punishments facing those with a criminal record, and the effects of criminal justice policies. Thus, when the women faltered, these failures were interpreted, by them and by others, through a lens of their own weaknesses and pathologies, not the barriers, stigma, and structural disadvantages they faced or an interaction between personal failings and structural barriers.

FUTURE RESEARCH

This research highlights the need to take seriously the narratives returning prisoners use, and to situate them historically, socially, and structurally. It also raises additional questions. Looking at the experiences of women, particularly qualitatively and inductively, expands our understanding of desistance. It highlights the importance of gender in shaping the experiences of returning prisoners and the value in making central the experiences of female returning prisoners. This focus can be extended to other research on reentry and desistance, including how others may respond differently to men and women with a criminal record. For example, women in this study were very invested in education and employment. They often had difficult experiences and faced significant barriers in achieving their goals, but the focus here was almost entirely on their perspectives, not those of potential employers. We have some evidence that the post-prison employment experiences of female prisoners differs from that of men (Cho and LaLonde 2008), but the question of how employers respond to women with a criminal record remains. Do women, and women of color in particular, with criminal histories experience the same types of labor market discrimination as men (Pager 2007; Pager, Bonikowski, and Western 2009)?

There are lessons to be learned and research questions to be raised about men's reentry and desistance experiences. Men and women prisoners are both disproportionately drawn from disadvantaged backgrounds, both have high rates of drug addiction, and both face stigma related to their criminal histories. Both are also likely to be exposed to twelve-step narratives. Yet there are also important differences in their self-conceptions and the expectations others hold for them. Male prisoners' roles as fathers have been less of a research focus than women's roles as mothers. In the interviews represented here, we see glimpses of complicated relationships between these women, their fathers, and the fathers of their children. Although there are important exceptions (for example, Curtis 2010; Edin, Nelson, and Paranal 2003; Nurse 2002), research on fatherhood, its role in desistance, and the ways in which it is impacted by incarceration is relatively rare. Similarly, more attention should be paid to the complexities in men's relationships with their families of origin (Martinez 2006; Martinez and Christian 2009). Both of these types of relationships shape self-perceptions and may be increasingly central to desistance efforts in the context of limited employment and other former social controls. It is possible that some of the factors that were central for these women will also be found to be important to men, if we ask the right questions.

The therapeutic discourse underlying twelve-step programs is not limited to drug treatment or desistance from offending (Bellah et al. 1985; Illouz 2008; Silva 2012; Wuthnow 1994). Still, questions remain about the use of twelve-step narratives by former prisoners without a history drug use, addiction, or treatment and how these narratives play out for those without this history. Do the many returning prisoners or criminal justice system–involved individuals who do not participate in programs like the Mercy Home also incorporate twelve-step narratives to the same extent in their own narratives? What other institutional narratives shape the experiences of other groups of former prisoners? Given their ubiquity in the contemporary United States, there is reason to think the influence of twelve-step programs reaches further than formal participation in these programs. But this is an empirical question to address with additional research.

Policy Implications

This research has several policy implications. The Mercy Home provides many valuable supports to returning prisoners—a free place to live, useful connections to employers, assistance navigating the free world and complex institutions like health care and educational systems. The women were given the space and the support to begin to rebuild key relationships and establish themselves in conventional life and roles. Many staff members served as role models and peer support. The women felt empowered and were dedicated to these redefinitional efforts. The Mercy Home also serves as an advocate for the women and as a signal to employers, parole officers, and loved ones that the person in question has changed and is a worthy risk. All of these are valuable functions, which many more returning prisoners and their families could benefit from. In this sense, programs like the Mercy Home should be more widespread and available to returning prisoners.

The Mercy Home and the women's experiences there also highlight problems with our current approach to returning prisoners. In some ways, these women are set up to fail if they believe the self-help and Mercy Home message of success through hard work. The societal appeal of twelve-step narratives in understanding addiction and offending is based in assigning responsibility to the individual. Twelve-step approaches universalize addiction and discourage a structural or institutional critique. Yet the women in this study became prisoners not only because of the behavior that led to their convictions but also because of their social context. Most were embedded in relationships, families, and neighborhoods in which rates of poverty were high, drugs were available, and policing and criminal justice responses were prevalent. Their social context also shaped their experiences when they attempted to reintegrate and desist from offending. They had limited resources on which to draw, particularly outside of supportive programming like the Mercy Home, and limited abilities to "knife themselves off" from their pasts. They also had limited desires to fully knife themselves off, as the negative aspects of their pasts were often closely intertwined with the positive aspects, like family support and familiar neighborhoods. When they started to experience the limits of their own efforts, they felt highly disempowered and defeated, which led to depression, recidivism, and drug use.

A focus on individual pathology allows us to avoid confronting the social inequalities that are created and exacerbated by current criminal justice, welfare, and drug policies (Garland 2001; Wacquant 2010; Western 2006). As long as we maintain the illusion of returning prisoners' unilateral control over their own reentry, we can continue to absolve ourselves of responsibility. Similarly, these narratives distract us from the ways in which social policies and stigma inhibit desistance. It can often be politically appealing to incorporate invisible or lifelong punishments into our criminal justice policies, but these are unlikely to encourage desistance.

A more productive approach would be to foster the desistance narratives and support the resulting behavior and relationship changes. This necessitates recognizing the social context and complex relationships and supporting efforts to work within those relationships, if that is what the returning prisoner desires. In addition, it necessitates allowing returning prisoners to continue to make meaningful progress towards their goals. Public acknowledgment of desistance efforts with ceremonies or rituals in which the state recognizes successful desistance efforts or an official end to punishment is one way to support desistance efforts and limit the lifetime consequences of a criminal history (Maruna 2001, 2011). Such rituals or "certificates of rehabilitation" might also increase the confidence of employers in hiring those with a criminal record (Solomon et al. 2004). In addition, time limits on the use of criminal records and otherwise restricting the use of criminal background checks in hiring decisions can allow former prisoners to secure employment and advance in their jobs (Blumstein and Nakamura 2009; Lucken and Ponte 2008; Stoll and Bushway 2008). These changes will not eliminate recidivism. Again, desistance is a process in which one is likely to experience setbacks. This should be expected, and the goal should be to minimize the deleterious consequences of these setbacks, rather than to expect that we can eliminate them altogether. Setbacks need not be permanent; as Shorty D said, "If you fall, you ain't gotta stay down." Our policies should support their efforts to get back up again.

Appendix A

Respondent Characteristics

Demographic Characteristics

		Current residents	Former residents	Total
Number of respondents		24	25	49
Age at first interview		39.8 years	42.8 years	41.3 years
Race	Black			87.5%
	White			6%
	Latina			6%
Marital status	Single			63.3%
	Married			8.1%
	Separated/divorced/ widowed			28.5 %
Current education	Less than high school	54.2%	4%	28.6%
	High school diploma/ GED	16.7%	28%	22.5%
	Some college	29.2%	68%	48.9%
Percentage with minor children				53.1% (average 1.08)

TABLE A.2

Offending Histories

	Total	
Number of incarcerations	2.54	
Total months in prison	40.5	
Average age at first incarceration (range)	31.7(19–57)	
Incarcerations	Drug-related (possession, delivery)	36%
	Theft or larceny	32%
	Forgery	10%
Self-reported offenses	Drug-related	76%
	Assault or battery	48%
	Theft or larceny	46%
	Prostitution	46%
	Driving without a license	46%

TABLE A.3
Respondents

	Number of interviews	Age at first interview	Age at Mercy Home	Age at first incarceration	Race	Number of children	Number of prison sentences	Total months incarceration
Caprice	4	47	47	34	Black	1	2	132
Shorty D	4	38	38	36	Black	2	1	16
Albany	4	45	45	27	Black	2	4	52
Sharon	4	34	34	30	Black	4	1	7
Tammy	4	33	33	19	Black	0	1	168
Danielle	4	47	47	n/a	Black	3	0	n/a
Sheila	4	48	48	44	Black	2	3	28
EJ	4	45	45	44	Black	1	1	9
Winifred	4	54	54	51	Black	1	2	20
Vivian	4	37	37	19	Latina	0	3	60
Sweetness	4	43	43	39	Black	4	3	39
Melvina	4	47	47	n/a	Black	3	0	n/a
Sunshine	4	35	35	30	Latina	3	1	66
Sugar	3	31	31	21	White	1	2	46
Heidi	2	28	28	25	Black	4	1	33
Shelly	4	38	38	32	Black	4	3	36
Patricia	1	42	42	41	Latina	3	1	4
Sasha	2	36	36	31	Black	0	2	37
Amanda	2	38	38	31	Black	1	3	36
Libra	3	45	45	45	Black	2	1	2
Millie	3	38	38	24	Black	1	3	18
Abra	1	42	42	n/a	Black	1	0	n/a
Starr	4	30	30	28	White	1	2	18
Carrie	1	34	34	27	Black	7	3	78
Jeanette	2	34	33	25	Black	5	3	54
Tasha	4	32	26	21	Black	0	3	27
Andrea	4	35	33	26	Black	1	3	57
April	4	48	40	38	Black	1	1	12
Allison	2	42	42	23	Black	3	10	93

(continued)

TABLE A.3
Respondents (continued)

	Number of interviews	Age at first interview	Age at Mercy Home	Age at first incarceration	Race	Number of children	Number of prison sentences	Total months incarceration
Mary	4	41	39	33	Black	1	2	19
Linette	4	34	34	27	Black	5	3	42
Marie	4	38	30	29	Black	2	1	10.5
Delilah	4	54	50	25	Black	4	5	156
Jane	2	55	53	37	Black	0	3	89
Victoria	1	37	35	26	Black	3	4	68
Bennie	4	48	41	28	Black	3	3	54
Dee Dee	4	39	39	24	Black	5	5	58
Edie	3	39	37	33	Black	1	2	48
Lisa D	4	46	41	38	Black	6	2	7.5
Carolyn	4	57	53	47	Black	2	1	54
Blanche	4	47	38	36	Black	1	2	28
Corinna	4	48	45	36	White	2	4	8.75
Angela	4	42	39	35	Black	0	2	24
Erica	4	33	30	20	Black	2	2	60
Lisa S	4	47	39	37	Black	3	1	9
Lauren	4	41	34	27	Black	1	3	51
Junelle	4	50	48	46	Black	1	1	4
Gertrude	3	38	33	30	Black	4	1	5
Adena	2	47	47	39	Black	3	4	23

Research Methods

As with all research, this project evolved from the original research proposal to the final product. And, as with all qualitative research, the researcher was an important aspect of the data collection and analysis. In this appendix, I detail the way this project unfolded and my role as researcher.

RESEARCH DESIGN AND RECRUITMENT

The original design of this study called for repeated interviews with women who were returning to the community from prison, along with interviews with their friends, family, and other members of their social networks. The purpose of this was threefold: tracking changes in the women's lives, especially over their key first year after prison; establishing greater rapport; and inductively identifying topics of interest and relevance to the women. Executing this plan was no small feat. I needed to be able not only to identify appropriate women but also to establish enough rapport and trust quickly so that they would talk with me again and refer me to others in their lives. I decided that working with a social service program geared toward a returning prisoner population might help increase access and establish an initial level of trust. This is a common approach when seeking access to a hard-to-reach population (Jones 2010; Maruna 2001; Miller 2001). Given that the nature of the study was to find a theoretically rich sample, rather than a generalizable one, this approach was well suited to my goals.

All of my interviews were recruited through the Mercy Home and included both current and former Mercy Home residents. Initially, however, I worked with another organization, which was both a residential program and a drop-in center whose target population was women engaged in prostitution. For about seven months, I volunteered there, helping women prepare for the GED, accompanying them on field trips, and doing street outreach.[1] One of the women I met was Delilah, who was then an outreach worker there and who told me about the Mercy Home, where she had lived when first released from prison several years before. I contacted the Mercy Home, first just to learn more about it, and arranged to meet with the executive director. At the same time, my progress at the first organization was faltering. I had the support of its executive director to conduct my study, but the service coordinator was more wary of allowing me to invite the women there to participate in interviews. In addition, the organization itself was struggling financially and organizationally. Soon, there were dramatic staff changes, including the replacement of the executive director, and numerous layoffs (including Delilah). I continued to volunteer and spend time there, but my hope that it would serve as a source of interview recruitment faltered, and eventually I drifted away. My interview with the Mercy Home's executive director was therefore particularly serendipitous. She was open and welcoming. The Mercy Home had participated in research projects before (most notably in a program evaluation conducted by a well-known and well-liked faculty member from the University of Illinois at Chicago who then served on its board). The director introduced me to several other staff members and asked if I wanted to conduct my research there. She suggested I come in and introduce the study to the women. They could then decide themselves whether to participate. We arranged a time, in September 2003, shortly after this initial meeting, for me to speak with the women.

I was nervous in this first meeting. If I made an unconvincing or unlikable first impression, the women could opt out (or, rather, not opt in). I knew there would be substantial social distance between us, and I was afraid this would affect their willingness to talk with me. I bumbled through my introduction, explaining what I wanted to do and what I wanted from them. I passed around informed consent forms and asked any interested women to sign them. I gathered the forms, thanked them, and left. I was tremendously relieved to see that most or all of the women who were at that meeting had indeed signed the form. Once the interviews were under way, more women, who had either moved in after that first meeting or had been out of the house that day, approached me and asked to join the project. Once the initial group had moved out of the house a few months later, I again recruited women in a formal meeting. I was at an advantage at those first meetings in that some of the women saw the initial interviews as a diversion from their "typical" day at the Mercy Home. In addition, I paid all respondents twenty dollars in cash for their time. This was not insignificant, especially for those women who were not yet working and who had fairly limited expenses while at the halfway house, though it did not seem to be a driving force for most.

In December 2003, I mailed an introductory letter to all former residents for whom the halfway house staff had current addresses, inviting them to join the study. This gave me a wider range of experiences with reentry, as I could learn what happened to some women months or years after they left the Mercy Home. I prepared the mailing and dropped it off at the halfway house, where staff added address labels.[2] This approach protected the privacy and confidentiality of the women who chose not to participate. Out of the approximately three hundred former residents since the time halfway house opened nine years earlier, the Mercy Home had what were believed to be current addresses for eighty-five. Ten of these were returned to me as undeliverable by the post office; a few women returned the form, but without a contact number or address, or they did not respond to my attempts to contact them. In all, I interviewed twenty-five former residents (33 percent of those with valid addresses), who had stayed at the Mercy Home from a few months earlier to up to nine years prior.

When I asked the women why they chose to participate in the project, most cited a desire to help others in similar positions, either individually or through policy changes, to give women like them a voice, or because they found the interviews therapeutic. First, they hoped that their experiences, through their inclusion in this project, might help others in a similar situation or help change policy. Carolyn said she participated "because no one tells the truth. Maybe somebody will be in charge and remember this." Some wanted to "get the word out" so that people had a better understanding of what they had gone through. For example, Caprice said that she agreed to participate "so you can know what we've gone through, how our lives have changed. Mostly where we're at and where we're going." Others hoped that their stories might directly help others who were going through similar experiences. Sharon said, "It sounded like it could help somebody else. . . . So people can really know." Sheila said, "Anything I can give or say to help someone. It might help, they may learn from my experience. Maybe if someone had sat me down to talk about this, maybe I wouldn't have been in hell as long as I was." Bennie said "Until we learn to channel this stuff, and know what's going on. . . . We have to start somewhere. Someone may turn the page and see themselves. . . . We learn we're only as sick as our secrets." Others specifically wanted to give something back to the halfway house and agreed to participate at least in part because I was somehow affiliated with them. April said she agreed to participate because "you asked. When I heard it was affiliated with the Mercy Home, I agreed. I wish I could spend more time there. . . . I need to give back what was freely given to me." Erica said that this is "my way of giving back, and helping someone else." Lastly, many women said they benefited personally from being able to talk about themselves, their struggles, and problems in a nonjudgmental setting. Linette, for example, said she participated because "when I talked to you, you sounded nice. . . . It gives you a chance to clear your thoughts, what's going on with you." A few women did say they wanted the money; still, in very few cases, including those who were open about the financial incentive, did I get the sense that participants were giving perfunctory answers or were going through minimal motions for a bit of extra cash.

Understanding Context

A key component of this study was to understand the women's social context and their relationships. I did not want to treat the women as individuals in isolation from their surroundings. In order to better understand their context, I did three things. First, I asked the women directly about their relationships, their jobs, and their neighborhoods in each interview, including changes in each from interview to interview. Second, in most cases, I interviewed the women at their homes. The primary purposes of this were to make the women comfortable and to conduct the interviews in a place that would be convenient to them. Occasionally, the women requested that I meet them at their place of work, which also gave some insight into their lives, and in a few cases, we met in a public place that they chose, such as a coffee shop or restaurant that was near their home or work. While the driving factor behind these decisions was the ease and convenience of the interview for the women, it also to gave me a glimpse into their lives and their communities. I saw firsthand where they lived and/or worked, which provided an additional layer to my understanding of their lives.

The third thing I did to understand social context was interview members of the women's social networks. During the course of my first interview with the women, I asked them to identify people they would feel comfortable with my interviewing. The women were free to refer anyone they were close to and comfortable with my talking to; referrals included friends, siblings, parents, adult children, romantic partners, and coworkers. This constrained the interviews to a doubly self-selected group (the women first choosing who to tell about the study and those people deciding whether to follow up), but through these interviews we can begin to better understand their social context and contacts. These interviews included questions about the respondent's background, his or her relationship with the woman that referred him or her, and his or her perceptions of the woman's offending and likelihood of desistance. I began these interviews several months into the project and interviewed these people twice when possible.

I interviewed twenty-six network members referred by fifteen women. I interviewed nineteen of these individuals twice and the remaining seven once. These interviews included boyfriends or husbands, siblings, cousins, mothers, one woman's adult daughter, friends, and coworkers. In addition, several of the women had significant relationships with other core respondents, in which cases I asked about these relationships in the context of the regular interview. For example, Sugar and Sasha developed a romantic relationship during the course of the interviews and were living together at our final interview. Sheila and Adena were cousins, and when I interviewed Adena's mother, daughter, and another cousin, I asked about their relationships with both Sheila and Adena. The women also developed friendships with one another and talked about these relationships in the course of the interviews. In one case, Jeanette referred me to Adena, as her friend. Because of Adena's history both with incarceration and the Mercy Home, I considered her a "core" interviewee, though she did not respond through my normal recruitment method. I also continued to also ask her about her relationship with Jeanette.

RESPONDENT ATTRITION

I planned to interview all women four times, approximately three months apart, and all network members twice. At each round of interviews, I lost contact with a few respondents. I interviewed forty-five of the forty-nine women at least twice and thirty-three women four times.[3] The most common timing of attrition was when the women moved out of the Mercy Home or to a new apartment (usually, but not always, within the Chicago region). Over the course of the year, twenty-seven women moved. Most of these (twenty-four) were residents of the halfway house moving into their own housing. I gave all respondents my name and phone number and encouraged them to let me know when they moved, but this often did not happen. I also left messages for them at the Mercy Home (as many stayed in especially close contact right after they moved) and had staff mail letters to those with forwarding addresses. Again, my connection to the Mercy Home was extremely beneficial in following the women over time. Nine women moved to the same single-room-occupancy building. In these cases, I knew where they were going before they left the halfway house and was able to keep track of all of them. I occasionally ran into them in common areas, or they left word with a woman I was visiting. This was more difficult for those who moved to SROs with a small number of interviewees, scattered-site locations, or private housing. In all, I lost contact with a third of the women (nine) after they moved, which is over half of the women who did not complete all four interviews. Some of these (as far as I know) did receive follow-up letters from me, and others were returned undeliverable. In a few cases, I missed one interview but interviewed them again later. For example, Sugar and Sasha moved out of town and I temporarily lost track of them. Eventually they did contact me and I made one trip to interview them again. I interviewed them three and two times, respectively, and covered all of the interview questions and roughly the same total time period as the others. Adena was incarcerated during the interview period. I interviewed her again after her release. Shelly contacted me months after I had completed the rest of the interviews; although this final interview was "off-schedule," we did complete the fourth and final interview.

INTERVIEWER AND INTERVIEW DYNAMICS

In conducting qualitative research, the researcher him- or herself is an important aspect of the data and thus it is useful to reflect on my role in the research.[4] There was significant social distance between the people in this study and myself. I was a young, white, middle-class, childless, unmarried female with a high level of education and I had never served time in prison or experienced a drug addiction. For the most part, the people I was interviewing knew these characteristics because they were clearly visible (race, age), they were the reason for my talking to them (my dissertation research), or because they asked (marital status and children). I shared one or two traits (for example, race, age, class background, lack of children, relationship status) with some of the women, but the only thing we consistently had in common was gender. In addition, all of the women had involvement with the criminal justice system, almost all had recently spent time in prison, and most self-reported criminal behavior and drug use. These details were salient because it was the reason I was there and the focus of many of the topics we discussed; thus regardless of demographic similarities or differences there was a clear and significant difference between us in almost all cases (with the exception of a few network members).

As stated at the outset, one of the reasons I chose to work with the Mercy Home was to help me establish initial access and mitigate some of this social distance. I do not know whether this was a necessary strategy, though my affiliation did help me gain initial access to a group of women and to track them over time. As I said earlier, many women mentioned this connection as a reason they first agreed to participate. Of course, there is a clear selection bias in that I was primarily talking to women who maintained enough contact with the Mercy Home that they had up-to-date contact information. Most of them had a positive experience and memory of their time at the Mercy Home, though this was not exclusively the case; some women did talk about frustrations and resentments from their time there. The women's involvement with the Mercy Home and previous treatment programs also meant that they were used to talking about their pasts and their future goals. For the most part, they were articulate, thoughtful, and reflective about their experiences, which is likely to be, in part, an outgrowth of their experience and comfort with counseling settings. Our discussions were another time in which to think about their lives and reflect on where they had been and where they were going. In some cases, the social distance between us led to greater explanations, as the women explained what black families, black women, prison, drug addiction, and so on were like, putting their own experiences in a broader context that I would not otherwise understand. When they didn't initially do this, such as when a woman offhandedly said, "You know what black families are like," it was easy to encourage her to elaborate. For the most part, I was the "acceptable incompetent" (Lofland and Lofand 1994).

The women often mentioned enjoying our discussion and they seemed comfortable (for the most part) talking to me. Still, as Kirsch (1999) writes, "unlike friendships, which are built in reciprocal trust and sharing of personal information, interviews only simulate this context. . . . In short, interviews represent an artificial, staged performance" (30–31). Perhaps because of this difference between "friendship and friendliness," my attempts at relating to them by mentioning similarities between us sometimes fell flat (Kirsch 1999). For example, I occasionally agreed with them on a certain point or experience, like a relationship dynamic or an insecurity over something, and told them that I had the same problem. A few women gave me a look back that seemed to say, skeptically and with mild irritation or dismissiveness, "We are not alike." Even though the perception of commonality was genuine on my part, it did not seem so to them. Another possible reason for this skepticism is that the women did see me as a therapist figure, something they often cited as a reason they agreed to participate or enjoyed talking to me. In this sense, any talk of me was time away from the topic at hand—themselves (Weiss 1994).

Other women expressed more interest in me, asking questions about myself, and seemed to view me more as a friend and social equal. I answered any questions they asked me, whether they were about my research or my life. I did, however, try to avoid giving them advice or offering my opinion, especially in terms of judging or validating their attitudes or behavior. In cases where I was directly asked my opinion, I would usually give it, though I tried to hedge and point out that I was unqualified to give advice (for example, when I was asked about what I would do in a certain parenting situation or with a romantic relationship). While some feminist researchers (Kirsch 1999; Miller 2001; Oakley 1981) may disagree with this somewhat more traditional interviewing approach, I did not feel comfortable judging or validating respondent's experiences or opinions. I do not think this hindered rapport, as few of the women ever seemed to seek validation, and they typically discussed their lives matter-of-factly, and occasionally with some regret. Occasionally they invited me to go to church with them, watch their choir performance, or socialize. When I was able to, I accepted these invitations, though I hesitated to encourage too close a relationship for fear of hurting a woman later. In a few cases, a woman pointed out similarities between us, particularly in terms of education or class. These varying interactions highlight the variability in their personalities and interaction styles, as well as the difficulty in predicting the influence of researcher characteristics or persona on a group of respondents.

Interviews most often took place at the woman's home. This meant that many of the interviews took place at the Mercy Home, especially early on. This helped me become a familiar presence to the residents in the early stages of the interviews, which helped with recruitment and retention. It also gave me the chance to see where the women lived (especially relevant in chapter 6), and demonstrated that I was not afraid or unwilling to travel to their neighborhoods and that their time and convenience were important. I wanted to minimize the clinical feel and the implied hierarchy that an interview in my office or a third-party place would elicit. Occasionally, we met in a common room in the woman's building (always the case at the halfway house) and sometimes at the woman's place of work or a mutually agreed upon restaurant or coffee shop. This was always at the request of the woman, and the only reason explicitly given for this was convenience or a desire to show me where she worked. In several cases, I went both to the woman's apartment and her place of work. A few woman expressed surprise that I was willing to go to her neighborhood without being afraid or that I was not afraid to leave my car parked outside. In at least one case, the woman herself was new to the neighborhood. This surprise, depending on the woman and the neighborhood, reflected either her own sense of insecurity in the neighborhood or a perception that "someone like me" might be afraid, though she herself was not. Rarely did I feel uncomfortable in a neighborhood, and never did anything significant happen. In addition, where possible, I tried to minimize displays of hierarchy in the interview itself. For example, I tried to sit in an equivalent chair, rather than behind a desk, if there was one. If the women directed me to a particular chair, I usually complied. If they were not familiar with the University of Chicago (many confuse it with the University of Illinois at Chicago), where I was then a graduate student, I would tell them it was "the one in Hyde Park," a neighborhood with which they were familiar.

Those I came into contact with—the interviewees and staff of residential programs—often viewed me in a case manager or therapist role. Often, staff members assumed I was a case manager and expressed surprise or confusion when I introduced myself as a friend or personal visitor. This mistake bothered me, as I was uncomfortable with the assumptions underlying it (for example, that I could not be a friend). It never caused a problem, however; most often it worked to my advantage or convenience (Duneier 2000). For example, I went to interview Danielle at the single-room-occupancy building shortly after she relapsed. As a result of this relapse, which was known to staff, she was not allowed any personal visitors in her room. Though I introduced myself at the reception desk as a friend, Danielle explained over the phone to the front desk worker that I was not a "friend" and convinced the front desk worker that I should be allowed up to her room. Although the front desk worker hesitated at first, she was easily convinced that an exception should be made for me. I made no attempt myself to convince her of this, and even after she said it was okay, I reiterated that I did not want to violate the rules or get Danielle in trouble. In this case, I was not violating the spirit of the restriction (if it was to minimize the likelihood someone would bring her drugs, rather than a simple "grounding"), and it gave Danielle an outlet during what was a difficult time for her. I always tried to remain aware of, and comply with, the rules of the different organizations with which I came in contact, both to maintain the cooperation of the staff and to avoid causing trouble for the respondents. The staff of the halfway house and the SROs I frequented got to know me by sight, even if they did not know not the reason for the visits; they often guessed who I was there to see and did not always make me follow regular sign-in procedures. Although I was a familiar and regular visitor at several buildings, their laxity was also likely because of my race, class, and gender position and the privileges it afforded. I never actively tried to take advantage of this, though I did benefit from it.

Being a frequent presence at the Mercy Home and the more common single-room-occupancy buildings helped me establish rapport and maintain contact with the women. Indeed, I felt the strongest collective bond with the first group of respondents, most of who moved to the same SRO building. I frequently ran into others while I was there for an interview. They would also leave messages for me with one another and seemed to know when I was coming. This allowed for more informal interactions outside the interview setting. I do not think it is a coincidence that I interviewed all but one of this group four times (and the one exception moved out of town).

Still, I was occasionally troubled by not feeling like more of an "insider" at the Mercy Home. I became a familiar and frequent presence but never felt a part of daily life there. I worried that not being invited to the anniversary celebration, for example, meant that I was not achieving the level of rapport to which I aspired, regardless of the richness of the interview data. However, over time, I came to believe that maintaining some distance from the house as a collective was beneficial. Several of the women said they told me things they would not say in group meetings, because they did not want other people "to know [their] business." Precisely because I remained something of an outsider—our relationship and interactions were slightly removed from the rest of their world—and because they could see over time that I maintained my promise of confidentiality, they were comfortable telling me things they did not want those in their circles to know. Had I been more of an insider— for example, if I participated in groups or Mercy Home events—I would have had to work hard to not be assigned a "staff" identity and they may have been more reluctant to open up to me. Maintaining some distance both from the staff and from other residents made me a truly "safe" person to talk with.

ANALYSIS

Writing about the process of qualitative data analysis, John Lofland and Lyn Lofland (1994, 181) note that "because analysis is the product of an inductive and emergent process in which the analyst is the central agent, achieving this order is not simply a mechanical process of assembly-line steps." This makes the analysis of a qualitative study particularly difficult to articulate (Miller 2008). The interview guides and original research proposal, grounded largely in literatures on female offending, prisoner reentry, and desistance, provided some structure for the initial coding of data and analysis. This included coding the interviews for descriptions of the women's pasts, their background of criminal and criminal justice system involvement, and their relationships at different levels of intimacy (intimate relationships with family, romantic partners, and friends, "parochial" relationships in neighborhoods and in jobs, and "public" relationships with criminal justice and other institutions). To some degree, this is reflected in some of the chapters.

New issues and themes emerged inductively in the data collection and early analyses (Becker 1998; Charmaz 2001; Glaser and Strauss 1967). This was reflected in new questions in subsequent interview guides, and also an increasingly large coding structure developed in NVivo (qualitative data analysis software), as I read and reread transcripts and field notes. The importance of phrases related to twelve-step programs and things like as aspiration to "normalcy" emerged only later and became an orienting theme in later analyses. At times, I also relied on low-tech methods of analysis, including writing key characteristics of the women on note cards, which I could then stack and move around, or entering aspects of their life histories in spreadsheets. These strategies made it easier to see the strength of patterns and which cases were outliers. I began to see common and important aspects of these women's lives that were not reflected in the previous research I was drawing on. Things like the ongoing importance of their families of origin, relationships with women (as romantic or sexual partners or as supportive friends), and their ability, and struggles, to navigate what were often described in the literature as undesirable situations and relationships were emerging as important dimensions of their lives. In many ways, these women were "succeeding" where the (especially quantitative) literature predicted they would not.

As time went on, I became more focused on analyzing the narratives that the women and members of their social worlds used. I was less concerned with these stories as statements of fact about their life histories than as reflections of ways in which they understood and described their lives and their social worlds. The foregrounding of twelve-step programs was very much an inductive interpretation that emerged over time. Over time, I began to recognize significant patterns in the ways the women talked about their experiences. Phrases like "avoiding people, places, and things," being powerless, giving over to God, and the importance of giving back were all prevalent in the women's narratives and reflect the tenets of twelve-step programs. Foregrounding this language, and the ways in which the women struggled with it, also allows us to see the ways in which individual lives are shaped by both culture and structure, or to "connect personal troubles to public issues" (Mills 1959). It is through this language that we can understand how their "core" selves and their human agency intersect with their social context and structural realities.

To present the data, I sometimes use extended examples of a single woman's life, perhaps with supplementary quotes from other women. This allows a more complete picture of some women to emerge, though at the cost of some women being less prominently included than others. This is an inevitable tradeoff of this type of research—in spite of what I believe are rich and compelling stories, they represent only a fraction of everything I heard and learned from these women. Still, the quotes and examples were chosen to be illustrative, either of common themes and patterns or of significant outliers (as noted). When I use percentages or words like "most" or "a majority," they should be read as an illustration of how widespread a phenomenon was among these women. No numbers should be interpreted as representative of a general population.

Notes

Introduction

1. The names of the women, members of their social networks, and the halfway house are pseudonyms. Women were asked to choose their own pseudonym; when they did not, I created one for them. A few women chose to use their real names.
2. In appendix B, I give a more detailed account of how I came to work with the Mercy Home and the research design, process, and analysis.
3. For example, over half (57.2 percent) of female state prison inmates and 16.1 percent of male state prison inmates reported prior abuse, and 36.7 percent of female prisoners and 14.4 percent of male prisoners reported abuse while under the age of eighteen (Harlow 1999) In addition, one study of incarcerated women in Ohio found that half reported child sexual violations or abuse and 70 percent reported sexual abuses that would qualify as rape or serious sexual assaults in most jurisdictions. Male family members were among the most prevalent abusers (McDaniels-Wilson and Belknap 2008).
4. Maruna (2001) also argues that those with this worldview may well have more realistic understandings of their life chances, given the many and significant barriers facing people with criminal histories and the often-accompanying drug addictions.

Chapter 1 The Mercy Home and the Discourse of Reentry and Desistance

1. In other words, this is not an evaluation of program effectiveness.
2. Occasionally a woman is accepted into the Mercy Home from residential drug treatment programs. Three of the women in this study came this way and had never been incarcerated but had served time on probation. All of the women were involved in the criminal justice system, and a non-prison pathway to the house is unusual. For simplicity, I refer to all the women as former prisoners.
3. While the number that returns to prison is not trivial, it is significantly lower than overall recidivism rates. One study found that 52 percent of women released from prison were rearrested within three years; this percentage was higher among women with more prior arrests (Greenfield and Snell 1999).
4. At EJ's request, I did not record her interviews. All quotes from her are paraphrased from handwritten notes.

Chapter 2 Introducing the Women and Their Pathways to Offending

1. The Audy Home for Children is the former name of the Cook County Juvenile Temporary Detention center in Chicago. It was named for former Superintendent Arthur Audy.
2. Class X is the most serious level of felony charge in Illinois.

CHAPTER 3   A YEAR IN THE LIFE: EVOLVING
PERSPECTIVES ON REENTRY AND DESISTANCE

1. See also Maruna's (2001) and Giordano and colleagues' (2008) discussion of persisting and desisting offenders and the difficulty in classifying people into meaningful categories of desistance.
2. A sixth woman had reportedly relapsed, and her behavior during our last interview was consistent with those rumors, though she did not admit it to me. I heard that she was selling drugs out of her apartment, had sold all of her furniture, was using drugs and did not want to stop, and would soon be asked to leave the Refuge Apartments. In our last interview, we met outside, rather than in her apartment as in previous interviews, and she gave very short and brusque answers (our final interview was under fourteen minutes, compared to forty-five to sixty minutes for previous interviews). Although she did not admit to any drug use to me, her strange behavior on that day was consistent with what I heard from several others.

CHAPTER 4   FAMILY DYNAMICS IN REENTRY AND DESISTANCE

1. This reflects the intersection of her financial status and her drug addiction. Not all drug users or addicts commit crimes to support their habit. Nonetheless, the combination was extremely common among this group of primarily low-income women, and in most cases the offending began or escalated after the addiction took hold. See also Steffensmeier and Allan (1996), but see Maruna (2001) for a different time order of addiction and offending (that is, most of the people Shadd Maruna interviewed began offending before drug use, and some even scaled back offending during periods of heavy drug use).
2. In contrast to these women, many male prisoners expect and often receive both emotional and financial support from family members (La Vigne, Visher, and Castro 2004; Martinez and Christian 2009). This difference likely reflects race and gender differences, especially among lower-income African American women who are less likely than white women to expect financial support from others (Bottcher 2001; McCorkel 2004; Rogers-Dillon and Haney 2005). This also may be, in part, an artifact of sample selection in this study. These women had alternative sources of support, largely through their Mercy Home connections, including subsidized housing, state-sponsored employment programs, and/or federal financial assistance for themselves or their children (see also Holtfreter, Reisig, and Morash 2004; Reisig, Holtfreter, and Morash 2002). Thus, they were better positioned to be financially independent from their families of origin than many ex-prisoners, male or female. However, when the women talked about their future plans, and when family members described them, most emphasized their self-reliance and their desire for independence, especially from romantic partners and from social service support.

CHAPTER 5   WOMEN'S CHOSEN RELATIONSHIPS
AND THEIR ROLE IN SELF-REDEFINITION

1. See Cherlin et al. (2004) for similar accounts among low-income women who had experienced physical and sexual abuse.
2. This is an important difference from the roles of romantic relationships in male offender's lives and their desistance. Women are often tangential to men's offending, and central to desistance process (Horney, Osgood, and Marshall 1995; King, Massoglia, and MacMillan 2007; Laub and Sampson 2003; Sampson and Laub 1993; Shover 1996; Warr 1998). Although not all desisting men are in a successful romantic

relationship with a law-abiding partner, researchers do not describe avoiding such relationships as a conscious or desistance-related choice that men make.

CHAPTER 6   EDUCATION, EMPLOYMENT, AND A HOUSE OF ONE'S OWN: CONVENTIONAL MARKERS OF SUCCESS

1. Almost 40 percent of state prison inmates have less than a high school diploma, though over half of female prisoners have a high school diploma or GED and 17 percent have some college (Greenfield and Snell 1999; Harlow 2003). Blacks (44 percent), Latinos (53 percent), inmates younger than twenty-four years old (52 percent), noncitizens (61 percent), and drug offenders (47 percent) are particularly unlikely to have earned a high school diploma or GED.
2. One concern of potential employers is their legal liability should an ex-prisoner commit a new crime at work (Holzer, Raphael, and Stoll 2001; Lucken and Ponte 2008; Petersilia 2003). Given the stereotypes of offenders as young men of color committing violent and drug-related offenses, this is likely to impact young black and Latino men disproportionately (Pager 2007).
3. About 40 percent of female inmates were working full time prior to their arrest, compared to 60 percent of male prisoners. Over one-third of female prisoners earned less than $600 a month prior to their arrests, compared to just over a quarter of men, and women were six times more likely than male inmates to be receiving welfare payments prior to their arrest (Greenfield and Snell 1999).
4. IDHS contracts with employers to hire individuals receiving food stamps for the Earnfare program, which is conceived as a welfare-to-work program for low-skill workers. The workers can then work off the value of their food stamps, at minimum wage, and earn up to an additional $294 a month (paid by the government) by working a maximum of eighty hours a month. Participation is limited to six out of twelve consecutive months and is designed to provide those receiving assistance with some work experience. The individual companies then may hire some participants on permanently (http://www.dhs.state.il.us, accessed August 31, 2004).
5. A few years after the data collection for this project ended, Corrina died of a drug overdose.
6. These percentages exclude seven women with whom I lost touch before or when they moved from the halfway house. I do not know where they moved.

CONCLUSION

1. See also the work of Peggy Giordano and colleagues for examples of the ways in which narratives of desistance and "objective" measures of such desistance do not match (for example, Giordano, Cernkovich, and Rudolph 2002; Giordano et al. 2008; Giordano, Schroeder, and Cernkovich 2007).

APPENDIX B   RESEARCH METHODS

1. The street outreach I did with them was for another study of which I was a part on HIV prevention programs.
2. The Mercy Home executive director and the University of Chicago Institutional Review Board (IRB) agreed upon all recruitment strategies.
3. Most of the interviews were tape-recorded. Two respondents did not want to be tape-recorded (one of whom was only interviewed once), and a third chose not to be recorded the first time but agreed for subsequent interviews. In addition, one network member did not want to be recorded. I accidentally deleted one interview recording. For those interviews that were not recorded (a total of nine interviews),

interview transcripts were based on handwritten notes only. For all other interviews, the recordings were transcribed verbatim. In addition, I took notes during each interview and wrote field notes after each to capture the setting, nonverbal communication, and interpersonal dynamics.

4. See Duneier (1999); Jones (2010); Miller (2001, 2008); and Twine and Warren (2000) for discussions of similar issues that shaped my thinking on them.

References

Abbott, Andrew. 2001. *Time Matters: On Theory and Method*. Chicago: University of Chicago Press.

Anderson, Elijah. 1990. *Streetwise: Race, Class, and Change in an Urban Community*. Chicago: University of Chicago Press.

———. 1999. *Code of the Street: Decency, Violence, and the Moral Life of the Inner City*. New York: W. W. Norton.

Archibald, Matthew E. 2007. *The Evolution of Self-Help: How a Health Movement Became an Institution*. New York: Palgrave Macmillan.

Baskin, Deborah R., and Ira B. Sommers. 1998. *Casualties of Community Disorder: Women's Careers in Violent Crime*. Boulder, CO: Westview Press.

Becker, Howard S. 1963. *Outsiders: Studies in the Sociology of Deviance*. New York: The Free Press.

———. 1998. *Tricks of the Trade: How to Think About Your Research While You're Doing It*. Chicago: University of Chicago Press.

Bellah, Robert N., Richard Madsen, William M. Sullivan, Ann Swidler, and Steven M. Tipton. 1985. *Habits of the Heart: Individualism and Commitment in American Life*. Berkeley and Los Angeles: University of California Press.

Berger, Peter L., and Thomas Luckman. 1966. *The Social Construction of Reality*. New York: Anchor Books.

Bersani, Bianca, John Laub, and Paul Nieuwbeerta. 2009. "Marriage and Desistance from Crime in the Netherlands: Do Gender and Socio-Historical Context Matter?" *Journal of Quantitative Criminology* 25 (1): 3–24.

Blee, Kathleen M., and Ann R. Tickamyer. 1995. "Racial Differences in Men's Attitudes about Women's Gender Roles." *Journal of Marriage and the Family* 57 (1): 21–30.

Bloom, Barbara, Barbara Owen, and Stephanie Covington. 2004. "Women Offenders and the Gendered Effects of Public Policy." *Review of Policy Research* 21 (1): 31–48.

Blumer, Herbert. 1969. *Symbolic Interactionism: Perspective and Method*. Berkeley: University of California Press.

Blumstein, Alfred, and Kiminori Nakamura. 2009. "Redemption in the Presence of Widespread Criminal Background Checks." *Criminology* 47 (2): 327–359.

Bottcher, Jean. 2001. "Social Practices of Gender: How Gender Relates to Delinquency in the Everyday Lives of High-Risk Youths." *Criminology* 39 (4): 893–931.

Braman, Donald. 2004. *Doing Time on the Outside: Incarceration and Family Life in Urban America*. Ann Arbor: University of Michigan Press.

Brown, J. David. 1991. "The Professional Ex-: An Alternative for Exiting the Deviant Career." *Sociological Quarterly* 32 (2): 219–230.

Brown, Marilyn. 2006. "Gender, Ethnicity, and Offending over the Life Course: Women's Pathways to Prison in the Aloha State." *Critical Criminology* 14 (2): 137.

Brown, Marilyn, and Barbara Bloom. 2009. "Reentry and Renegotiating Motherhood." *Crime & Delinquency* 55 (2): 313–336.

Cain, Carole. 1991. "Personal Stories: Identity Acquisition and Self-Understanding in Alcoholics Anonymous." *Ethos* 19 (2): 210–253.

Carr, E. Summerson. 2011. *Scripting Addiction: The Politics of Therapeutic Talk and American Sobriety.* Princeton, NJ: Princeton University Press.

Charles, Camille Zubrinsky. 2000. "Neighborhood Racial-Composition Preferences: Evidence from a Multiethnic Metropolis." *Social Problems* 47 (3): 379–407.

Charmaz, Kathy. 2001. "Grounded Theory." In *Contemporary Field Research: Perspectives and Formulations*, edited by Robert M. Emerson, 335–352. Long Grove, IL: Waveland Press.

Cherlin, Andrew J., Linda M. Burton, Tera R. Hurt, and Diane M. Purvin. 2004. "The Influence of Physical and Sexual Abuse on Marriage and Cohabitation." *American Sociological Review* 69 (6): 768–789.

Chesney-Lind, Meda. 1997. *The Female Offender: Girls, Women, and Crime.* Thousand Oaks, CA: Sage Publications.

———. 2002. "Imprisoning Women: The Unintended Victims of Mass Imprisonment." In *Invisible Punishment: The Collateral Consequences of Mass Imprisonment*, edited by Marc Mauer and Meda Chesney-Lind, 79–94. New York: The Free Press.

Cho, Rosa, and Robert LaLonde. 2008. "The Impact of Incarceration in State Prison on the Employment Prospects of Women." *Journal of Quantitative Criminology* 24 (3): 243–265.

Collins, Patricia Hill. 2000. *Black Feminist Thought: Knowledge, Consciousness, and the Politics of Empowerment.* New York: Routledge.

———. 2005. *Black Sexual Politics: African Americans, Gender, and the New Racism.* New York: Routledge.

Comfort, Megan. 2008. *Doing Time Together: Love and Family in the Shadow of the Prison.* Chicago: University of Chicago Press.

Covington, Jeanette. 1985. "Gender Differences in Criminality among Heroin Users." *Journal of Research in Crime and Delinquency* 22 (4): 329–354.

Covington, Stephanie. 2003. "A Woman's Journey Home: Challenges for Female Ex-Offenders." In *Prisoners Once Removed: The Impact of Incarceration and Reentry on Children, Families, and Communities*, edited by Jeremy Travis and Michelle Waul, 67–104. Washington, DC: Urban Institute Press.

Curtis, Anna. 2010. "'Little Me' versus 'My Princess': Incarcerated Fathers and Gender Expectations for Children." Paper delivered at the American Sociological Association Annual Meeting, Atlanta, GA.

Duneier, Mitchell. 1999. *Sidewalk.* New York: Farrar, Strauss, Giroux.

———. 2000. "Race and Peeing on Sixth Avenue." In *Racing Research and Researching Race: Methodological Dilemmas in Critical Race Studies*, edited by France Winddance Twine and Jonathan Warran, 215–226. New York: New York University Press.

Ebaugh, Helen Rose Fuchs. 1988. *Becoming an Ex: The Process of Role Exit.* Chicago: University of Chicago Press.

Edin, Katheryn, and Maria Kefalas. 2005. *Promises I Can Keep: Why Poor Women Put Motherhood before Marriage.* Berkeley: University of California Press.

Edin, Kathryn, Timothy J. Nelson, and Rechelle Paranal. 2003. "Fatherhood and Incarceration as Potential Turning Points in the Criminal Careers of Unskilled Men." In *Imprisoning America: The Social Effects of Mass Incarceration*, edited by Mary Patillo, David Weiman and Bruce Western, 46–75. New York: Russell Sage Foundation.

Elder, Glen H., Jr. 1998. "The Life Course as Developmental Theory." *Child Development* 69 (1): 1–12.

Enos, Sandra. 2001. *Mothering from the Inside: Parenting in a Women's Prison.* Albany: State University of New York Press.

Erikson, Erik. 1950. *Childhood and Society.* New York: W. W. Norton.

Fagan, Jeffrey. 1994. "Women and Drugs Revisited: Female Participation in the Cocaine Economy." *Journal of Drug Issues* 24 (1/2): 179–225.

Farrall, Stephen, Gilly Sharpe, Ben Hunter, and Adam Calverley. 2011. "Theorizing Structural and Individual-Level Processes in Desistance and Persistence: Outlining an Integrated Perspective." *Australian & New Zealand Journal of Criminology* 44 (2): 218–234.

Fitch, Catherine A., and Steven Ruggles. 2000. "Historical Trends in Marriage Formation: The United States 1850–1990." In *The Ties That Bind: Perspectives on Marriage and Cohabitation*, edited by Linda Waite, Christine Bachrach, Michelle Hindin, Elizabeth Thomson, and Arland Thornton, 59–88. New York: Aldine de Gruyter.

Flavin, Jeanne. 2001. "Of Punishment and Parenthood: Family-Based Social Control and the Sentencing of Black Drug Offenders." *Gender and Society* 15 (4): 611–633.

Gaarder, Emily, and Joanne Belknap. 2002. "Tenuous Borders: Girls Transferred to Adult Court." *Criminology* 40 (3): 481–517.

Garland, David. 2001. *The Culture of Control: Crime and Social Order in Contemporary Society.* Chicago: University of Chicago Press.

Gilfus, Mary E. 1992. "From Victims to Survivors to Offenders: Women's Routes of Entry and Immersion into Street Crime." *Women and Criminal Justice* 4 (1): 63–89.

Giordano, Peggy C., Stephen A. Cernkovich, and Jennifer L. Rudolph. 2002. "Gender, Crime, and Desistance: Towards a Theory of Cognitive Transformation." *American Journal of Sociology* 107 (4): 990–1064.

Giordano, Peggy C., Monica A. Longmore, Ryan D. Schroeder, and Patrick M. Seffrin. 2008. "A Life Course Perspective on Spirituality and Desistance from Crime." *Criminology* 46 (1): 99–131.

Giordano, Peggy C., Ryan D. Schroeder, and Stephen A. Cernkovich. 2007. "Emotions and Crime over the Life Course: A Neo-Median Perspective on Criminal Continuity and Change." *American Journal of Sociology* 112 (6): 1603–1661.

Glaser, Barney, and Anselm Strauss. 1967. *The Discovery of Grounded Theory: Strategies for Qualitative Research.* Aldine Transaction.

Goffman, Erving. 1963. *Stigma: Notes on the Management of Spoiled Identity.* New York: Simon and Schuster.

Greenfield, Lawrence A., and Tracy L. Snell. 1999. *Women Offenders.* Washington, DC: Bureau of Justice Statistics, U.S. Department of Justice.

Griffin, Marie L., and Gaylene S. Armstrong. 2003. "The Effect of Local Life Circumstance on Female Probationers' Offending." *Justice Quarterly* 20 (2): 213–239.

Gubrium, Jaber F., and James A. Holstein. 1998. "Narrative Practice and the Coherence of Personal Stories." *Sociological Quarterly* 39 (1): 163–187.

———. 2000. "The Self in a World of Going Concerns." *Symbolic Interaction* 23 (2): 95–115.

Hagan, John, and Juleigh Petty Coleman. 2001. "Returning Captives of the American War on Drugs: Issues of Community and Family Reentry." *Crime and Delinquency* 47 (3): 352–367.

Haney, Lynne A. 2010. *Offending Women: Power, Punishment, and the Regulation of Desire.* Berkeley and Los Angeles: University of California Press.

Harlow, Caroline Wolf. 1999. *Prior Abuse Reported by Inmates and Probationers.* Washington, DC: U.S. Department of Justice, Bureau of Justice Statistics.

———. 2003. *Education and Correctional Populations.* Washington, DC: U.S. Department of Justice, Office of Justice Programs.

Harris, David R. 1999. "'Property Values Drop When Blacks Move In, Because . . .': Racial and Socioeconomic Determinants of Neighborhood Desirability." *American Sociological Review* 64 (3): 461–479.

Haynie, Dana L. 2001. "Delinquent Peers Revisited: Does Network Structure Matter?," *American Journal of Sociology* 106 (4): 1013–1057.

Haynie, Dana L., and Danielle C. Payne. 2006. "Race, Friendship Networks, and Violent Delinquency." *Criminology* 44 (4): 775–805.

Heimer, Karen, and Stacy De Coster. 1999. "The Gendering of Violent Delinquency." *Criminology* 37(2): 277–318.

Hill, Gary D., and Elizabeth M. Crawford. 1990. "Women, Race, and Crime." *Criminology* 28 (4): 601–626.

Hill, Shirley A. 2001. "Class, Race, and Gender Dimensions of Child Rearing in African American Families." *Journal of Black Studies* 31 (4): 494–508.

Holtfreter, Kristy, Michael D. Reisig, and Merry Morash. 2004. "Poverty, State Capital, and Recidivism among Women Offenders." *Criminology and Public Policy* 3 (2): 185–208.

Holzer, Harry, Paul Offner, and Elaine Sorensen. 2005. "Declining Employment among Young Black Less-Educated Men: The Role of Incarceration and Chid Support." *Journal of Policy Analysis and Management* 24 (2): 329–350.

Holzer, Harry, Steven Raphael, and Michael Stoll. 2001. *Will Employers Hire Ex-Offenders? Exployer Prefereences, Background Checks, and Their Determinants.* University of California, Los Angeles.

Horney, Julie, D. Wayne Osgood, and Ineke Haen Marshall. 1995. "Criminal Careers in the Short-Term: Intra-Individual Variability in Crime and Its Relation to Local Life Circumstances." *American Sociological Review* 60 (5): 655–673.

Huebner, Beth M., Christina DeJong, and Jennifer Cobbina. 2010. "Women Coming Home: Long-Term Patterns of Recidivism." *Justice Quarterly* 27 (2): 225–254.

Illouz, Eva. 2008. *Saving the Modern Soul: Therapy, Emotions, and the Culture of Self-Help.* Berkeley and Los Angeles: University of California Press.

Irwin, John. 1970. *The Felon.* Englewood Cliffs, NJ: Prentice Hall.

Jayakody, Rukmalie, Linda M. Chatters, and Robert Joseph Taylor. 1993. "Family Support to Single and Married African American Mothers: The Provision of Financial, Emotional, and Child Care Assistance." *Journal of Marriage and the Family* 55 (2): 261–276.

Jones, Nikki. 2010. *Between Good and Ghetto: African American Girls and Inner City Violence.* New Brunswick, NJ: Rutgers University Press.

Kane, Emily W. 2000. "Racial and Ethnic Variations in Gender-Related Attitudes." *Annual Review of Sociology* 26:419–439.

Katz, Alfred H. 1993. *Self-Help in America: A Social Movement Perspective.* New York: Twayne Publishers.

Katz, Rebecca S. 2000. "Explaining Girls' and Women's Crime and Desistance in the Context of Their Victimization Experiences: A Developmental Test of Revised Strain Theory and the Life Course Perspective." *Violence Against Women* 6 (6): 633–660.

King, Ryan D., Michael Massoglia, and Ross MacMillan. 2007. "The Context of Marriage and Crime: Gender, the Propensity to Marry, and Offending in Early Adulthood." *Criminology* 45 (1): 33–65.

Kirk, David S. 2012. "Residential Change as a Turning Point in the Life Course of Crime: Desistance or Temporary Cessation?" *Criminology* 50 (2): 329–358.

Kirsch, Gesa E. 1999. *Ethical Dilemmas in Feminist Research: The Politics of Location, Interpretation, and Publication*. Albany: State University of New York Press.

Kirschenman, Joleen, and Kathryn M. Neckerman. 1991. "'We'd Love to Hire Them, But . . .': The Meaning of Race for Employers." In *The Urban Underclass*, edited by Christopher Jencks and Paul E. Peterson, 203–232. Washington, DC: The Brookings Institute.

Kruttschnitt, Candace. 2010. "The Paradox of Women's Imprisonment." *Daedalus* 139 (3): 32–42.

La Vigne, Nancy G., Cynthia A. Mamalian, Jeremy Travis, and Christy Visher. 2003. *A Portrait of Prisoner Reentry in Illinois*. Washington, DC: The Urban Institute.

La Vigne, Nancy G., Christy Visher, and Jennifer Castro. 2004. *Chicago Prisoners' Experiences Returning Home*. Washington, DC: The Urban Institute.

Langan, Patrick, and David Levin. 2002. *Recidivism of Prisoners Released in 1994*. Washington, DC: U.S. Department of Justice, Bureau of Justice Statistics.

Laub, John H., Daniel S. Nagin, and Robert J. Sampson. 1998. "Trajectories of Change in Criminal Offending: Good Marriages and the Desistance Process." *American Sociological Review* 63 (2): 225–238.

Laub, John H., and Robert J. Sampson. 2003. *Shared Beginnings, Divergent Lives: Delinquent Boys to Age 70*. Cambridge, MA: Harvard University Press.

Leverentz, Andrea. 2006. "The Love of a Good Man? Romantic Relationships as a Source of Support or Hindrance for Female Ex-Offenders." *Journal of Research in Crime and Delinquency* 43 (4): 459–488.

———. 2010. "People, Places, and Things: How Female Ex-Prisoners Negotiate Their Neighborhood Context." *Journal of Contemporary Ethnography* 39 (6): 646–681.

———. 2011. "Being a Good Daughter and Sister: Families of Origin in the Reentry of African American Female Ex-Prisoners." *Feminist Criminology* 6 (4): 239–267.

Lofland, John, and Lyn Lofand. 1994. *Analyzing Social Settings: A Guide to Qualitative Observation and Analysis*. Belmont, CA: Wadsworth Publishing.

Lucken, Karol, and Lucille M. Ponte. 2008. "A Just Measure of Forgiveness: Reforming Occupational Licensing Regulations for Ex-Offenders Using Bfoq Analysis." *Law & Policy* 30 (1): 46–72.

Maher, Lisa, and Kathleen Daly. 1996. "Women in the Street-Level Drug Economy: Continuity or Change?" *Criminology* 34 (4): 465–491.

Maher, Lisa, and Susan L. Hudson. 2007. "Women in the Drug Economy: A Metasynthesis of the Qualitative Literature." *Journal of Drug Issues* 37 (4): 805–826.

Makarios, Matthew D. 2007. "Race, Abuse, and Female Criminal Violence." *Feminist Criminology* 2 (2): 100–116.

Martinez, Damian J. 2006. "Informal Helping Mechanisms: Conceptual Issues in Family Support of Reentry of Former Prisoners." *Journal of Offender Rehabilitation* 44 (1): 23–37.

Martinez, Damian J., and Johnna Christian. 2009. "The Familial Relationships of Former Prisoners: Examining the Link between Residence and Informal Support Mechanisms." *Journal of Contemporary Ethnography* 38 (2): 201–224.

Maruna, Shadd. 2001. *Making Good: How Ex-Convicts Reform and Rebuild Their Lives*. Washington, DC: American Psychological Association.

———. 2011. "Reentry as a Rite of Passage." *Punishment and Society* 13 (1): 3–28.

Maruna, Shadd, and Kevin Roy. 2007. "Amputation or Reconstruction? Notes on the Concept of "Knifing Off" and Desistance from Crime." *Journal of Contemporary Criminal Justice* 23: 104–124.

Massoglia, Michael, Glenn Firebaugh, and Cody Warner. 2013. "Racial Variation in the Effect of Incarceration on Neighborhood Attainment." *American Sociological Review* 78 (1): 142–165.

Matsueda, Ross L., and Karen Heimer. 1987. "Race, Family Structure, and Delinquency: A Test of Differential Association and Social Control Theories." *American Sociological Review* 52 (6): 826–840.

McAdams, Dan. 2006. *The Redemptive Self: Stories Americans Live By*. New York: Oxford University Press.

McCorkel, Jill. 2004. "Criminally Dependent? Gender, Punishment, and the Rhetoric of Welfare Reform." *Social Politics—International Studies in Gender State and Society* 11 (3): 386–410.

McDaniels-Wilson, Cathy, and Joanne Belknap. 2008. "The Extensive Sexual Violation and Sexual Abuse Histories of Incarcerated Women." *Violence Against Women* 14 (10): 1090–1127.

Mead, George Herbert. 1934. *Mind, Self, and Society: From the Standpoint of a Social Behaviorist*. Chicago: University of Chicago Press.

Miller, Gale, and David Silverman. 1995. "Troubles Talk and Counseling Discourse: A Comparative Study." *Sociological Quarterly* 36 (4): 725–747.

Miller, Jody. 1995. "Gender and Power in the Streets." *Journal of Contemporary Ethnography* 23 (4): 427.

———. 1998. "Up It Up: Gender and the Accomplishment of Street Robbery." *Criminology* 36 (1): 37–66.

———. 2001. *One of the Guys: Girls, Gangs, and Gender*. New York: Oxford University Press.

———. 2008. *Getting Played: African American Girls Urban Inequality and Gendered Violence*. New York: New York University Press.

Mills, C. Wright. 1959. *The Sociological Imagination*. Oxford: Oxford University Press.

Neckerman, Kathryn M., and Joleen Kirschenman. 1991. "Hiring Strategies, Racial Bias, and Inner-City Workers." *Social Problems* 38 (4): 433–447.

Nurse, Anne M. 2002. *Fatherhood Arrested: Parenting from within the Juvenile Justice System*. Nashville, TN: Vanderbilt University Press.

Oakley, Ann. 1981. "Interviewing Women: A Contradiction in Terms." In *Doing Feminist Research*, edited by Helen Roberts, 30–61. London: Routledge & Kegan Paul.

O'Brien, Patricia. 2001. *Making It in the "Free World": Women in Transition from Prison*. Albany: State University of New York Press.

———. 2007. "Maximizing Success for Drug-Affected Women after Release from Prison—Examining Access to and Use of Social Services During Reentry." *Women & Criminal Justice* 17 (2): 95–113.

O'Halloran, Seán. 2005. "Symmetry in Interaction in Meetings of Alcoholics Anonymous: The Management of Conflict." *Discourse & Society* 16 (4): 535–560.

Owen, Barbara. 1998. *"In the Mix": Struggle and Survival in a Women's Prison*. Albany: State University of New York Press.

Pager, Devah. 2005. "Walking the Talk: What Employers Say versus What They Do." *American Sociological Review* 70 (3): 355–380.

———. 2007. *Marked: Race, Crime, and Finding Work in an Era of Mass Incarceration*. Chicago: University of Chicago Press.

Pager, Devah, Bart Bonikowski, and Bruce Western. 2009. "Discrimination in a Low-Wage Labor Market." *American Sociological Review* 74 (5): 777–799.

Paternoster, Ray, and Shawn Bushway. 2009. "Desistance and the "Feared Self": Toward an Identity Theory of Criminal Desistance." *Journal of Criminal Law & Criminology* 99 (4): 1103–1156.

Petersilia, Joan. 2003. *When Prisoners Come Home: Parole and Prisoner Reentry.* Oxford: Oxford University Press.

Reckdenwald, Amy, and Karen F. Parker. 2008. "The Influence of Gender Inequality and Marginalization on Types of Female Offending." *Homicide Studies* 12 (2): 208–226.

Reisig, Michael D., Kristy Holtfreter, and Merry Morash. 2002. "Social Capital among Women Offenders." *Journal of Contemporary Criminal Justice* 18 (2): 167–187.

Richie, Beth. 1996. *Compelled to Crime: The Gender Entrapment of Battered Black Women.* New York: Routledge.

———. 2001. "Challenges Incarcerated Women Face as They Return to Their Communities: Findings from Life History Interviews." *Crime and Delinquency* 47 (3): 368–389.

———. 2002. "The Social Impact of Mass Incarceration on Women." In *Invisible Punishment: The Collateral Consequences of Mass Imprisonment*, edited by Marc Mauer and Meda Chesney-Lind, 136–149. New York: The New Press.

Rogers-Dillon, Robin, and Lynne Haney. 2005. "Minimizing Vulnerability: Selective Interdependencies after Welfare Reform." *Qualitative Sociology* 28 (3): 235–254.

Sampson, Robert J., and John H. Laub. 1993. *Crime in the Making: Pathways and Turning Points through Life.* Cambridge, MA: Harvard University Press.

Sampson, Robert J., John H. Laub, and Christopher Wimer. 2006. "Does Marriage Reduce Crime? A Counterfactual Approach to Within-Individual Causal Effects." *Criminology* 44: 465–508.

Sampson, Robert J., and Charles Loeffler. 2010. "Punishment's Place: The Local Concentration of Mass Incarceration." *Daedalus* 139 (3): 20–31.

Sarkisian, Natalia, and Naomi Gerstel. 2004. "Kin Support among Blacks and Whites: Race and Family Organization." *American Sociological Review* 69 (6): 812–837.

Sered, Susan, and Maureen Norton-Hawk. 2011. "Whose Higher Power? Criminalized Women Confront the 'Twelve Steps.'" *Feminist Criminology* 6 (4): 308–332.

Shover, Neal. 1996. *Great Pretenders: Pursuits and Careers of Persistent Thieves.* Boulder, CO: Westview Press.

Silva, Jennifer M. 2012. "Constructing Adulthood in an Age of Uncertainty." *American Sociological Review* 77 (4): 505–522.

Simpson, Sally. 1991. "Caste, Class, and Violent Crime: Explaining Difference in Female Offending." *Criminology* 29 (1): 115–135.

Solomon, Amy L., Kelly Dedel Johnson, Jeremy Travis, and Elizabeth C. McBride. 2004. *From Prison to Work: The Employment Dimensions of Prisoner Reentry.* Washington, DC: The Urban Institute.

Steffensmeier, Darrell J. 1983. "Organization Properties and Sex-Segregation in the Underworld: Building a Sociological Theory of Sex Differences in Crime." *Social Forces* 61 (4): 1010–1032.

Steffensmeier, Darrell, and Emilie Allan. 1996. "Gender and Crime: Toward a Gendered Theory of Female Offending." *Annual Review of Sociology* 22: 459–487.

Sterk, Claire E. 1999. *Fast Lives: Women Who Use Crack Cocaine.* Philadelphia: Temple University Press.

Stewart, Eric A., Christopher J. Schreck, and Ronald L. Simons. 2006. "'I Ain't Gonna Let No One Disrespect Me': Does the Code of the Street Reduce or Increase Violent Victimization among African American Adolescents?" *Journal of Research in Crime and Delinquency* 43 (4): 427–458.

Stoll, Michael A., and Shawn D. Bushway. 2008. "The Effect of Criminal Background Checks on Hiring Ex-Offenders." *Criminology & Public Policy* 7 (3): 371–404.

Sutherland, Edwin H. 1947. *Criminology*. Philadelphia: Lippincott.

Swann, Christopher A., and Michelle Sheran Sylvester. 2006. "The Foster Care Crisis: What Caused Caseloads to Grow?" *Demography* 43 (2): 309–335.

Swora, Maria Gabrielle. 2004. "The Rhetoric of Transformation in the Healing of Alcoholism: The Twelve Steps of Alcoholics Anonymous." *Mental Health, Religion & Culture* 7 (3): 187–209.

Taub, Richard, D., Garth Taylor, and Jan D. Dunham. 1984. *Paths of Neighborhood Change: Race and Crime in Urban America*. Chicago: University of Chicago Press.

Terry, Charles. 2003. *The Fellas: Overcoming Prison and Addiction*. Belmont, CA: Wadsworth.

Thompson, Melissa, and Milena Petrovic. 2009. "Gendered Transitions: Within-Person Changes in Employment, Family, and Illicit Drug Use." *Journal of Research in Crime and Delinquency* 46 (3): 377–408.

Travis, Jeremy. 2002. "Invisible Punishment: An Instrument of Social Exclusion." In *Invisible Punishment: The Collateral Consequences of Mass Imprisonnment*, edited by Marc Mauer and Meda Chesney-Lind, 15–36. New York: The New Press.

———. 2005. *But They All Come Back: Facing the Challenges of Prisoner Reentry*. Washington, DC: The Urban Institute Press.

Turner, Clevonne E. 1997. "Clinical Applications of the Stone Center Theoretical Approach to Minority Women." In *Women's Growth in Diversity*, edited by Judith V. Jordan, 74–90. New York: Guilford Press.

Twine, France Winddance, and Jonathan W. Warren. 2000. *Racing Research, Researching Race: Methodological Dilemmas in Critical Race Studies*. New York: New York University Press.

Uggen, Christopher. 1999. "Ex-Offenders and the Conformist Alternative: A Job Quality Model of Work and Crime." *Social Problems* 46 (1): 127–151.

———. 2000. "Work as a Turning Point in the Life Course of Criminals: A Duration Model of Age, Employment, and Recidivism." *American Sociological Review* 65 (4): 529–546.

Uggen, Christopher, and Candace Kruttschnitt. 1998. "Crime in the Breaking: Gender Differences in Desistance." *Law and Society Review* 32 (2): 339–366.

Uggen, Christopher, and Melissa Thompson. 2003. "The Socioeconomic Determinants of Ill-Gotten Gains: Within-Person Changes in Drug Use and Illegal Earnings." *American Journal of Sociology* 109 (1): 146.

Vaillant, George E. 1988. "What Can Long-Term Follow-up Teach Us about Relapse and Prevention of Relapse in Addiction?" *British Journal of Addiction* 83:1147–1157.

Wacquant, Loïc. 2010. "Class, Race, and Hyperincarceration in Revanchist America." *Daedalus* 139 (3): 74–90.

Warr, Mark. 1998. "Life-Course Transitions and Desistance from Crime." *Criminology* 36 (2): 183–216.

Weiss, Robert S. 1994. *Learning from Strangers: The Art and Method of Qualitative Interviewing*. New York: The Free Press.

Western, Bruce. 2002. "The Impact of Incarceration on Wage Mobility and Inequality." *American Sociological Review* 67 (4): 526–546.

———. 2006. *Punishment and Inequality in America*. New York: Russell Sage Foundation.

Western, Bruce, and Becky Pettit. 2010. "Incarceration and Social Inequality." *Daedalus* 139 (3): 8–19.

Wilson, William Julius. 1987. *The Truly Disadvantaged: The Inner City, the Underclass, and Public Policy.* Chicago: University of Chicago Press.

Wuthnow, Robert. 1994. *Sharing the Journey: Support Groups and America's New Quest for Community.* New York: The Free Press.

Yeung, King-To, and John Levi Martin. 2003. "The Looking Glass Self: An Empirical Test and Elaboration." *Social Forces* 81 (3): 843–879.

Index

ABLA homes, 48–49

Abra (pseud.), 115, 146, 151, 164–166, 168, 187

abuse, 7–8, 201n3; child abuse, 21, 29, 42–44, 46–48, 54, 102, 107, 145, 177; emotional abuse, 43, 46–47, 54, 107, 115; in family relationships, 41–47, 52, 54, 81, 100, 102, 107, 113, 128, 145; in foster homes, 42; as "kill or be killed," 115; as pathway to offending, 40–48, 52, 54–55; physical abuse, 4, 41, 43–44, 102, 115; in romantic relationships, 54–55, 81, 115, 129; sexual abuse, 41–43, 201n3

acquaintances. *See* associates, drug-using

addictions, 2–3, 5, 175, 177–178; addiction studies, 3; cross-addiction, 83; and desistance, 11, 58, 62–63, 65, 69–70, 74, 76; and education, 151; and employment, 142, 144–145; and family relationships, 62–63, 82–92, 96, 100, 104–106, 108–111, 202n1 (ch4); and friendships, 83, 132–137; high rates of, 13; and Mercy Home, 27, 31, 38, 69, 104, 149; and motherhood, 82–92, 96, 105; and neighborhoods, 157, 169; pathways to, 40–41, 43–44, 48–50, 52, 54; and romantic relationships, 115–119, 121, 123–124, 127, 129; and "selfishness," 84, 137; and twelve-step/self-help programs, 12–14, 76, 109, 181–182. *See also* alcohol use/alcoholism; drug use

Adena (pseud.), 22, 26, 31, 39, 48–51, 55, 69, 86–88, 108–110, 113, 134–135, 160, 163, 178, 188, 192–193

adoption, 94–96, 129–130

African American women, 8–9; and desistance, 61–62; and employment, 141, 155; and family relationships, 81, 202n2 (ch4); and neighborhoods, 157–158, 165–167, 169–173; and pathways to offending, 40–42, 45–46, 48, 51, 53–54; and romantic relationships, 114, 129; structural/contextual factors influencing, 8–9

age, 175, 187–188, 194; age-graded theory of social control, 10; of children, 41, 82, 86, 88, 90–91, 96; and desistance, 62, 69, 71–72, 86; and education, 152; and employment, 153–154; and Mercy Home, 21–22; and motherhood, 82, 86; and neighborhoods, 172; and pathways to offending, 41, 49–52, 54; and romantic relationships, 124–126

agency, personal, 7, 51, 56, 68, 162, 164, 166, 172–173

Albany (pseud.), 32, 160, 187

Alcoholics Anonymous (AA), 5, 12–14, 120, 123, 126, 180

alcohol use/alcoholism, 1; beer, 71; and desistance, 59, 71–72, 75; and employment, 147–149; and family relationships, 41, 82, 85, 87, 91, 105; and Mercy Home, 27, 36–37; and motherhood, 82, 85, 87, 91; as pathway to offending, 41, 44–46, 53–54; "recovering alcoholic," 14; and relapses, 71–72; and romantic relationships, 120; structural/contextual factors influencing, 8; and twelve-step/self-help programs, 12–14, 75. *See also* addictions; relapses/reoffending

About the Author

Andrea M. Leverentz is an associate professor of sociology at the University of Massachusetts Boston. She received her PhD in sociology from the University of Chicago. Her research interests include gender and crime, prisoner reentry, communities and crime, urban sociology, and qualitative research methods.

CPSIA information can be obtained at www.ICGtesting.com
Printed in the USA
BVOW09s0800110214

344552BV00002B/2/P